John Pickering Putman

The Open Fireplace in All Ages

John Pickering Putman

The Open Fireplace in All Ages

ISBN/EAN: 9783337251680

Printed in Europe, USA, Canada, Australia, Japan

Cover: Foto ©ninafisch / pixelio.de

More available books at **www.hansebooks.com**

LARGE VENTILATING FIREPLACE.
IN MEDIÆVAL STYLE.
(*See pages 189 and 190.*)

THE OPEN FIREPLACE

IN ALL AGES.

BY

J. PICKERING PUTNAM,
ARCHITECT.

ILLUSTRATED BY 300 CUTS, INCLUDING 55 FULL-PAGE PLATES.

NEW EDITION, REVISED AND ENLARGED.

CONTAINING OVER

TWENTY NEW PLATES OF DESIGNS OF CHIMNEY-PIECES AND INTERIOR DECORATION, CONTRIBUTED BY AMERICAN ARCHITECTS.

BOSTON:
TICKNOR AND COMPANY
1886.

INTRODUCTION TO THE SECOND EDITION.

No part of the interior of a building offers so broad a field for the exercise of the taste and skill of the designer as the Open Fireplace and Chimney-Piece. The friendly warmth of the fire renders it the immediate centre of attraction. Its ever-varying, cheerful flame enchains our attention as a living and sympathetic companion, long after the surrounding inanimate objects have ceased to occupy our thoughts. Hence the Chimney-Piece has, for ages, been honored and treated as the focus of interest; the key-note of the interior decoration of the apartment; and, so long as our physical natures remain the same, it is likely to continue to be so treated. No one object has assumed a greater and more interesting variety of forms at different hands, and none shows to better advantage the peculiar character and individuality of the designer. By adding to our collection already formed in the first edition, a number of the best modern designs executed or prepared for execution in this country, we have obtained an interesting index of the gradual and comparative development of interior decoration and household art, both mediæval and modern, at home and abroad.

Many thanks are returned to the well-known artists whose names will be recognized in the descriptions of the designs contributed by them for this purpose.

We render, also, hearty thanks to Messrs. Ducher & Co., 51 Rue des Écoles; Messrs. A. Morel & Co., 13 Rue Bonaparte, Paris, France, and to Messrs. Harper & Bros., Franklin Square, New York, Publishers, for their liberality in permitting the reproduction of their engravings, as acknowledged in detail in the descriptions of the illustrations. Also, to Messrs. J. Baxdry, 15 Rue des Saints-Pères; Ernest Lachand, 4 Place du Théâtre-Français; Noblet, et Baudry, 20 Rue Jacob; Victor Masson, Place de l'École de Médecine; A. Lévy, 29 Rue de Seine, Paris, France; and to Messrs. Virtue, Brothers, & Co., London, England, and to others from whom extracts have been made, and acknowledged in the body of the book.

The knowledge of the decimal system of Weights and Measures has now become so general in this country of decimal currency that every educated man will appreciate the advantages of its use in a work where accuracy and simplicity, in the expression and calculation of quantities, is desired. To facilitate the translation of meters into feet and inches, however, for those still unaccustomed to thinking in the former, a comparative diagram of centimeters and inches, together with a general table of conversion, has been added in the Appendix.

4 PEMBERTON SQUARE, October, 1881.

TABLE OF CONTENTS.

CHAPTER I.

THE OPEN FIREPLACE AS IT IS.

	PAGE
Direct Radiation	1
Waste of Heat by Open Fires	2
Dangerous Draughts and Imperfect Ventilation	2
Practical Experiments on the Waste Heat and Air Currents	3
Result of Experiments	7
The Ideal Fireplace	8

CHAPTER II.

HISTORICAL.

The Chimney-Flue a Modern Discovery	12
Earliest Forms of the Open Fireplace	14
Braziers and Portable Fires	16
Origin of the Chimney	18
First Fireplaces of the Middle Ages	19
Further Development of Mediæval Fireplaces	22
Efforts to Improve the Draught and Economize the Fuel	29
The Ventilating Fireplace	34
Smoke-consuming Fireplaces	36
Improvement in the Form of the Chimney-Throat	41
The Sliding Blower	46
The Movable Grate	48
Fireplaces with Inverted Smoke-Flue	48
Ventilating Stove Fireplaces with Direct Smoke-Flue and Fresh-Air Circulation	54
Ventilating Fireplaces Manufactured in this Country	64
Experiments with the "Fire on the Hearth" Heater	69
The "Dimmick" Heater	70
Experiments with the "Dimmick" Heater	71
Other American Fireplaces	75
Jackson's Ventilating Fireplace	78
The Franklin Reflector	83
General Remarks	87
Description of Plates.	

CHAPTER III.

SUGGESTIONS FOR THE IMPROVEMENT OF THE OPEN FIREPLACE.

	PAGE
Introductory Remarks	89
Combination of Furnace and Fireplace	94
Furnaces	95
Moisture in the Air	97
Special Forms of Furnace Construction	97
Material of Furnaces	100
Experiments on Cast Iron	101
Examples of Furnaces	105
Fresh Air in our Dwellings	110
Simple Test to ascertain the Purity of the Air	114
Amount of Fresh Air required per Head per Minute	115
Natural Ventilation	116
The Position of the Fresh-Air Inlet	122
Ventilation of Gas-Burners	127
The Furnace Ventilation Fireplace	137
The "Distributor" in Ventilating Fireplaces	141
Various Examples of the Use of the "Distributor"	152
The "Distributor" as an Open Radiator	157
Cost of the Furnace Ventilating Fireplace	161
Heating Power of the Furnace Ventilating Fireplace	166
Effect on the Draught of Abstraction of Heat from the Flue	167
Ventilating Chimney	170
Chimney-Tops	173
Range Flue	174
Furnace Flue	174
Decorative Treatment of the Ventilating Registers	175
Improved Smoke-consuming Fireplace	177
Large Fireplaces	177
Formulæ for Discovering the Cause and Effecting the Cure of Smoky Chimneys	180
Recapitulation	186
The "Real Fireplace"	186
Description of Plates.	

APPENDIX.

Heating and Ventilation of Private Houses	189
The "Fire on the Hearth," Heater, No 2.	191
The Jackson Fireplace	194
The Metric System	195
Tables	196

LIST OF ILLUSTRATIONS.

PLATES.

	Large Ventilating Fireplace in Mediæval Style	*Frontispiece Following Title.*
I.	Fireplace in a Studio at Terre Neuve (Vendée), France	"
II.	Fireplace in a Peasant's Cottage in Brittany	"
III.	Fireplace in the Council Chamber of Courtray	"
IV.	Fireplace in the "Salle de Mars," Château of François I.	"
V.	Gothic Mantel in Palace of the Dukes of Burgundy, Dijon, France	"
VI.	Turkish Fireplace at Kéresoun	"
	Vignette	
VII.	Gothic Fireplace of the Fifteenth Century	*End of Chap. II.*
VIII.	Fireplace at the Hôtel de Ville at Lyons	"
IX.	Renaissance Fireplace	"
X.	Moorish Fireplace	"
XI.	Fireplace in the Bed-chamber of King Louis XIII., France	"
XII.	Modern French Fireplace	"
XIII.	Fireplace in the Château de Tanlay, France	"
XIV.	Fireplace in the Castle of Heidelberg	"
XV.	Fireplace in the Château de Cormatin	"
XVI.	Fireplace in the Museum of Cluny, Paris	"
XVII.	Fireplace in a house at Sarlat, France	"
XVIII.	Fireplace in the Hôtel d'Alluyer, Blois, France	"
XIX.	Fireplace in the Château de Tanlay, France	"
XX.	Fireplace in the Château de Baynac	"
XXI.	Dining-room Fireplace in Modern English Gothic Style	"
XXII.	Fireplace in the Hôtel de Vogué, at Dijon	"
XXIII.	Fireplace in the Smoking-room of the House of M. Le Comte Branicki, Paris	"
XXIV.	Fireplace in the "Salon des Médailles," in the Palace of Versailles, France	"
XXV.	Renaissance Fireplace	"
XXVI.	Fireplace in a House in the Rue de Berlin, Paris	"
XXVII.	Fireplace in the Grand Drawing-room of the Bishop's Palace at Beauvais, France	"
XXVIII.	Fireplace exhibited at the Centennial Exhibition, 1876	"
XXIX.	Old Fireplace at Morlaix, France	"
XXX.	Fireplace at San Germano, Italy	"
XXXI.	Fireplace in the National Museum at Florence, Italy	"
XXXII.	Fireplace in the Hotel Cluny, Boston	*End of Chap. III.*
XXXIII.	Stone Fireplace for a Modern Dining-room	"
XXXIV.	Rustic Fireplace between two Window-niches	"
XXXV.	Hall Mantel for a House in Salem, Mass	"
XXXV.	Hall Mantel for a House in Andover, Mass.	"
XXXVI.	Library Mantel. House on Commonwealth Avenue, Boston	"

x   LIST OF ILLUSTRATIONS.

XXXVII.	Hall Mantel for a House at Nahant, Mass. . . .	End of Chap. III.
XXXVIII.	Parlor Fireplace for a House on Commonwealth Avenue, Boston .	"
XXXIX.	Dining-room Fireplace for a House on Commonwealth Avenue, Boston	"
XL.	Hall Fireplace in the House of Mr. Marcus Sayer, Montrose, N.Y.	"
XLI.	Fireplace in the House of Mr. Pierre Lorillard, Newport, R.I. .	"
XLII.	Fireplace in a Private Residence	"
XLIII.	Dining-room Alcove Fireplace	"
XLIV.	Fireplace at Lenox, Mass.	"
XLV.	Hall Fireplace designed for Residence at Chestnut Hill, near Philadelphia	"
XLVI.	Fireplace in the Private "Counting-room" of Messrs. Harper & Brothers, Publishers, N.Y.	"
XLVII.	Hall Fireplace in the House of C. H. Joy, Esq., Boston .	"
XLVIII.	Fireplace in a Residence in Boston	"
XLIX.	Hooded Mantel in Oak, for Henry I. Sheldon, Esq., Chicago .	"
L.	Hall Fireplace	"
LI.	Saloon Fireplace in the House of D. Jackson Steward, Goshen, N.Y.	"
LII.	Fireplace in House of Dr. Greenleaf, Lenox, Mass. . .	"
LIII.	Dining-room Fireplace	"
LIV.	Hall Fireplace.	"
LV.	Fireplace in the Reading-room of the Equitable Life Insurance Building, Boston	

FIGURES.

NO.		PAGE
1.	Modern Office Fireplace used in Experiments. Front View .	3
2.	Modern Office Fireplace. Section	3
3.	Diagram giving Dimensions of Office Fireplace used in Experiment .	5
4.	Primitive Smoke-flue. (From Viollet-le-Duc) . . .	13
5.	Backwoodsman's Log Cabin	14
6.	Chimney of Logs. (From Viollet-le-Duc) . . .	15
7. 8. }	Brazier. (From Joly)	16
9.	Spanish Portable Brazier. From Joly	16
10.	Origin of the Chimney. (From Labarthe) . . .	18
11. 12. }	Fireplace in Conisborough Castle. (From Tomlinson) .	18
13.	Fireplace of the Fourteenth Century. (From Viollet-le-Duc) .	19
14.	Fireplace of the Fifteenth Century. (From Viollet-le-Duc) .	20
15.	Fireplace in the House of Jaques Coeur. [From Gailhabaud (except figures)]	21
16.	Old Fireplace. [From "Antient Domestick Architecture" (except figures)]	22
17.	Hooded Mediæval Fireplace of Thirteenth Century. (From Viollet-le-Duc)	23
18.	Fireplace in the Ville de Cluny. [From Viollet-le-Duc (except figures and accessories)]	24
19.	Fireplace in Roslin Castle. [From "Antient Domestick Architecture" (except figure and accessories)]	24
20.	Kitchen Fireplace of Granite. (From Viollet-le-Duc) . .	25
21. 22. }	Fireplace of the Fifteenth Century. (From Viollet-le-Duc) .	{ 26 { 27

LIST OF ILLUSTRATIONS.

NO.		PAGE
23.	Section of Fireplace of the Fifteenth Century. (From Viollet-le-Duc)	28
24.	Details of the Construction of Fireplace of the Fifteenth Century. (From Viollet-le-Duc)	28
25.	Stone Fireplace in the Château d'Armay-le-Duc, Sixteenth Century. (From Sauvageot)	29
26.	Fireplace in Linlithgow Palace. [From "Antient Domestick Architecture" (except figure)]	30
27.	Fireplace in the Château de Coucy, France. (From Viollet-le-Duc)	30
28.	Fireplace in the Grand Hall of the Palais des Comtes of Poitiers. (From Viollet-le-Duc)	31
29.	Fireplace at the Louvre. Front elevation. (From Tomlinson)	32
30.	Fireplace at the Louvre. Section. (From Joly)	32
31.	Savot's Fireplace	33
32.	Winter's Fireplace	33
33.	Fireplace with "Bellows"	33
34.	Gauger's Ventilated Fireplace	34
35. 36.	Diagram showing Direction of Reflected Rays	35
37.	Perspective of Gauger's Fireplace	35
38.	Fresh-air Supply Valve	35
39.	Delesme's "Furnus Acapnos"	37
40.	Leutmann's Vulcanus Famulans	37
41.	Smoke-consuming Fireplace. (From Peclet)	37
42. 43.	Smoke-consuming Fireplace of Touet-Chambor. (From Peclet)	38
44.	Franklin's Smoke-consuming Grate. (From Labarthe)	38
45.	Cutler's Smoke-consuming Grate. (From Edwards)	39
46.	Dr. Arnott's Smokeless Fireplace. (From Tomlinson)	39
47. 48.	Atkins & Marriot's Smoke-consuming Grate. (From Edwards)	40
49.	Rumford's Fireplace. Vertical Section. (From Peclet)	42
50.	Rumford's Fireplace. Horizontal Section. (From Tomlinson)	42
51.	Another form of Rumford's Fireplace	43
52.	Modern Improvements on Rumford's Fireplace	43
53. 54.	Sylvester's Fireplace. (From Edwards)	44
55. 56.	Stephen's Fireplace. (From Edwards)	45
57. 58.	King's Patent Grate. (From Edwards)	46
59.	Lhomond's Fireplace	47
60.	Lhomond's Blower	47
61.	Lhomond's Fireplace. Front Elevation. (From Peclet)	47
62.	Lhomond's Fireplace. Section. (From Peclet)	47
63.	Bronzac's Movable Grate	48
64.	Franklin's Pennsylvanian Fireplace	48
65.	Desarnod's Fireplace. (From Joly)	49
66.	Montalembert's Fireplace	49
67. 68.	Douglas Galton's Fireplace	49
69.	Fireplace of Descroizilles	50
70.	Sheet-iron Ventilating Fireplace. (From Peclet)	51
71.	Ventilating Fireplace, with Vertical Fresh-air Tubes behind the Back. (From Peclet)	52
72.	Ventilating Fireplace, with Vertical Fresh-air Tubes behind the Back. (From Peclet)	53
73.	Taylor's Fireplace. (From Taylor)	53

No.		Page
74.	Suggestion of Smoke Circulation. (From Joly)	54
75.	Fireplace of Leras. (From Peclet)	54
76.) 77.)	Ventilating Fireplace, with Vertical Air Tubes. (From Peclet)	55
78.	Section of Ventilating Fireplace, with Horizontal Fresh-air Tubes. (From Peclet)	55
79.	Front Elevation of same. (From Peclet)	55
80.	Vertical Section of Fireplace with Metallic Heat-conducting Plates. (From Peclet)	56
81.	Horizontal Section of same. (From Peclet)	56
82.	Section of Plates. (From Peclet)	56
83.	Vertical Section of Ventilating Fireplace, without Plates. (From Peclet)	57
84.	Fournet's Fireplace. Front Elevation	57
85.	Fournet's Fireplace. Section	57
86.	Section of Cordier's Fireplace. (From Bose)	58
87.	Perspective View of Cordier's Fireplace. (From Bose)	59
88.	Back of Cordier's Fireplace. (From Bose)	59
89.	Metallic Fire-back of Cordier's Fireplace. (From Bose)	59
90.	Fire-back in Profile of Cordier's Fireplace. (From Bose)	59
91.) 92.)	Lloyd's Tubular Fireplace. (From Tomlinson)	60
93.) 94.) 95.)	Details of Lloyd's Tubular Fireplace. (From Tomlinson)	60
96.	Joly's Fireplace. (From Joly)	62
97.) 98.) 99.)	Dampers in Joly's Fireplace. (From Joly)	62
100.	Section of Dampers in Joly's Fireplace. (From Joly)	62
101.	Plan of Dampers in Joly's Fireplace. (From Joly)	63
102.	English Ventilating Fireplace. (From Douglas Galton)	63
103.	Plan of Ventilating Fireplace. (From Tomlinson)	63
104.	Section of Ventilating Fireplace. (From Douglas Galton)	64
105.	Double Ventilating Flue. (From Peclet)	64
106.) 107.)	Morin's Fireplace. (From Bose)	64
108.	Douglas Galton Fireplace. (From Peclet)	65
109.	The "Fire on the Hearth" Heater	66
110.	The "Fire on the Hearth" Heater. Plan	66
111.) 112.)	The "Fire on the Hearth" Heater. Smoke and Ventilating Flues	67
113.	The "Fire on the Hearth" Stove	70
114.	The Dimmick Fireplace	71
115.	Section of the Dimmick Fireplace	72
116.	English Ventilating Fireplace. (From Johnson's Encyclopedia)	75
117.) 118.)	Stove Radiator	76
119.	Jackson's Ventilating Fireplace. Section	78
120.	Jackson's Ventilating Fireplace. View of Hot-air Chamber	78
121.	Jackson's Ventilating Fireplace. Front View	79
122.	Jackson's Ventilating Fireplace. Plan	79
123.	Fireplace with Ash Pit	82
124.	The "Franklin Reflector" (so called)	83
125.	Ventilating Fireplace described by Peclet. (From Peclet)	84
126.	"Another Country Parson's" Grate	85
127.	"Another Country Parson's" Grate. Sectional View	86
128.	Persian Fireplace	88

LIST OF ILLUSTRATIONS.

xiii

NO.		PAGE
129.	Diagram of Furnace for utilizing the Heat of the Smoke	95
130.	Furnace in which the Smoke passes between Perpendicular Hot-air Pipes. (From Peclet)	98
131.	Furnace in which the Smoke circulates round Horizontal Hot-air Pipes. (From Peclet)	98
132.	Magee's Furnace	98
133.	The Peerless Furnace	99
134.	The Chilson Furnace	100
135.	Cast-iron Cup tested for Permeability	101
136.	Experiment on the Permeability of Cast-iron	101
137.	Test of Gas-pressure by means of a Manometer	103
138.	Section of Pig Iron	103
139.	The Reynolds Furnace	105
140.	Dunklee's Golden-Eagle Furnace	105
141.	Chubbuck's Furnace	106
142.	The Gothic Furnace	106
143.	Crary's Clay Heater	107
144.	The Soapstone Furnace	107
145.	Apparatus for testing the Porosity of Building Materials	119
146.	Movement of Hot Air from Furnace Flues	123
147.	Exhaust Register placed too high	124
148.	Movement of Air about a Stove	125
149.	Ventilating Chandelier	128
150.	Ventilating Chandelier	128
151.	Ventilating Chandelier	129
152.	Ventilating Chandelier	128
153.	Ventilating Chandelier	130
154.	Ventilating Chandelier	131
155.	Ventilating Bell	130
156.	Ventilating Drop-light	130
157.	Ventilating Drop-light	130
158.	The Faraday Gas-ventilator	129
159.	The Faraday Gas-ventilator	129
160.	The Faraday Gas-ventilator	131
161.	The Faraday Gas-ventilator	131
162.	The Faraday Gas-ventilator	131
163.	Ventilating Gas-burner used in England	129
164.	Ventilating Gas-burner used in England	132
165.	Ventilating Gas-burner used in England	132
166.	Ventilating Gas-burner used in England	132
167.	Ventilating Gas-burner used in England	132
168.	Ventilator for Bracket-burners	133
169.	Ventilator for Bracket-burners	133
170.	Ventilator for Bracket-burners	133
171.	Ventilator for Bracket-burners	133
172.	Ventilator for Stage Foot-lights	134
173.	Ventilator for Stage Foot-lights	134
174.	Ventilator for Stage Foot-lights	134
175.	Ventilator for Stage Foot-lights	134
176.	Ventilator for Stage Foot-lights	134
177.	Plan of City House	138
178.	Plan of City House	138
179.	Plan of City House	138
180.	Plan of City House	138
181.	Parlor Ventilating Fire-place	137
182.	Horizontal Section of same	139
183.	Front Elevation of House on Dartmouth St.	140

LIST OF ILLUSTRATIONS.

NO.		PAGE
184.	Vertical Section of Terra-cotta Distributor	141
185.	Vertical Section of Terra-cotta Distributor	141
186.	Terra-cotta Distributor	142
187.	Ventilating Chimney	140
188.	Vertical Section of Iron Distributor	146
189.	Vertical Section of Iron Distributor	146
190.	Dining-room Ventilating Fireplace	149
191.	Fire-place with Iron Distributor	150
192.	Fire-place with Iron Distributor	150
193.	Fire-place with Iron Distributor	150
194.	Fire-place with Iron Distributor	150
195.	Distributor with "Fire on the Hearth" Heater	152
196.	Distributor with "Fire on the Hearth" Heater	152
197.	Distributor with "Fire on the Hearth" Heater	152
198.	Distributor with "Fire on the Hearth" Heater	152
199.	Distributor with "Fire on the Hearth" Heater	152
200.	Distributor with Downward Draught	153
201.	Hood	153
202.	Hood	153
203.	Library Ventilating Fireplace	154
204.	Distributor	154
205.	Distributor	154
206.	Distributor	155
207.	Distributor	155
208.	Perspective View of Dining-room Ventilating Fireplace	155
209.	Hall Ventilating Fireplace	156
210.	Drain-pipe Distributor	156
211.	Drain-pipe Distributor	156
212.	Distributor as Open Radiator	158
213.	Distributor as Open Radiator	158
214.	Diagram showing Direction of Heat Rays and Air Currents	159
215.	Diagram showing Direction of Heat Rays and Air Currents	159
216.	Distributor as Open Radiator	160
217.	Distributor as Open Radiator	160
218.	Distributor as Open Radiator. Horizontal Section	161
219.	Model of House	168
220.	Ventilating Chimney	171
221.	Smoke-flue Joint	171
222.	Registers and Valves	172
223.	Registers and Valves	172
224.	Van Noorden Chimney-top	173
225.	Diagram showing Movement of Air Currents	173
226.	Range-flue Ventilating Registers	174
227.	Parlor Fireplace in Hotel Cluny, Boston	176
228.	Dining-room Ventilating Register	178
229.	Large Fireplace for Reading-room	179
230.	Ornamental Terra-cotta Chimney-tops on Public Buildings	185
231.	Ornamental Terra-cotta Chimney-tops on Private Houses	186
232.	The "Fire on the Hearth" Heater, No. 2	Appendix
233.	The "Fire on the Hearth" Heater, No. 2	Appendix
234.	The "Fire on the Hearth" Heater, No. 2	Appendix
235.	The Jackson Fireplace	Appendix
236.	The Jackson Fireplace	Appendix
237.	The Jackson Fireplace	Appendix
238.	The Jackson Fireplace	Appendix

PLATES.
I.-VI.

PLATE 1.

Fireplace of a studio at Terre Neuve (Vendée), France. From *L'Eau Forte de*, 1847.

PLATE I.

PLATE II.

Fireplace in a peasant's cottage in Brittany. The abode of the farmer often consists of a single room on the ground-floor, in which it is no uncommon thing to find the beds of eight or ten persons, the room serving as kitchen, parlor, bed-room, and cattle-stall at once. The room shown in our plate has been somewhat modernized, the colossal fireplace and mantel alone preserving its original appearance. The woodwork is of the period of Louis XIV. or XV. The cut is from the *Revue Générale de l'Architecture et des Travaux Publics*, 1873. Vol. xxx. Ducher & Co., Publishers, Paris.

PLATE II.

PLATE III.

Fireplace in the Council Chamber of Courtray. Elizabethan style.

PLATE III

PLATE IV.

Fireplace and chimney in the "Salle de Mars," Château of François I. at St. Germain en Laye, France. From Sauvageot "Palais et Chateaux de France." A. Morel & Co., Publishers, Paris.

PLATE IV.

PLATE V.

Gothic mantel of stone in the Guard Chamber of the ancient palace of the Dukes of Burgundy at Dijon, France; fifteenth century. The style is late Gothic or Flamboyant; the decorative screen-work is designed to screen the pyramidal flue of masonry behind it from sight. There are several ancient Gothic fireplaces with pyramidal upper part existing in England; but they are all undecorated. In France, a small concealed place or chamber was often constructed behind the fireplace. The Duchess de Berry and her attendants were captured in one of these hiding-places, having crowded more into it than the place was intended to hold, and the soldiers having made a large fire in front of them. The cut is from *The Builder*, London, 1847.

PLATE V.

PLATE VI.

Turkish fireplace at Kérésoun. This specimen of the Oriental Art of the seventeenth century is in the Pacha's Palace in the city of Kérésoun (ancient Cerafonta), which stands on a rock on the southern coast of the Black Sea.

The entire central frame of the fireplace is of a hard grayish stone, somewhat resembling granite. The decoration of the mantel and of the two sides, or wings, ornamented with niches, is moulded plaster-work vigorously retouched with the chisel. The whole is fitted in the wooden facings of the wall, which are garnished with divans and cushions. The climate of this country demanding often a speedy and bright flame, the fuel is placed vertically, as in Persia. The lighting is effected by means of dry aromatic herbs. From *L'Art pour Tous*, for 1861. A. Morel & Co., Publishers, Paris.

PLATE VI.

THE OPEN FIREPLACE

IN ALL AGES.

THE OPEN FIREPLACE.

CHAPTER I.

THE OPEN FIREPLACE AS IT IS.

That Great Radiator of heat to all living beings, the sun, furnishes those beings with the kind of heat best suited to support the life which it has developed, namely, that of direct radiation.

If we would only accept this lesson, repeated every day, as if for the purpose of giving it all possible emphasis, in a manner the most impressive and with apparatus the most magnificent that nature can furnish or the mind of man imagine; if we would accept the lesson, and endeavor to heat our houses after the same principles, these houses might be made as healthy as the open fields. We should be prompted to respect more the open fireplace, as furnishing the best substitute for the life and health giving rays of the sun, and to discard all such systems of heating as are opposed in principle to that employed by nature.

With direct radiation the body is warmed, while the air breathed is cool and refreshing. With the hot-air principle of heating the reverse is the case, and it is found that, when this method is long employed to the total exclusion of the more natural, serious discomfort and disease are the results. That warm air is less effective than cold in purifying the blood by removing the carbonic acid from the lungs is demonstrated both by our own experience and by the investigations of science. Experiments made on birds and animals have shown that the amount of carbonic acid exhaled when breathing air heated from $30°$ to $41°$ Centigrade ($86°$ to $106°$ F.) is less than one-half that exhaled when the temperature is near the freezing-point.

The open fire, while it radiates an agreeable heat upon our bodies, animating us with a cheering and healthy glow or excitement, like that produced by a bright sun on a frosty morning, leaves the air comparatively cool, concentrated, and invigorating for breathing.

Now, although from the earliest times of which we have record the open fireplace seems to have been the favorite device for heating and ventilating the habitations of man; although no modern house is considered complete without it either for use or for ornament; although the physician regards it as a most valuable ally in the mastery of disease;

and although its improvement has at all times claimed the attention of the most distinguished scientists and philanthropists, as well as of the practical mechanic, — yet we find it to-day so little understood and generally so incorrectly constructed that at least seven-eighths of the heat of the fuel is lost, and its capabilities as a ventilator are almost entirely neglected, so that our fireplaces may be properly described as devices contrived in the interest of the coal-merchant for the purpose of carrying up to the roof, in the form of smoke, the greatest possible amount of money, and of leaving the smallest possible amount of comfort behind. My definition of the word "chimney" would be this: A long tube open at both ends, the lower opening, called a "fireplace," being used to receive fuel and to emit smoke; the upper, to direct upon the roof from 85 to 95 per cent. of the heat and smoke generated below; generally so constructed as to carry off as much of the warm air of the room as is pure enough to be breathed, and cause large draughts of cold air to supply its place by rushing across the feet of the occupants in the manner best calculated to give them rheumatism, consumption, pneumonia, and other diseases. To complete the apparatus, screens are sometimes added to obstruct the circulation in the apartment.

WASTE OF HEAT.

In the city of Paris, according to M. V. Ch. Joly, there are used annually, for heating purposes, over 500,000 cubic meters of firewood alone, costing about 25,000,000 francs, and of this only 8 to 10 per cent., or in value about 2,000,000 francs, are actually turned into serviceable heat. The remainder, to the value of about 23,000,000 francs, annually disappears in the air without profit to any one. "What must we estimate the total amount of annual loss," says an eminent writer on ventilation, "in fuel, both of wood and coal, throughout the entire world, when we consider that the open fireplace is used to-day by over 50,000,000 of people!"

DANGEROUS DRAUGHTS AND IMPERFECT VENTILATION.

The "Encyclopædia Britannica" has on ventilation the following: "An open fireplace, unless the air enters from the ceiling, often produces little or no ventilation above the level of the chimney-piece, and, even then, it does not afford the best and purest atmosphere. The air above may be comparatively stagnant, and offensive in the extreme from the products of combustion and respiration, while a fresh current moves along the floor to the fireplace."

So great is the danger from cold draughts occasioned by open fireplaces as they are now constructed that one is said to be less liable to take cold standing in the open air, with the thermometer at freezing-point, than sitting on such a day in a room heated only by a bright open fire. So unequal is the distribution of heat in such a room that water may be frozen in one corner near the window-draughts, and boiled in another near the fire, and it has even been found possible to roast a goose in front of such a fire, while the air flowing by it into the chimney was freezing cold.

"I have no doubt in my own mind," said Count Rumford, "that thousands die in this country every year of consumption, occasioned solely by this cause."

In short, it would be difficult to point out any part of our usual domestic edifices which would show such a total absence of scientific principles as the construction of our fireplaces and chimneys.

PRACTICAL EXPERIMENTS ON THE WASTE HEAT AND AIR-CURRENTS.

The best authorities put the waste heat of our fireplaces at from 80 to 95 per cent., depending upon the shape of the fireplace, the nature of the fuel, the amount of the draught, and the size and nature of the flue; but I have been unable to find any satisfactory records of experiments made to corroborate their statements. Those made by General Morin answer most nearly, but still not entirely, our questions. I have, therefore, made a number of careful experiments, the results of some of which are given in the accompanying tables.

The first 6 experiments were made in houses built on the new land on Marlborough street, and the second series of 5 on the house No. 4 Pemberton square, Boston. The grates, fireplaces, and flues tested were of the so-called "most approved" modern construction, and calculated to utilize the greatest amount of heat possible without employing the peculiar or patented forms invented by Franklin, Galton, Winter, Gauger, Fondet, Joly, and others. The fireplace and grate used in the second series of experiments 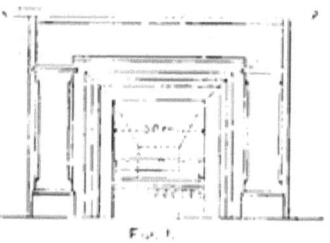 recorded in the accompanying tables are represented in front elevation in Fig. 1, and in section in Fig. 2. The dotted lines show the form of the back only of the fireplace used in the first series of experiments, the sides forming an angle of 135 degrees with the back, to improve their reflecting power. In the second series the fireplace was smaller, shallower, and the sides were at right angles with the back, the upper half of which inclined forward as shown in Fig. 2.

The entire length of the flue in this case was 22 meters (70 feet). Half-way up, or 11 meters from the fireplace, an opening was made in the flue large enough to receive a chemist's Centigrade thermometer, and the heat was tested at this point during the experiments in order to ascertain the amount lost by absorption in the upper half of the chimney. The thermometer was surrounded by putty to render it air-tight. When the readings were taken it was drawn out through the putty far enough to see the head of the mercury column, and then pushed back into its place. These readings were recorded by an assistant in columns 6 and 16 of the tables. (See Appendix, Tables I. and II.)

For want of space only two of the tables are given, the others agreeing substantially with them, and the results being nearly the same.

The anemometer used was one of Casella's most delicate instruments, lately imported from London. A careful test previously to making the experiments proved it to be exceedingly accurate and reliable. Where possible the observations were made every minute; but where this was impracticable the intervals were made as small as possible, and the figures for the intervening moments were obtained by calculation. The amount of wood burned in each experiment was exactly 3 kilograms.[1]

From these tables it will be seen that the amount of heat dissipated in the open air through the mouth of the chimney, from the combustion of 3 kilograms of dry pine wood, is sufficient to raise the temperature of nearly 16,000 cubic meters of air 1° Centigrade, according to the first experiment, or 16,980 cubic meters according to the second experiment; giving an average of 16,488 cubic meters raised 1°. This is equivalent to 5,070 units of heat, or enough to raise the temperature of over 5 tons of water 1° C., or to raise 50 kilograms of water from freezing to boiling point.

The greatest possible amount of heat which 3 kilograms of dry pine wood is capable of yielding being, according to Rumford, $3,590 \times 3 = 10,770$ units, we see that one half of the heat generated passes at once up through the chimney, and out at its mouth. Of the remainder we shall hereafter see that about four-fifths is absorbed in the brickwork, and either given out from the surfaces of the outer walls, or carried up in the air-space between the studding and the brickwork to the roof, whence it radiates into space.

By columns 2 and 12, Table I., we see that before the fire is lighted a ventilating draught of 73 meters per minute is caused by a difference of but 2 or 3 degrees in the temperature of the air in the chimney flue or house, and that of the outside air. But as this difference increases after the fire is lighted until it reaches 70° and 75°, as given in columns 4 and 14, we

---

[1] In this article I shall use the metric weights and measures, both because the calculations are made easier by so doing, and because these units have been adopted by most of the writers on the subject whose works we have occasion to consult.

1 kilogram or kilog. = 2,2046 or 2.2 pounds avoirdupois.

1 meter = 3.28 feet; 1 square meter = 10.8 square feet; 1 cubic meter = 35 cubic feet.

1° Centigrade = 1.8° Fahrenheit.

1° Fahrenheit = 0.55° Centigrade.

1 metric heat unit or calorie is the amount of heat required to raise 1 kilogram of water 1° Centigrade.

1 calorie = 3.968 English heat-units.

find the velocity of the draught rising to 285 meters per minute. Thus we have a chimney throwing out hot air raised nearly to the boiling-point of water at the rate of 285 meters or nearly 1,000 feet a minute! Yet in some of the chimneys tested on the Back Bay the waste was found to be much greater, one chimney giving out heated air at the rate of over 1,600 feet per minute raised to about the boiling-point! What might the saving be, if all this heated air could be separated from the smoke, partially cooled by dilution with fresh cool air, and brought into the house for use!

Returning to our table, we find by columns 6 and 16 the temperature of the draught at the middle of the flue, and, by calculation, an average of 885 heat units absorbed in the upper half of the chimney.

Now we know that the heat generated by our fuel is of two kinds, of which one is given up to the air supporting combustion, and passes entirely away with this air up chimney in combination with smoke and vapor; while the other, and by far the smaller part, is sent off from the fire in rays in all possible directions. This latter part may be considered as *uncombined* heat, or heat combined only with light as distinguished from that combined with smoke and air. Thus only the *radiated* heat of the fire is used in our rooms. The experiments of Peclet show that the radiating power of wood is, under the best possible circumstances, when the rays are all collected, only 23 per cent., leaving 77 per cent. to pass off with the air of contact. Therefore $.23 \times 10,770 = 2,477$ units radiated in the case of our 3 kilograms of wood.

In the average fireplace only one-third of these rays, or in our case 826 units, pass directly into the room, the rest falling upon the back, sides, or bottom of the fireplace, or entering the flue through the throat of the chimney.

In the fireplace represented in Figs. 1 and 2 (see page 3, *ante*) the back measures 2,500 sq. cm., the sides 500 each, the bottom 500, and the top 350, as per accompanying diagram, making in all 4,350 sq. cm., against 2,500 for the opening in front, so that the rays entering the room directly amount to $\frac{2,500}{4,350+2,500}$; or, considering the portion intercepted by the grate, to about one-third of the whole, or less than 8 per cent. of the entire heat generated by the fuel.

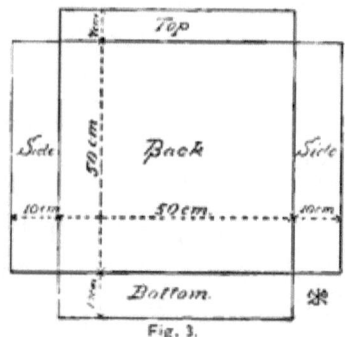

Fig. 3.

To this 8 per cent. must be added something for the return radiation from the brickwork, because, although a large portion of the radiated heat, striking the walls of the fireplace, is carried off by contact of the cold air entering the chimney under the influence of the draught, which, as we have seen, amounts to from 5 to 1,500 feet a minute, and part is absorbed by the brickwork, yet a certain portion is returned by radiation and reflection into the room. A simple calculation will give us the amount accurately enough for our purposes. The fireplace represented in our figures being small and blackened with smoke on its sides as well as back, no *reflected* heat could be counted upon. Moreover the radiating power of these walls being inversely as their reflecting power, what we lose in reflection we shall gain in radiation. The surface of the back, sides, and bottom measures 4,000 sq. cm. According to Peclet 1 sq. meter of brickwork radiates 3.59 units of heat per hour for 1° C. difference of temperature between the radiating and the receiving surfaces. Therefore 0.4 sq. m. would radiate 1.44 units per hour per 1° C. The temperature of the walls of the fireplace is shown in the second column of Table II., thermometers being placed in different parts of the back of the fireplace and the average temperature being taken. While the fire is burning brightly, the radiation from the walls of the fireplace would be partially intercepted by the fire itself; but taking the average temperature of these walls during the first 20 minutes at 220° C., and supposing that only one-half the radiation of these walls was intercepted by the fire, fuel, grate, etc., and finding 20° C. to be the average temperature of the objects in the room, we have $\frac{220-20}{2} = 100°$.

$$1.44 \times \frac{1}{3} \times 100 = 48 \text{ heat units.}$$

During the next 6 minutes the average temperature per minute being according to the table 210°, we have $210 - 20 = 190°$, from which we have, by calculating as before, 27.3 units radiated. Continuing the calculation in this way for each portion of the time, we have, for the total amount of radiation from the walls of the fireplace, 270 heat units.

Of this we may assume that one-half was radiated into the room and the other half lost, and we have 135 units ($=\frac{135}{1222}$ or $\frac{1}{2}$ of the radiated heat striking the walls of the fireplace) returned into the room to be added to the 826 units, or 8 per cent., of direct radiation. This gives 961 units, or a little less than 9 per cent. of the whole heat generated, for our result. According to Peclet only 6 per cent. is realized instead of this 9 per cent.

As for reflected heat, under certain circumstances a small amount may be added to the above results when the sides of the fireplace are kept white, or are tiled, and of the proper inclination for reflecting the rays. Inasmuch, however, as the radiation diminishes as the reflection increases, this may here be neglected.

Duelot's experiments show that the radiation from heated bodies is much greater in proportion at very high temperatures than at moderate temperatures. But we have not added anything to our figures for this, because we consider it more than balanced by losses in other ways, such as that due to imperfect combustion of the fuel, for which we have also made no account. It is estimated that with the ordinary fireplace, about ⅛th of the fuel is wasted in unconsumed smoke.

Our 9 per cent. so far found must, however, again be modified, in consideration of the heat taken from the room by the cold air entering the doors and windows under the influence of the draught.

In our case we have by Table I. an average of 833 cubic meters of air, which must have passed through the room, and into the fireplace from the outside. The average temperature of the room and objects contained in it having been raised one degree by the combustion of our 3 kilograms of wood (the doors and windows having been kept closed during the experiment), we have $833 \times 1 \times 1.29 \times .24 = 258$ units, or $\frac{258}{961}$ = about $\frac{1}{4}$ of the whole. Deducting 258 from 961 we have 703 units, or only 6 per cent. of the heat generated by the fuel, for the total amount of heat which can possibly be utilized from wood fires under the best conditions and most perfect form of ordinary fireplace, to say nothing of the fact that where the rooms are provided with the so-called ventilators near the ceiling, even this little heat is carried off almost as fast as it is formed!

Deducting from the 10,770 units generated by the fuel the 703 units utilized by radiation, and the 5,070 units escaping through the chimney mouth into the atmosphere, together with the eighth lost in unconsumed smoke, capable of generating 1,340 units, we have 3,660 units for the amount absorbed in the brickwork. Of this nearly 1,000 units were absorbed in the upper half. The remaining 2,660 must have been taken up by the lower half. In these experiments, however, the flues were cold at the outset, and the absorption on the part of the masonry was at its maximum. In winter, when the flues are kept constantly heated, but little is absorbed by the brickwork, its power of absorption being limited by the low conducting power of the material, and the amount lost at the top of the chimney is correspondingly greater.

With coal-fires more of the heat of combustion is utilized. Supposing that, under the best of circumstances and with coal having the greatest radiating power, we adopt the figure of Peclet of 50 per cent. for the radiating power, we have, as before, $.50 \times \frac{1}{2} + (\frac{2}{3} \times \frac{1}{2}) .50 = .24$. From this 24 per cent. deduct, as before, one quarter for the amount returned up chimney by the draught, and we have 18 per cent. for the total amount utilized, under the best possible circumstances, with the best possible fuel. According to Peclet only 12 per cent. instead of 18 per cent. is realized from a coal-fire.

RESULTS OF EXPERIMENTS.

Our experiments present the following curious results:—

1. Our 3 kilograms, or 6½ pounds, of wood served to raise the average temperature of our room less than 1° Centigrade, although the heat generated by the wood was sufficient to raise the temperature of 14 rooms of equal size from freezing to 68° Fahrenheit. (The room measured $20 \times 20 \times 10$ feet.)

2. While our fireplace was only sufficient, with 3 kilograms of dry wood, to maintain the temperature of the room at 1° C. (supposing the outside air stood at 0° C.) for a few minutes, the heat actually generated was sufficient to maintain the temperature at a little below 20° C., or 68° F., and to pass fresh air, raised from freezing to 68° F., through the room for ventilating purposes at the rate of one cubic meter a minute for 2 days of 12 hours each.

3. Supposing, again, that the outside air stood at the freezing-point,

we shall see by consulting the third column of Table II. that a person or object standing 50 cms. distant from the fire would have been heated by radiation up to $75° — 20° = 55°$ C., or $131°$ F., while the air flowing by him into the fire would have stood scarcely a degree above the freezing-point. At this distance three men would intercept nearly all the heat of the fuel, and all other parts of the room would fall to the freezing-point. This radiated heat itself would last at $55°$ only about 5 minutes, when it would fall $15°$, after which it would continue to fall as shown in the table.

At a distance of 1 meter, a person would be warmed only to $48° — 20° = 28°$ C., and 6 men would appropriate the greater portion of the heat of the fire, which would last, say, 5 minutes, and then fall $9°$. At a distance of 2 meters a person would be warmed (according to another experiment not here recorded) only $7°$ C., and at a distance of 4 meters only about $2°$ C. But if he happened to stand anywhere in the room sheltered from the direct radiation of the fire, he would enjoy a temperature scarcely half a degree above the freezing-point of water.

4. According to our table 3 kilograms of dry wood cut small served to give a bright fire only 10 minutes, and burned out entirely in 20 minutes. To keep a bright fire burning, as in this experiment, or, as is done in many houses in cold weather, for a day of 12 hours, would therefore require 144 kilograms of wood, which, according to Rumford, are capable of producing $3,590 \times 144 = 516,960$, or over a half million units of heat, which, if all were utilized in the proper manner, would be enough to keep the temperature of the room up to $68°$ F. in freezing weather for about 30 days of 12 hours each, equal to one month in midwinter, and give a change of pure air equal to one cubic meter a minute, heated, say, up to $60°$ F., for ventilation, during the whole time, it being supposed that the adjoining rooms and those above and below were inhabited and maintained at the same temperature, that the outside wall was double as well as the window, and that the door and window fitted well and were kept closed.

5. Finally, to raise the temperature of the room in which our experiment was made up to $68°$ F. and maintain it at this temperature, during a single day of 12 hours, would (even supposing the entrance of cold air were prevented in some way from increasing with the increased heat of the fire) require $20 \times 144 = 2,880$ kilogs. of wood, or sufficient, if all were utilized, to maintain the room at the same temperature and add to it a ventilation of 1 cubic meter of fresh air per minute raised to $60°$ F. for 20 months of freezing weather, or, allowing 3 months of such weather per year, it would accomplish the heating and ventilation of the room for *over 6 years!*

THE IDEAL FIREPLACE.

What now would be the action of a fireplace and flues ideally perfect?

Ideal perfection would imply: —

1. That all the heat generated by the combustion of the fuel be utilized in heating and ventilating the house, and that the combustion of the fuel be complete.

2. That the supply of fresh air introduced into the house to take the place of the foul air removed be guaranteed perfectly pure; warmed in winter to a temperature somewhat below that of the room; moistened enough to give it its proper hygrometric condition; abundant enough to supply amply the fire and the occupants; so distributed and located at its entrance as to cause no perceptible draught at any point; the gentle air current so directed that it should reach every part of the room; so steady that no part of it should pass over the some spot twice or be twice breathed by the occupants; and so regulated by simple valves as to be under perfect control.

3. That the flues include a special gas ventilator so arranged that all the heat generated by the combustion of the gas should be retained in the room and utilized, while the injurious products of combustion should be carried off.

4. That a complete ventilation of the rooms be effected, both in summer and in winter, without opening doors or windows.

5. That the chimney never smoke.

6. That the construction of the fireplace and flues be simple, durable, inexpensive, safe, and unobjectionable in appearance.

The open fireplace as ordinarily constructed, so much overestimated as a ventilator, satisfies the requirements above enumerated to the following extent: —

1. Only from 5 to 15 per cent. of the heat generated by the fuel is utilized in heating and ventilating the house. It must be borne in mind that that is not ventilation which provides only for the outlet of the air and ignores the inlet, and that a hundredth part of the heat of the fuel would be ample to abstract the bad air far more efficiently, if properly applied, than is done by the 85 or 95 per cent. now used.

2. The air introduced to take the place of the foul air removed is not guaranteed pure, but its purity or impurity is left entirely to chance. If the windows are tight, the fire draught will be supplied from the halls, neighboring chambers, or even water-closets and toilet-rooms, or, in other words, from soil and drain pipes, bringing poisonous gases and perhaps disease into the house; or, if disease be already there, distributing the noxious air from the sick-chamber into other parts of the house.

If the windows are not tight, the air entering will be too cold in winter, too hot in summer, and always loaded with whatever dust, dampness, or impurity may happen to be in the outer air, to the detriment of the lungs as well as of the furniture of the inmates.

Or, finally, if both doors and windows are closed and tight, as may sometimes happen with careful carpentry, and especially at night in bedrooms, either the air must come in through the chimney itself, causing the fire to smoke, or else no air is admitted, and suffocation is the result.

The history of ventilation furnishes numerous sad cases of such suffocation, cases where the smouldering fire and the sleeper, rendered insensible by smoke or gas, have evidently long struggled for life before either or both succumbed to the want of air.

We may add here that even when the supply of air chances to be pure enough, and abundant enough, and warm and moist enough, and otherwise satisfactory in its quality, it is still unable to ventilate the apartment properly because it is drawn directly up the chimney before it has had time to receive the necessary amount of heat to cause it to rise to the level of the heads of the occupants; while the impure air formed above the level of the mantel, and heated by the lungs and by the gas-burners, rises to remain a long time in the room and be breathed over and over again. Or, if special openings are provided above to carry off this upper stratum, what little pure air warmed by contact with the walls, heated by radiation manages to rise above the mantel, is, as before said, carried off with the impure air almost as fast as it is formed. Thus it often happens with large fireplaces and flues that the cold air enters faster than the warm air is produced, so that the more the fuel is piled on and the fiercer the fire, the more powerful become the freezing draughts and the lower the temperature of the room.

3. The gas-burners are seldom properly ventilated, and sometimes not at all. Breathing foul air is as injurious as drinking foul water, yet, while we would shrink with disgust from the idea of drinking water into which the drainage from our houses was known to flow, we allow our gas-burners to pour forth a continual stream of carbonic acid and other poisonous gases into our small reservoirs of breathing air, already sufficiently polluted by the exhalations from our bodies and lungs, without giving the matter a passing thought.

4. Complete ventilation in summer as well as in winter is, under the average construction, impossible without opening doors or windows.

5. The chimney often smokes.

6. In one respect our fireplaces and flues appear to approach the ideal, and that is in their simplicity; but is it not the simplicity of ignorance rather than that of science?

In order to be able to judge as to how far we may expect to approach our ideal, it will be necessary first to familiarize ourselves with some of the most important devices already tried or recommended by those who have given the subject most attention, and to study the causes which have thus far rendered their adoption so limited.

Many of these devices appear so excellent that it is hard to understand why they were not seized upon at once. But we must bear in mind that the majority of the public are aware neither of the waste of fuel they actually experience, nor of the importance of good ventilation. The style and color of the grate and mantel are of more importance than the construction of flues and all parts which are out of sight. That the pattern and color should be in accordance with the latest fashion is more important than either; and to expect fashion to yield to mere sanitary considerations would bespeak ignorance of one of the most marked peculiarities of human nature.

Then, too, we know how prone every Yankee builder is to avail himself of his liberty "to follow his own nose by way of a guidepost in the matter of a little science," and how loath he is to leave the beaten track.

These considerations, and the fact that many reject on principle all novelties, on account of the difficulty of distinguishing the good from the bad, are sufficient to render any persistent effort to improve our time-honored forms of building construction most onerous and discouraging, and it would be folly to expect even the most evident improvement, in a matter of this kind, to meet with anything more than a slow and partial recognition.

CHAPTER II.

HISTORICAL.

It is remarkable that, while the open fireplace was one of the earliest contrivances invented to contribute to the health and comfort of man, the upright flue for carrying off the injurious products of combustion should have remained one of the latest.

It is true that the principle of the modern chimney was probably understood long before the practice of constructing it became general; but it was so rare an object, even in the sixteenth century, as to have excited the surprise of Leland, who, speaking of Bolton Castle, in his "Domestic Architecture," thus expressed himself: "One thynge I muche notyd in the hawle of Bolton, how chimneys were conveyed by tunnells made on the syds of the walls betwyxt the lights in the hawle, and by this means, and by no covers, is the smoke of the harthe in the hawle wonder strangely conveyed."

According to Peclet, chimneys appear to have been unknown to writers of the early part of the fourteenth century.[1] But, once introduced, their merits appear to have been rapidly appreciated; since we find it stated that, in the reign of Queen Elizabeth, apologies were made to visitors if they could not be accommodated with rooms provided with chimneys, and ladies were frequently sent out to other houses where they could have the enjoyment of this luxury.

Thus the general use of the chimney is quite recent, and it was not until the time of Savot, Franklin, and Gauger, that we have record of any serious attempts to combine the cheerfulness of an open fireplace with the economy of an enclosed stove.

The science of the proper ventilation of buildings is still more recent. "Till the discoveries of modern science," says Dr. Reid, "revealed the nature and composition of atmospheric air, and the reciprocal action that ensues between it and the blood, the architect was, in respect to this question, like a traveller without a guide, and had no distinct appreciation of the position in which man is placed in respect to the atmospheric ocean in which he lives." Even where these facts are understood by scientific men, the great mass of the people still remain in ignorance of them, and the rough treatment to which our lungs are subjected

---

[1] "L'époque à laquelle il faut placer l'origine des cheminées est assez incertaine ; les auteurs du commencement du quatorzième siècle semblent ne les pas connaître. La date la plus ancienne, et en même temps la plus certaine où il ait été question des cheminées, est l'année 1347."

in the form of draughts, poisoning and vitiated air, and sudden changes of temperature, often inducing fatal diseases of the organs of respiration,— diseases which might be prevented if the elements of physics and hygiene were more generally taught,— shows how little the value of pure air is appreciated by the public. This want of knowledge and appreciation of the subject explains in a measure why the progress of improvement is so slow. The time has been too short to make men believe that an atmos-

Fig. 4. Primitive Smoke Flue. From Viollet-le-Duc.

phere apparently pure and transparent, as well as agreeable to the senses, may be filled with the most subtle poison. A hundred years is insufficient to work a revolution in the habits and prejudices of men for the sake of a thing which they can neither see, smell, feel, hear, nor understand.

What progress has been made will be seen from the following historical sketch:—

EARLIEST FORMS OF THE OPEN FIREPLACE.

In the earliest ages the chimney consisted of the entire house, the fire being built in the middle of the building or hut, and the smoke escaping from the roof, as is shown in Fig. 4. Barbarous as this arrangement may seem, it nevertheless has certain advantages we should not lose sight of in making our improvements. The heat of the fire is utilized to a far greater extent than is the case with that burning under our modern chimney. All the radiated heat is obtained and a large part of the heat of contact of air. As a ventilator it is superior to our modern apparatus, since no impure air can remain for a moment in the room, and the cold draughts entering are not drawn to a single spot limited by the height and size of the mantel, as with us, and being, therefore, less concentrated, are less dangerous.

In its manner of disposing of the smoke it is, of course, inferior, notwithstanding the statement of the owner of the hunter's cabin represented

Fig. 5. Backwoodsman's Log Cabin.

in the accompanying sketch, that the smoke never troubled him in the most unfavorable weather.

A central flue, constructed of sticks smeared on the inside with mud or clay, and descending from the opening in the roof to within a safe distance of the fire below, would improve the draught and prevent the smoke from blackening the roof, though at the expense of some of the heat.

The next step made to improve the draught by means of a flue is described by Viollet-le-Duc, in his "Habitations of Man," Fig. 6. But the description must have been purely imaginary, as no evidence exists of the use of such flues at the early age indicated by the writer. The fire was in this case supposed to be built against the wall of the house. Thus a large part of the radiated heat of the fire was cut off and no corresponding change was made to regain the proportion of heat thereby lost.

Fig. 6. Chimney of Logs. From Viollet-le-Duc.

Gradually, for the purpose of avoiding lateral currents of air, jambs were built on each side of the fire, to direct the air upon the fuel, and the chimney-flue was brought down to within a few feet of the fire. By this step another large portion of the radiant heat was lost, and the whole of the heat of contact of air, without an effort to obtain a corresponding compensation.

BRAZIERS AND PORTABLE FIRES.

In milder climates we find the portable brazier without any provision whatever for the outlet of the smoke. This system of heating was generally employed by the Greeks and Romans. It is still used in Spain, Italy, Algeria, and other warm countries. The braziers of the Greeks and Romans formed elegant pieces of furniture, often beautifully sculptured, as in Figs. 7 and 8. The Spanish portable brazier, Fig. 9, in which charcoal is burned, is rolled from room to room, warming each in succession. By this system the entire heat of the fuel is realized, but, on the other hand, the products of combustion, always disagreeable to the occupants, and highly injurious to the paintings and furniture, are extremely dangerous for the health.

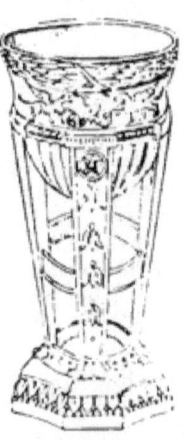

Fig. 7. Brazier.

Fig. 8. Brazier.

The combustion of 1 kilogram of coal, for instance, converts into carbonic acid all the oxygen contained in 9 cubic meters (or yards) of air. This, according to Peclet, renders 27 cubic kilograms of air unfit to breathe, so that the air of our room 20 × 20 × 10 feet, or of about 110 cubic meters capacity, deducting furniture, would be rendered irrespirable and would suffocate the persons attempting to breathe it, by the combustion of about 4 kilograms of coal. It is true that the heat generated by this quantity of fuel burned in the middle of a closed chamber, without chimney or other opening, would soon be so excessive as to require the opening of the windows. The 4 kilograms would raise the temperature of our room to $\frac{4\times 7000}{110\times 1.3\times 0.2377}$ = 823 degrees Centigrade, or about 1,500 degrees Fahrenheit, which would be nearly hot enough to melt brass. (In the equation, 7,000 represents the heating power of coal in units; 1.3 the weight of 1 *m. c.* of air at 0° C.; and 0.2377 the specific heat of air.)

Fig. 9. Spanish Portable Brazier.

The real danger results from the production of carbonic oxide, which gives much less heat. It is calculated that a hundredth part of this gas in the air is sufficient to kill warm-blooded animals. Hence the danger of using charcoal for fuel, as in the Spanish brazier, the products of combustion being largely carbonic oxide. A remarkable instance of death by charcoal fumes is given by the suicide of the son of the celebrated chemist Berthollet. He left us a vivid account of his own destruction by asphyxia in an air-tight chamber. Locking the door of the room and closing up all the cracks which might admit fresh air, he prepared a charcoal fire on a brazier, seated himself at a table with writing materials and a seconds marking-watch, marked the precise hour and then lighted the charcoal on the brazier before him. With all the method and precision of a scientific experiment, he recorded the various sensations he experienced, detailing the approach and rapid progress of delirium, and as suffocation began the language became more and more confused, the writing larger and more illegible, until the writer fell dead upon the floor.

In colder climates, where greater heating power is necessary, the brazier is of course insufficient. In the frigid zones, however, where wood and coal cannot be obtained, the brazier reappears in the form of the smoky lamp of the Laplander and Esquimau. Here economy approaches its maximum, the heating, lighting, and ventilation being effected by one and the same inexpensive agent, namely, putrid oil, burned under a hole in the roof of the hut. "The Greenlander," says Tomlinson, "builds a larger hut and contrives it better, but it is often occupied by half-a-dozen families, each having a lamp for warmth and cooking, and the effect of this arrangement, according to the remark of a traveller, 'is to create such a smell that it strikes one not accustomed to it to the very heart.'" The effect of this great economy, however, is shown in the bleared eyes and the stunted growth of the natives.

Finally, the last degree of economy in warming, if we can call that economy which saves fuel at the expense of health, is reached by the lace-makers of Normandy, who work warmed by the natural fires burning in the bodies of their domestic animals. They rent the close sheds of the farmers who have cows in winter-quarters. "The cows are tethered in a row on one side of the shed, and the lace-makers sit cross-legged on the ground on the other side, with their feet buried in straw. The cattle being out in the fields by day, the poor women work all night for the sake of the steaming warmth arising from the animals."[1]

We wonder at the backwardness of the civilized Greek and Roman in the use of their tripods, smile at the Spaniard with his barbarous rolling brazier, pity the Esquimau with his feeble and smoky lamp, and sympathize with the wretched lace-makers of Normandy in their close and sickly atmosphere, yet all the time forget that we ourselves allow the air of our rooms to be impoverished in the very same manner, and often to an even greater extent, by the noxious vapors pouring from our unventilated gas-burners.

---

[1] Tomlinson, *Warming and Ventilation.*

ORIGIN OF THE CHIMNEY.

The idea of building the fireplace against the side wall probably originated in England in the eleventh century, at the time of the Norman Conquest. Previously the chimney consisted merely of a hole in the roof, with a small wooden tower above to carry up the smoke. At the time of the Conquest, fortresses were constructed and the roofs used for defence, so that the central opening for smoke was rendered impossible. The fireplace was removed to an outside wall, and an opening made in this wall above the fire for the passage of the smoke, as in Fig. 10. The oblique opening in the wall gave place soon after the Conquest to the ordinary

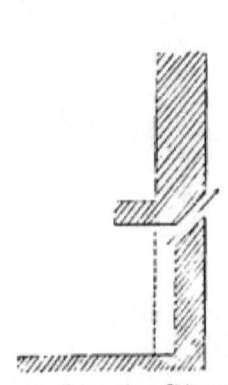

Fig. 10. Origin of the Chimney.

Figs. 11 and 12. Fireplace in Conisborough Castle.

chimney-flue. Figs. 11 and 12 represent the fireplace and flue in the great guard-room of Conisborough Castle, erected in or near the Anglo-Saxon period.

This form of flue naturally led to the ordinary chimney as it is now constructed. The fireplaces and flues were at first very large. In France a royal edict, as late as 1712 and 1723, fixed the size of the flue at 3 feet wide and deep enough to admit the chimney-sweep. In this country we have seen old-fashioned fireplaces 8 feet long and 3 feet deep. These caused such a draught that screens were necessary in the room to protect the inmates from powerful currents of cold air; but although the waste of heat was enormous, on account of the cooling effect of these strong draughts of outside air, it was nevertheless much less in proportion to the fuel burned than is the case with the smaller modern fireplace. Provided usually with a large hood projecting boldly into the room, and placed at a considerable height, sometimes 6 or 8 feet, above the hearth (Figs. 13 and 14), they radiated the heat generously into the room, and, although they did not pretend, any more than do our ordinary modern fireplaces, to heat the air of the apartment, they at least sufficed to warm amply the persons grouped around them or seated on the hospitable benches built upon the hearth itself.

As for smoke, it is undeniable that where but a small fire is required, as is usual in our smaller modern rooms, and the fireplace and flues are large, the hot-air current is greatly cooled by the cold air entering above the fire, and the rapidity of the draught is proportionally diminished. It is of course thereby rendered less capable of resisting any impediments to its passage which may be offered in the form of defective construction of the flue or imperfect ventilation of the apartment. But where the flue was perfect, and where sufficient air was brought into the room to supply the place of that drawn up the chimney, and where the hood projected well over the fire, a smoky chimney was found to be a rare occurrence, even with the largest fireplaces and with the smallest fires.

It is the custom when one of these ample fireplaces, built after the old-fashioned style, is found to smoke, to lay the blame to the size of the opening and flue, although nine times out of ten the real fault will be found to be in an insufficient ventilation of the apartment, or in a careless or irregular construction of the flue. Hebrard, in his "Caminologie," wrote in 1756 as follows: "It is surprising that we should allow these old chimneys to be changed in order to follow the fashion of the day, without taking the pains to examine whether the utility is as great as the novelty. It appears that it is not. It has been observed, on the contrary, that of the few old chimneys which have escaped remodelling there is scarcely one which smokes. Old men testify to the same effect in regard to those which existed in their time, while we have no hesitation in saying of the majority of our new chimneys that they do smoke."

The cause of this change was the suppression of the hood which had been built and recommended as of the utmost importance by Alberti,

Fig. 13. Fireplace of the Fourteenth Century. From Viollet-le-Duc.

Philibert Delorme, and others. The hood was dropped, partly because it was thought to interfere with the decoration of the apartment, and partly on account of the desire for novelty. (Figs. 15 and 16.) Unfortunately this modification involved a second, which had a still more injurious effect upon the heating power of the fire. The smoke, being no longer properly conducted to the flue, would, under adverse circumstances, enter the room, and the device of lowering the mantel was adopted to obviate the difficulty. This was done at first by adding a simple band of leather or of some other material below the mantel-shelf, then by movable registers

Fig. 14. — Fireplace of the Fifteenth Century. From Viollet-le-Duc.

or blowers of metal, and finally by lowering the mantel and shelf itself, which modification in the course of the eighteenth century brought the fireplace down to the form commonly met with in our day, — a form which, objects Labarthe, "utilizes neither the radiant nor the transmitted heat." Still another reason was given for the lowering of the mantel. It was urged by Serlio and Savot that this new disposition had only been introduced to protect the eyes from the heat of the fire. It was, however, argued with all apparent reason, by Hebrard, that the object sought could not in the least degree be obtained by this means, since it would be necessary for the purpose to give up chairs and warm one's self standing up.

I shall endeavor to show in the next chapter in what way these large, old-fashioned chimneys may be constructed, either with or without the hood, so as to render the draught, in all cases, both ample and unfailing.

The hearth in the middle of the hall still existed as late as the fourteenth century as a general custom. The great logs were simply

Fig. 15. Fireplace in House of Jacques Cœur, Bourges.

piled on andirons, and the smoke escaped through the louvre on the roof. Major J. S. Campion, an English traveller, gives the following description of a Spanish kitchen fireplace, showing that this rude form even now exists: "Almost in the middle of the room was a rough hearth, about 4 feet square and a foot high, and composed of tiles, flat stones, pieces of iron,—anything that would not consume. In its centre burned a fire of three sticks, laid star-fashion, with a blazing brushwood heaped on them. A large wooden hood, supported by massive rafters, caught and conducted such portion of the smoke as did not circulate about the room to a hole in the roof furnished with a rough louvre, through which it escaped; and from a cross iron of the hood hung a stout chain, terminating in a hook, by which was suspended a large pot full of potatoes slowly simmering." Wood was the ordinary fuel till the seventeenth century, and this was burnt on the capacious hearth, resting on the two standards, or *andirons*, a name which may have come from the Anglo-Saxon *brand-isen*, or brand-iron, or from the words *hand* or *end* iron.

Fig. 17.— English Mediæval Fireplace.

For the large kitchen fire the standards were strong and massive, but quite plain. "In the hall, that ancient seat of hospitality," says Tomlinson, "they were also strong and massive, to support the weight of the huge logs; but the standards were kept bright, or ornamental, with brass rings, knobs, rosettes, heads and feet of animals, and various grotesque forms. In the kitchen and in the rooms of common houses the standards were of iron, but in the halls, of copper, brass, or even silver."

FURTHER DEVELOPMENT OF THE OPEN FIREPLACE OF THE MIDDLE AGES.

In its primitive form it consisted of a simple niche cut in the thickness of the wall, the sides terminating in small piers supporting the massive hood, as shown in perspective view by Fig. 17, from Viollet-le-Duc. The oldest fireplaces of the Middle Ages were often circular in plan, the back of the fireplace forming one segment of the circle, and the mantel and hood the other. Those supposed to be of the twelfth century were not so large as those of a century later, and the mantel was apt to be formed of a single piece or of two pieces of material, as in that of the Cathedral of Puy en Velay, shown above, or in that of the private house in the old town of Cluny, France, represented in Fig. 18. Here the hood is supported by a single curved timber. In this example the entire thickness of the wall is used, the back of the fireplace being on a line with the outside of the wall, so that the masonry of the chimney shows in projection on the exterior. The hood is elliptical and resolves itself, as it ascends, into a circular flue. On the right and left are little shelves for lamps, corresponding to our modern gas-burners on the chimney-breast.

Fig. 17.— Hooded Mediæval Fireplace of the Thirteenth Century.

The low windows near the fireplace enabled the occupants to see what was going on in the street, while they sat by the fire.

Fig. 19 represents the old fireplace in Roslin Castle, of colossal dimensions and extreme simplicity of design. In these great fireplaces huge trunks of trees 6 or 8 feet long were sometimes burned. Seats were placed on and about the hearth, and the screens and jambs of the fireplace formed together a complete antechamber, as it were, apart from the large halls in which they were built, and here the family united to pass the long winter evenings and listen to the famous legends of olden times.

After the thirteenth century the kitchen, forming part of the main

Fig. 18. Fireplace in the Ville de Cluny, Rue d'Avril, No. 13. From Viollet-le-Duc (except figures and accessories).

Fig. 19. Fireplace in Roslin Castle.

house, and no longer a separate establishment, in which whole sheep and oxen were cooked at one time, was furnished with one or more of these massive fireplaces, of which Fig. 20 furnishes a beautiful example. It belonged to the Abbey Blanche de Mortain, was built of granite, and still bears the arms of the abbey and the triple pothanger with the iron plate behind the fuel.

Fig. 20. Kitchen Fireplace of Granite. From Viollet-le-Duc.

Here we have no piers at all, the hood resting on heavy corbels of granite, and the fireplace is built, as usual, in the thickness of the wall.

Up to the fourteenth century the fireplaces of private houses and châteaux were generally of great simplicity, and it was only later that we see any attempt at decoration.

Figs. 21 and 22 represent two fireplaces of the fifteenth century, with jambs of stone and hoods of wood plastered and curiously decorated. They are in the little town of Saint Antonin (Tarn-et-Garonne).

Fig. 23 gives a section of the first fireplace, showing the construc-

Fig. 21. From Viollet-le-Duc.

tion of the hood, which stands 1.77 meters (about 5 feet 9 inches) above the hearth. Fig. 24 gives a detail of a lower corner of the framework. The hood, being plastered, and having therefore the appearance of stonework, seemed to the eye too heavy to be self-sustaining. The artist has therefore taken the pains to carve upon the surface heavy cables, in the hopes of being able thereby to diminish in a measure this disagreeable effect of weakness.

The second fireplace is more profusely decorated, and chains are added, as well as man-power, on the right and left, to assist the cable in supporting the heavy hood.

Fig. 25 represents one of the richly sculptured fireplaces in the Château d'Arnay-le-Duc, of the sixteenth century. It is 2.50 meters long by nearly 2 meters high, and stands in a room 4.20 meters high.

Chapter III. contains a figure of the great fireplace in the Council Chamber of Courtray, built in the Elizabethan style. Although decorated with the finest sculpture, it has nevertheless a bold and massive as well as

Fig. 22. Fireplace of the Fifteenth Century. From Viollet-le-Duc.

a highly picturesque effect, and must be considered as one of the most beautiful examples of its style and period.

The fireplaces thus far described have not exceeded 8 or 10 feet in width. When very large halls or saloons in palaces or public buildings were to be heated they sometimes measured 30 or 40 feet, and were decorated in a most sumptuous manner. In this case, however, it was necessary to support the mantel by intermediate piers, as shown in Fig. 26. When these piers extended from the front to the back they formed, under a single mantel, separate fireplaces, each having a distinct flue of its own, as shown in Figs. 27 and 28, the former being from the Château de Coucy, France, and the latter from the Grand Hall of the Palais des Comtes of Poitiers.

The subdivision of the opening and flue into several parts had other objects besides that of properly supporting the mantel. The ties or withes strengthened the walls, and the draught of each was materially improved by having its own small, independent flue. When the fire was first lighted, or when less than the ordinary amount of the heat was required, it was possible to confine the fire to a single section. By this arrangement each part, besides having sufficient draught of itself, served also to heat and improve that of the rest.

The fireplace represented by Fig. 28 was built in the 15th century, and occupies one end of the hall in which it stands. "It is," says Viollet-le-Duc, "no less than 10 meters long and 2.30 meters (7 feet) high under the mantel. .... In the interior of the public buildings as well as in the exterior, the Middle Age understood how to produce imposing effects of architecture, which make the treatment even of our most important modern buildings seem weak and insignificant by comparison.

"When the counts of Poitiers, in their grand robes of state, sat enthroned in this hall, surrounded by their officers; when behind the feudal court blazed the three fires on their three hearths; and when, to complete the picture, the assistants were seated on benches before the gorgeous windows above the mantel, one can imagine the respect that a scene of such nobility and grandeur ought to have inspired in the minds of the vassals assembled around the court of their lord. Certainly one should feel himself triply in the right to be able to defend his cause before a tribunal so nobly seated and surrounded."

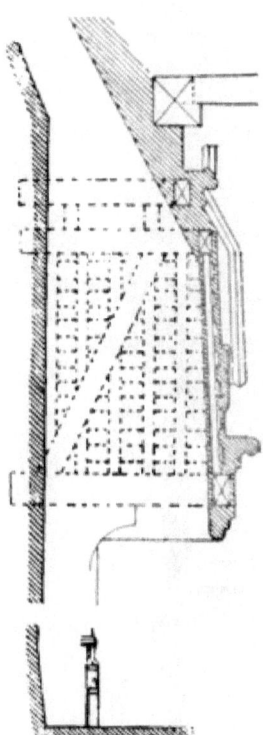

Fig. 23. Section of Fireplace of the 15th century. From Viollet-le-Duc.

Fig. 24. Details of the construction of the Hood. From Viollet-le-Duc.

Fig. 25 Stone Fireplace in the Château d'Arnay-le-Duc. Sixteenth Century. From Sauvageot.

EFFORTS TO IMPROVE THE DRAUGHT AND ECONOMIZE THE FUEL.

Interesting and beautiful as were these immense fireplaces of the Middle Ages, they were, as then constructed, open to the objection of being too expensive for ordinary use both in first cost and in their large consumption of fuel. For the majority of our modern rooms they would be altogether out of proportion in size, and about as much in place as would be a smelting-furnace for a domestic oven, or the grand portal of a cathedral for the entrance of an ordinary dwelling. Their capacious throats engulfed huge quantities of air from the room,— much more than

30   THE OPEN FIREPLACE.

Fig. 26   Fireplace in Linlithgow Palace.   From "Antient Domestick Architecture" (except figure).

Fig. 27.   Fireplace in the Château de Coucy, France.   From Viollet-le-Duc.

was necessary to support the combustion of the fuel,[1] — and, as this air could not conveniently be allowed them, where no economical means of warming it as it entered the room was known, they smoked (as any sensible chimney would do under the circumstances), and the only way that could be imagined to diminish the smoking was to diminish the size of the fireplace opening. This diminution took place as has already been described, and the fireplace assumed its present economical proportions.

The chimney continued to smoke, however, and it was seen that the cure had not as yet been discovered.

The first recorded effort to study the matter seriously on a scientific basis was that of Louis Savot, a physician of Paris, born in 1579, and died in 1640. Savot made a study of architecture from a sanitary point of view, and, having found in the smoky chimney an unusually troublesome patient, he set to work, like a true physician, to investigate the

Fig. 28. Fireplace in the Great Hall of the Palais des Comtes de Poitiers.

causes of the disease. But his success was only partial. The treatment he administered was quieting and salutary; but he failed to discover the real trouble and the secret of its cure. He improved the form of the fireplace opening by diminishing its width, so that less cold air could enter on each side of the fire, and he showed that the flue should be smooth to lessen the friction of the ascending smoke.

His is the first recorded attempt to save the waste heat of the smoke and the back of the fire. The famous fireplace at the Louvre, of which

---

[1] To support the combustion of say 3 kilograms of wood about 30 cubic meters of air are necessary, whereas we have seen by our Table I, that over 800 cubic meters passed up our small chimney. Thus over 20 times as much as is necessary to support combustion, and 10 times as much as would generally be necessary for ventilation, are used even with our small fireplaces.

Fig. 29 gives the front elevation, and Fig. 30 the section, was first brought into public notice by him, and shows the manner in which this was done. The room is warmed not only by direct radiation, as is usual with the ordinary fireplace, but also by the heat of contact of air. The air of the room enters the opening shown under the grate, passes behind the back of the fireplace and above the top, as shown by the arrows, and returns heated into the room through the round openings just under the mantel moulding. The ornamental bands passing in front of these openings appear to have been designed to deflect the warmed air upwards as it issued from them, and prevent its returning at once into the fireplace. To admit of this circulation of air the fireplace was, of course, made double, as shown, and the inner box was made of iron. In this way a portion of the cold air at the bottom of the room was heated and tended to rise to the top, and a certain amount of heat was saved. This ingenious con-

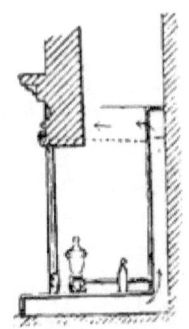

Fig. 29. Fireplace at the Louvre. Front Elevation. Fig. 30. Fireplace at the Louvre. Section.

trivance does not appear to have been appreciated or successful, though, since the time of Savot, the arrangement has, with slight modifications, been patented over and over again as a new invention. By it neither was the air of the room changed nor was the draught of the chimney improved, and the saving of heat does not appear to have been sufficient to bring about its introduction. A simple modification in the nature of its air supply, however, would have rendered this invention of the greatest value. By taking the supply of air to be heated from the outside instead of from the room itself, we have the principle of the so-called ventilating fireplace, hereafter to be described, and in consideration of its simplicity it would have formed one of the best of its class known. To secure the air-space below the hearth the fire was raised 3 or 4 inches above the general floor level. This rendered the fire more efficient in warming the floor of the room, inasmuch as a greater number of rays of heat would evidently strike the floor, and all at a better angle.

Fig. 34 shows, in section, another form of Savot's invention.

When the column of air in an upright flue is heated and becomes lighter than the surrounding air, it is no longer able to maintain its equilibrium with the colder and denser column outside, which, therefore, rushes into the house through the cracks and crevices, driving the warm air up the chimney until the balance is restored. If, now, these cracks are all closed, the cold air will force its way into the room through the chimney itself, descending on one side of the flue, while the hot air and smoke ascend on the other. A struggle will ensue between the two opposite currents, causing the cold air to enter spasmodically, or in puffs, bringing part of the smoke with it.

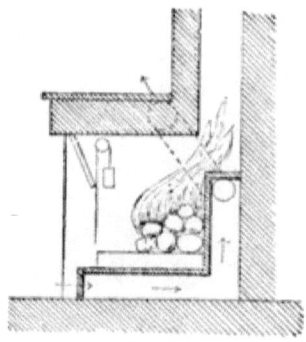

Fig. 31. Savot's Fireplace.

But let a separate inlet be made for the outside air and it will enter the room in a steady stream, and drive the smoke smoothly and rapidly up the flue. In a great many cases a smoky chimney may be cured by observing this simple law. The first really important step in improving the chimney draught, then, was made when this principle was recognized, and a sufficient opening provided for the admission of the outside air. The manner, however, in which the renewal of the air was at first accomplished was such as to improve the draught only at the expense of the ventilation of the room, as will be seen by examining the accompanying Fig. 32. It represents the apparatus of Sir John Winter, invented in 1658.

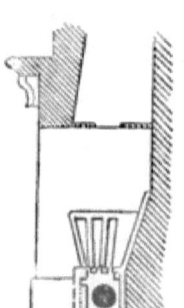

Fig. 32. Winter's Fireplace.

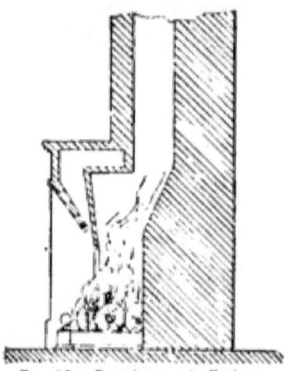

Fig. 33. Fireplace with Bellows.

Fresh air was brought in under the grate from the outside and acted on the fire as a powerful blower. A valve was placed in the supply-pipe, and by it the amount of entering air was regulated to the requirements of the fire. It will be seen at once that when the supply-pipe was large enough and the valve was opened the fire would be supplied with air entirely by this pipe, and all objectionable draughts through window and door cracks be effectually debarred. But it must also be borne in mind that by just as far as the draught was supplied from this source, by just so far would the ventilation of the room be reduced, and if the pipe supplied all the air necessary the ventilation would be nothing.

Fig. 33 represents the section of another form of the "blower" chimney, almost entirely abandoned at the present day, but at the time of its invention much in vogue. The fresh air is brought in a canal from the outside and turned on the fire from above, passing between the two plates represented in section under the mantel. This has all the objections and none of the advantages of the blower of Winter. The ventilation of the room is destroyed; a cold current of air is produced in the neighborhood of the fire; and the point of delivery of cold air is not located favorably for stimulating the fire.

Still another form has been much praised, though without a shadow of merit. By it the fresh air is introduced into the room directly from the outside at the level of the floor, just in front of the fireplace, under a fender perforated for the purpose. The form of the fender is such as to direct the incoming air forward upon the fire as it enters. This is the worst possible form of fireplace; and besides having all the objections enumerated above is liable to clog with dirt, and is difficult and expensive to construct.

A modification in the *manner* of supplying the fresh air, so that it could be used to ventilate and warm the room before feeding the fire, would have rendered Winter's invention of the greatest value.

His contrivance was, therefore, also a failure, though it has, since his time, after having undergone slight modifications not affecting its general principle, been frequently patented as a new idea. It only remained to combine the inventions of Savot and Winter to produce most useful results.

THE VENTILATING FIREPLACE.

This combination was made, in 1713, by Gauger, the real inventor of the ventilating fireplace, and, indeed, of almost all the most important principles of improvement in the form of the fireplace since the time of Savot. He gave the fireplace the elliptic form as shown in Fig. 34, instead of the square form hitherto used, for the purpose of improving its reflecting power. He showed that, with the rectangular jambs, very few of the rays of the fire are reflected into the room. Thus,

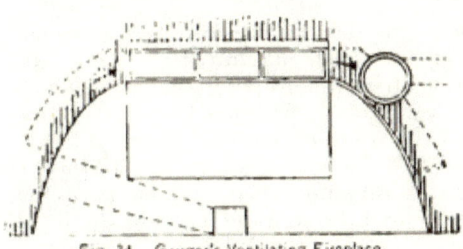

Fig. 34 Gauger's Ventilating Fireplace.

if we suppose a fire to be at F in Fig. 35, in an ordinary fireplace, only two of the rays represented by dotted lines as striking the jamb would be reflected into the room, the rest being thrown upon the opposite side, or upon the fuel or back of the fireplace, or up the flue. With the curved back, however, all the rays come into the room. "Geometricians," he says, "are sensible that all radii which set out from the focus of a parabola and fall upon its sides are reflected back parallel to its axis." So any ray falling from the fire or parabolic focus F or F'. Fig. 36, and striking the back of the fireplace, will come into the room. The same will happen to any ray coming from any part of the fire intermediate between the two foci F and F'.

The fireplace of Gauger, besides the parabolic jambs and a small *soufflet*, or blower, of Winter, had also, after the principle of Savot, hollow back, jambs, hearth, and mantel, for the pur-

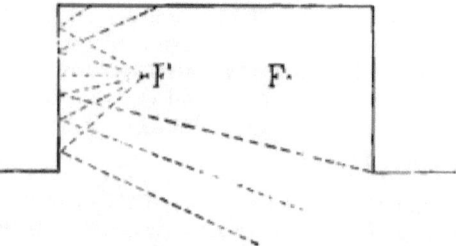

Fig. 35. Diagram showing the Direction of Reflected Rays.

pose of pouring into the room a copious supply of fresh air heated in these hollow walls. But, unlike Savot, he brought the air direct from the outside for ventilation. These spaces were called caliducts or meanders, and are shown in Fig. 37. They contained perpendicular or horizontal divisions or baffles, so arranged as to cause the air to circulate in the hollow spaces, in

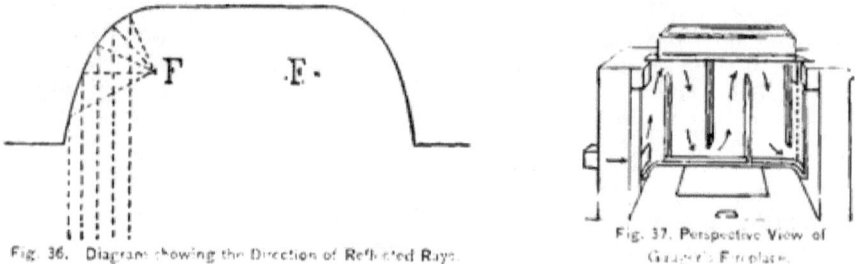

Fig. 36. Diagram showing the Direction of Reflected Rays.

Fig. 37. Perspective View of Gauger's Fireplace.

the direction of the arrows, as much as possible, before entering the room.

The temperature and amount of the fresh air introduced into the room was regulated by a valve in the air-channel acting like a two-way water-cock. A small cylinder, Fig. 38, revolved within a larger fixed one

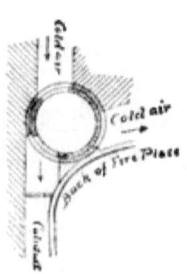

Fig. 38. Fresh-air Supply Valve.

in such a way that the cold air could be passed directly into the room, or first into the caliducts and thence into the room, or shut off altogether. The axis of the revolving cylinder passed through the cover of the fixed cylinder, and had a small lever attached to it by means of which it was turned by the hand into certain positions marked on a small dial. The caliducts were made of iron or brass. He preferred to place them only in the back of the fireplace, as shown in Fig. 34, leaving the sides solid and lined with metal.

The object of the *soufflet* was to bring a small column of air directly under the fire to act as a blower in lighting it. The fire once lighted, the *soufflet* could be closed by a valve, and all the fresh air turned into the room through the regular openings above. This fireplace of Gauger is the legitimate ancestor of scores of modern patents, whose authors are either ignorant of or have failed to acknowledge their descent therefrom.

In reading his work "La Méchanique du Feu," we see that the author was in want of a proper word to express his idea. The word "ventilation" did not then exist. Dr. Desaguliers, the translator of Gauger's treatise, was the first to use it.

The objection to the fireplace of Gauger is, that it is somewhat expensive, and difficult to cleanse or repair when out of order.

To give the sloping back the parabolic form is almost too much of a refinement, and the *soufflet* is unnecessary where sufficient air is provided by the caliducts. Moreover, the hottest part of the fireplace is just above the flame rather than behind or at either side. Therefore the caliducts of Gauger do not occupy the most advantageous position with respect to the fire. By modifying these details and improving the form of the chimney-throat the arrangement might be made much more perfect. The external air, in passing through the caliducts, is, nevertheless, raised to a temperate heat, rises and spreads itself through the chamber, again cools, descends, and, after ventilating the room, supplies the fire with air, and escapes up chimney. The Gauger fireplaces were constructed for the combustion of wood fuel. Dr. Desaguliers modified them for coal, and put up a considerable number of them in London. For a time they were appreciated, and rose rapidly into favor; but, unfortunately, an outcry was raised against them by scientific opponents of Dr. Desaguliers, who declared that these fireplaces "burnt the air, and that burnt air was fatal to animal life;" and the death-warrant of the new fireplace was signed. When used again they appeared under a different name, and protected by patent rights. The unfortunate Dr. Desaguliers mournfully remarked, "As I took so much pains and care, and was at some expense to make this arrangement of air useful, I can't help complaining of those who endeavored to defeat me in it."

SMOKE-CONSUMING FIREPLACES.

In 1682 the savants of Paris were attracted by the exhibition of the "Furnus Acapnos" (smokeless stove), invented by Dalesme.

It was simply a fireplace resembling a large clay pipe, Fig. 39, and its object was to consume its own smoke by causing it to pass downwards through the burning fuel before entering the chimney-flue. In the ordinary fireplace a large portion of the fuel escapes unconsumed in the form of smoke, which, in large cities like London, becomes a serious nuisance, hanging over the city in the form of a dark cloud, and filling the atmosphere with soot and impurity. To consume this smoke it is only necessary to bring it in contact with the glowing cinders of the fire, when it will at once ignite and give out its heat. The fuel, wood or coal, is placed in the vase over the grate bars. From the ash-box below the grate bars an iron smoke-pipe leads into the brick flue, which has no other inlet for air than through the fuel in the vase. The upper part of the iron smoke-pipe is then heated by a lamp, in order to establish a draught through the fuel. Brushwood is lighted at the top of the coal, and this, burning downwards, ignites the entire mass. The smoke of any new fuel supplied from above is consumed in passing through the glowing coals already ignited.

Justel, who described this arrangement to the Royal Society in 1681, says that "the most fetid things, matters which stink abominably when taken out of the fire, in this engine make no ill scent, neither do red herrings broiled thereon. On the other hand, all perfumes are lost, and incense makes no smell at all when burned therein."

The invention of this device was claimed by a German named Leutmann, who called his fireplace the "Vulcanus Famulans,"— of which Fig. 40 gives the appearance.

But it is difficult to see how the draught could be effected in

Fig. 39. Dalesme's "Furnus Acapnos."

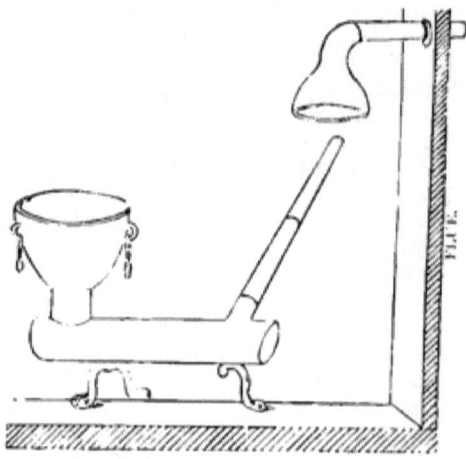

Fig. 40. Leutmann's "Vulcanus Famulans."

this machine, both on account of the break at the end of the iron smoke-flue, which would admit the external air, and on account of the small size of this flue. For these reasons Franklin gives it as his opinion that the invention not only did not belong to the German at all, but that he did not even understand the principle and working of the machine he claimed as his own.

Fig. 41 represents another smoke-consuming apparatus, similar in principle to the preceding, but placed against the wall like an ordinary fireplace. To establish a draught it is necessary to burn some kindlings within the little door placed above the grate before lighting the

Fig. 41. Smoke-consuming Fireplace.

fuel in the latter. This form of fireplace is objectionable, on account of its liability to smoke upon slight provocation.

Mr. Touet-Chambor attempted to overcome this objection by placing

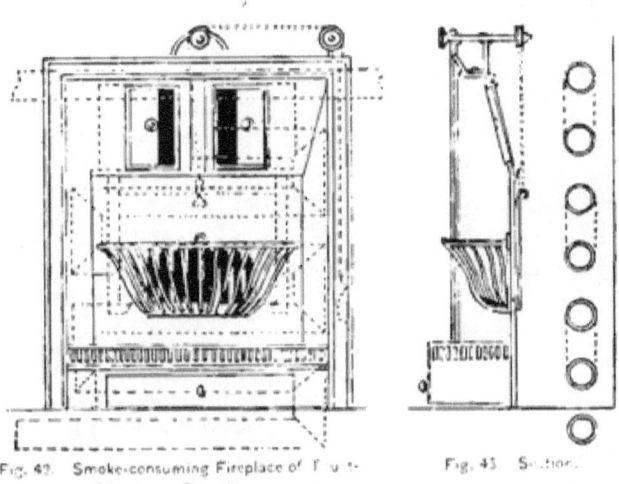

Fig. 42. Smoke-consuming Fireplace of Touet-Chambor. Front View.   Fig. 43. Section.

the grate in a niche, as in Figs. 42 and 43, and having two openings into the flue, one above, as in the ordinary fireplace, to use when the fire is first

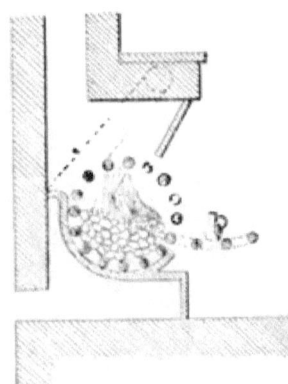

Fig. 44. Franklin's Smoke-consuming Grate.

lighted, and one below to reverse the flame. He added the tubes behind the fire-back to save the heat of the smoke and flame, by warming in them fresh air from the outside. The position of the upper openings, however, is such that their presence is far from being an infallible cure to smoking, and the objectionable appearance of the fireplace, when partially blackened by smoke, can easily be imagined.

These objections may be removed by certain modifications hereafter to be shown.

Franklin accomplished the same result, of consuming the smoke, in a different manner. Instead of reversing the flame, he reversed the grate. The device is shown in Fig. 44. The grate is cylindrical in form and revolves upon a fixed seat. The fresh fuel is thrown in through the door, represented in the figure as opened and supporting a pitcher. This door is opened for the purpose by means of a poker. The door is then closed, and the grate revolved by means of the poker, so as to bring the fresh coals underneath those already burning.

By this means the smoke of the fresh fuel is obliged to pass through the fire or red-hot coals, and is ignited.

In 1815, a Mr. Cuttler took out a patent for a smoke-consuming grate, with a chamber or magazine attached, for containing sufficient fuel to last all day. (Fig. 45.) The following description is from Rees's "Cyclopedia:" "The bottom plate of the chamber is movable, and, by means of a wheel and axle, the fuel contained in the chamber can be raised so as to bring a portion of it into the grate at the lower part or from beneath, and thus from time to time replace the fuel that is consumed without the trouble of throwing on coals. To make the fuel burn, the flue must be so constructed as to produce a strong draught through and across the top of the fire. Introducing the fresh coals from beneath causes the smoke therefrom to be consumed in passing through the superposed hot coals. Another improvement is to reduce or extinguish the fire ; the fire is lowered into the chamber beneath the grate, and is thus deprived of a supply of fresh air, and is consequently soon extinguished." If by this means the smoke could be entirely consumed, soot and chimney-sweeping would be unknown, and smoke could not enter the room, because it would cease to exist, and a fire so readily extinguished would be a great source of comfort to the anxious house-keeper.

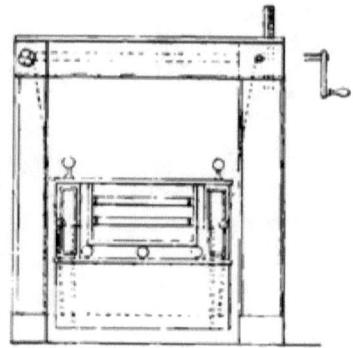

Fig. 45. Cuttler's Smoke-consuming Grate.

Dr. Arnott effected the same object by a somewhat simpler means in his "Smokeless Fireplace." (Fig. 46.) His coal chamber has, like Cuttler's, a false bottom or piston supported by a piston-rod with notches, in which a catch engages so as to support the piston at any required height. By placing the poker in one of these notches, and resting its point on some fixed support, it may be used as a lever for raising the piston, and bridging a fresh supply of fuel into the grate. Should it be necessary to replenish the coal-box, while the fire is burning, as when the piston has been raised to its full height, a shovel or spade, which may be made for the purpose, is pushed in over the piston to take its place, while the piston is lowered. The spade is then raised in front by its handle, presses upwards the two front bars of the grate, which bars are arranged loose for the pur-

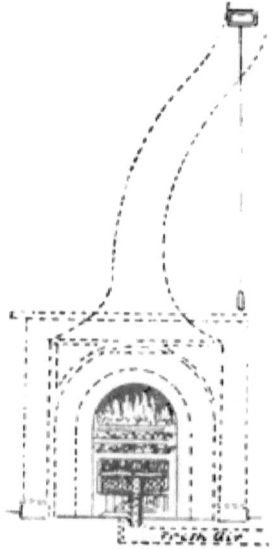

Fig. 46. Dr. Arnott's Smokeless Fireplace.

pose, and exposes the mouth of the coal-box, and a new charge of coal is shot in. It is, of course, important that the piston should fit accurately in the coal-box to prevent ingress of air from below, or, in other words, to limit the combustion to that part of the fire which is visible from the room. In recommending this device, Dr. Arnott stated that the cost of washing the clothes of the inhabitants of London was greater by two and a half million pounds sterling a year than for the same number of families resident in the country, to say nothing of the injury of such articles as carpets, curtains, female apparel, books and paintings, decorations of

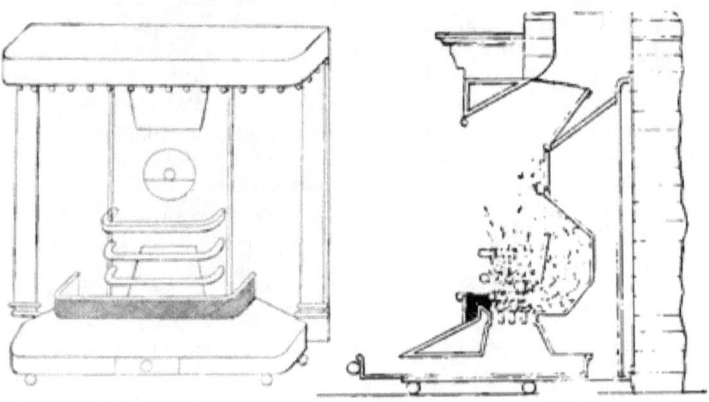

Fig. 47   Atkins & Marriot's Smoke-consuming Grate.   From Edwards   Fig. 48.

walls and ceilings, and even the stones and bricks of the houses themselves, from the same cause. He also urged that the frequent washing of hands and face led to an increased consumption of soap; and that many trees and shrubs could not live in a smoky atmosphere like that of London.

Nevertheless the complete combustion of the smoke will not render it wholesome to breathe. Some injury is no doubt caused by inhaling soot; but by passing the smoke through the fire in some smoke-consuming apparatus, while we save the heat, we convert the visible soot into invisible acids, carbonic, sulphurous, and pyroligneous, and ammonia, etc., of which, with water, it is composed.

Figs. 47 and 48 represent the smoke-consuming grate of Atkins and Marriot, an ingenious contrivance, which introduced fresh coal at the bottom of the grate as it was wanted. The section shows clearly how this was done. The order was to obviate the possibility of the whole body of coal getting into a state of active combustion, as in Cutler's grate. It either was not understood, or was for some reason practically objectionable, for it does not appear to have met at any time with success, and was soon forgotten.

These smoke-consuming fireplaces never came into general use on account of their awkward appearance, and the inconvenience of managing them. They involve machinery which is a little liable to get out of order, and few house-keepers are philosophers enough to be willing to undertake the management of a machine requiring especial mental effort, where the advantages are not directly visible to the senses. The average servant is thoughtless and impatient enough to prefer the primitive method of "discharging an avalanche of coals" upon the fire from the hod, to going through the experiments with the lever, ratchet, wheel and axle, recommended by Cuttler and Arnott.

Moreover, the complete combustion of the smoke, and, indeed, everything else connected with the fire, has been considered of minor importance, compared with obtaining a "good draught" at any sacrifice. If we assume that but an eighth or a tenth part of the fuel takes the form of unconsumed smoke, and consider that a tenth part of the entire heat generated by the fuel is more than we ordinarily realize, the saving by the use of a smoke-consuming apparatus would, in an ordinary fireplace, amount to only about a hundredth part. It is evident, therefore, that such a refinement on the score of *economy* is absurd, *so long* as we allow the waste in other ways to be so large. If we throw away nine-tenths of the fuel consumed, we cannot complain of the loss of the one-tenth of the remainder which is unconsumed.

IMPROVEMENT IN THE FORM OF THE CHIMNEY-THROAT.

The next important step made was in the improvement of the form of the smoke-flue where it connects with the fireplace. Cold air, being heavier than warm, will fall below the latter, and press it upwards to make way for itself. Thus the air in the neighborhood of the fireplace will press the hot smoke up into the chimney-throat. If this throat is only large enough to take the smoke, hot air only will enter the flue, and the draught will be rapid. But if the throat is larger than necessary, that part of the cool air of the room which enters the fireplace and becomes most heated by the fire, and next in buoyancy to the smoke, will, in its turn, be pressed up by the cooler air behind it, and enter the flue alongside of the smoke. Indeed, the entire volume of the air of the room, being warmer than the outside air, will tend to enter the flue with the smoke, so long as there be room provided for its entrance. The heat of the column, and consequently the rapidity of its rise, will therefore be proportionately diminished. For this reason the throat of the chimney should be contracted until it is no larger than is sufficient to carry off the products of combustion. A similar contraction throughout the entire length of the flue would be desirable, were it not that an allowance must be made for clogging up by soot, and for the resistance by friction to the passage of the air offered by the rough walls of the flue.

The first to recognize and apply this principle was Count Rumford (1796–1802). He published a number of valuable and interesting essays on various matters of domestic economy, one of which was devoted entirely to fireplaces and chimneys. But he is to be blamed for not investigating or at least acknowledging the progress made by his predecessors in this particular. He says, "It is, however, quite certain that the quantity of heat which goes off combined with the smoke vapor and heated air is much more considerable, perhaps three or four times greater, at least, than that which is sent off from the fire in rays; and yet, small as the quantity is of this radiant heat, it is the only part of the heat generated in the combustion of the fuel burned in an open fireplace, which is ever employed, or which can ever be employed, in heating a room;" and again, "As it is the radiated heat alone which can be employed in heating a room, it becomes an object of much importance to determine how the greatest quantity of it may be generated from the combustion of fuel." Thus, however much good he may have done in improving the form of the chimney-throat, and in calling public attention to the advantages of bevelled over rectangular jambs, he certainly also did much to discourage any further effort in economizing the waste heat of the smoke, and should therefore be considered as having really done more than any other one man to *retard* the proper development of the subject. He complains of the enormous waste of heat, and regrets that no means of saving it can be invented, in the face of the discoveries of both Savot and Ganger. Even his bevelled jambs for better reflecting the rays into the room had long since been recommended by Ganger. They were brought forward as quite new by Rumford. In speaking of the waste in unconsumed smoke, he says, "I never view from a distance, as I come into town, this black cloud which hangs over London, without wishing to be able to compute the immense number of chaldrons of coal of which it is composed; for, could this be ascertained, I am persuaded so striking a fact would awaken the curiosity and excite the astonishment of all ranks of the inhabitants, and *perhaps* turn their minds to an object of economy to which they had hitherto paid little attention." Yet he gives no way of consuming the smoke, or of alleviating the evil.

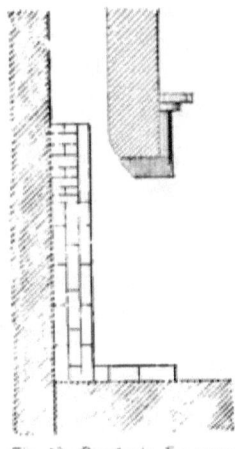

Fig. 49. Rumford Fireplace.

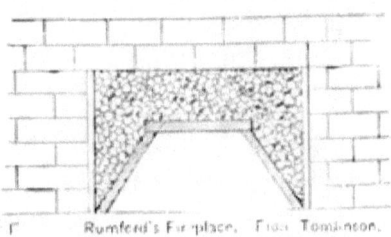

Rumford's Fireplace. From Tomlinson.

Figs. 49 and 50 represent the so-called Rumford stove or fireplace. He contracted the area of the fire-chamber, and gave the sides an angle of 135° with the back, or, which is the same thing, of 45° with the front of the fireplace, in order, as he said, to reflect the greatest possible amount of heat into the room. He considered the best proportions for the chimney recess to be when the width of the back was equal to the depth from front to back, and the width of the front or opening between the jambs three times the width of the back. These proportions are used to-day, and are undoubtedly the best. He objected to the use of iron for these surfaces on account of its great heat-conducting power, which wasted the heat and cooled off the fire; but advocated some non-conducting substance, such as fire-clay. He also objected to circular covings, on the ground that they produced eddies or currents, which would be likely to cause the chimney to smoke.

But his chief, or perhaps only, real improvement consisted in the reduction of the size of the chimney-throat, and the rounding off of the lower edge of the chimney-breast, as shown in Fig 51, in order, as he said, to afford less obstruction to the ascent of the smoke. When the chimney required sweeping, the plate or flagstone opposite this rounded edge could be removed so as to open the throat, and be replaced after the operation. This form, as given by Rumford, is, however, still defective. The smallest part of the flue should be at the bottom, as shown in Fig. 52, so as to prevent the entrance into the flue of unburnt air from the room.

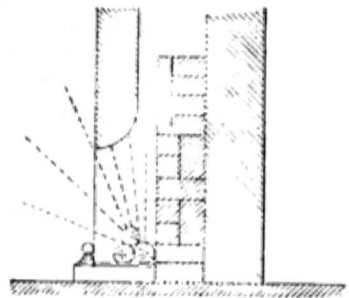

Fig. 51. Another form of Rumford's Fireplace.

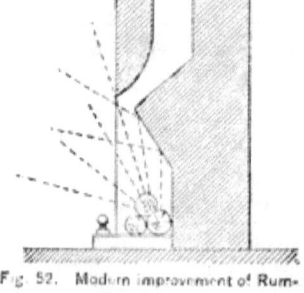

Fig. 52. Modern improvement of Rumford's Fireplace.

From this point it should increase somewhat, to allow of a slight expansion of the heated column and to diminish its friction against the walls of the flue, as well as to allow for a partial clogging by soot and for the resistance to its passage offered by the roughness of the plaster. The back of the fireplace should also incline forwards, as shown, in order to increase its radiating effect as well as that of the flame.

The simple and earnest style of Count Rumford's essays, the substantial nature of his acknowledged improvement, the facility with which it could be tested, and the enthusiasm with which he urges its importance, the detailed directions he gives for the guidance of the builder, and the liberality with which he offered the free use of his invention and services to the public,—all tended to make a permanent impression, and not only to give the Rumford fireplace precedence over all others, but even to place the latter altogether in the shade. So much in the shade that, though infinitely more important as tending to improve the ventilation of the apartment and the draught of chimney, as well as to save the waste heat of the fuel, they were almost forgotten, and, so far as the mass of the public is concerned, remain so up to the present day. So great was the influence of Count Rumford as a man of science, and his ability as a writer, that his failure to acknowledge the value of the efforts of his predecessors seemed like a tacit condemnation of them, and proved the severest blow to the cause.

Almost all modern grates are based upon the principles explained by Count Rumford, and a fireplace was considered perfect which was made in accordance with them. It was a rare exception when anything beyond this was thought possible.

The modern grate represented in Figs. 53 and 54, called Sylvester's patent, formed one of these exceptions, and was introduced about twenty years ago. In this the fire was put lower down than it had been at any time since coal became the staple fuel. The bottom of the grate was

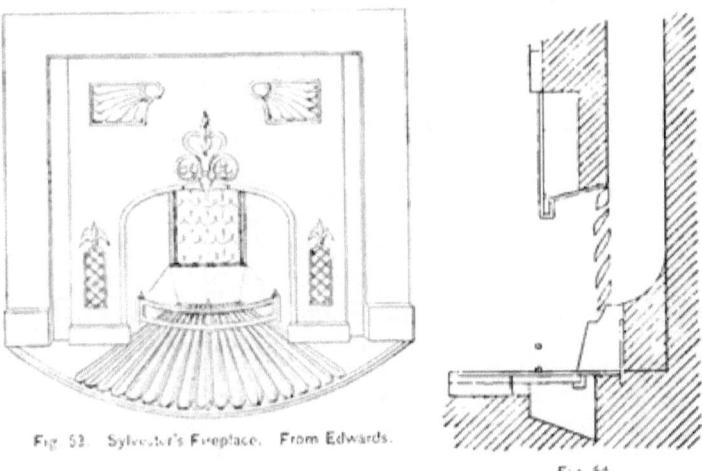

Fig. 53. Sylvester's Fireplace. From Edwards.

Fig. 54.

formed of separate bars, which extended considerably into the room. A curb of iron and a raised bar of circular form were used to enclose the bars, and answer the purpose of a fender. The back and sides of the fireplace were formed of fire-brick. Instead of the register door above, Venetian plates were provided at the back of the grate for the escape of the smoke, which could be opened more or less by a touch with the poker. This grate is quite common with us to-day; but it is rare that we see it with the ventilating attachment shown in the figure, and operating on the old principle of the fireplace at the Louvre, described by Savot. The air from the room was warmed against the back and top of the fireplace, in the spaces shown in the section, and afterwards returned into the room.

The contraction of the chimney-throat by means of the Venetian plates, which could easily be regulated, was an excellent application of the principle advocated by Rumford. The projecting bars reflected considerable heat, but there were certain disadvantages. The apparatus was necessarily expensive. It required more than usual care in setting. The fire was injudiciously low, and the necessity of removing the bars individually for the purpose of taking away the dust, and of then replacing them, was objected to, from the fact that the operation was an unusual one, and one, therefore, which domestics were certain to object to.

Figs. 55 and 56 represent the so-called Stephen's grate. This has

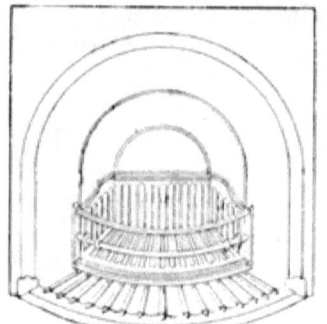 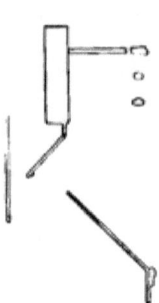

Fig. 55. Stephen's Fireplace. From Edwards.   Fig. 56.

no ventilating flues. It was simply built after the Rumford principles, and may be taken as a type of what was and is considered a perfect grate or fireplace. As in Sylvester's device, the smoke passes away from behind, but through a single arched aperture instead of between Venetian plates. A polished surface of iron fills up the space between the aperture and the front of the grate. A pan to receive the ashes is fitted below the fire-bars, and is made to project a few inches in front of them, where it is covered by an open grating. Fire-brick is used behind the bars to enclose the fire, and a door to move backwards and forwards is used to regulate the opening into the chimney. The iron-work is ground and stained black for dining-rooms and libraries, and is ground and polished bright for drawing-rooms.

Burnished steel and ormolu are introduced, of course, for those who can afford to pay for them, and the ash-pan itself is sometimes constructed of stamped and highly burnished steel bars, which, according to Edwards, the grate-manufacturer, gratify the ladies by their brightness. Two curious circumstances attending the introduction of this grate are, that it was not made of a semicircular form by the inventor, but elliptical, and that the notion was given over for a small sum of money to a manufacturer, who called it a patent, and retained the sole privilege of using it for many years, till it was discovered that there was no such thing as a patent in existence. Even before the introduction of Stephen's grate, another one, known as King's patent, and shown in Figs. 57 and 58, was introduced, which combined several similar qualifications, but only succeeded in becoming very little known. The form of the upper part was square instead of semicircular, and the door at the back of the grate, instead of being suspended from the bottom, as in Stephen's apparatus, was suspended from above and balanced by chains and weights, so that a slight touch with the poker could move it up or down at pleasure, and increase or diminish the draught. This fireplace was, scientifically speaking, superior to Stephen's. The amount of reflecting surface was greater than in the semicircular form, and the draught into the chimney was far more perfectly regulated than by the Stephen's door. It is curious to observe how instantaneously the draught is affected as the door is brought in proximity to the fire or is

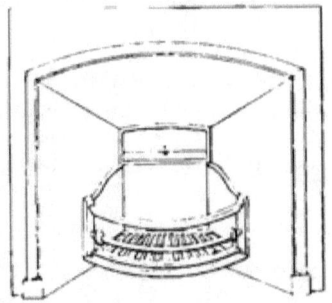

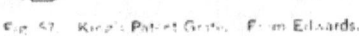

Fig. 57. King's Patent Grate. From Edwards.   Fig. 58.

removed from it, and how perfectly all the products of combustion are carried off when the opening into the chimney is exceedingly contracted. The grate, however, failed to excite much attention for one reason, and one only, namely, that the square form was not at that time calculated to be so popular as the arched form. "It is," says Edwards, "of no use to attempt to reason upon matters of taste. It suffices to state that the arched form was at that time novel, and that few would look at any other. King's grate was subsequently made of the semicircular form, but not until the other had got the run, and it had become practically impossible to supplant it."

THE SLIDING BLOWER.

Soon after the improvement made by Rumford, Lhomond added a movable blower, as shown in Figs. 59, 60, 61, and 62, allowing the opening of the fireplace to be increased or diminished at will. In this way the entire current of air could be turned upon the fuel, and the open fireplace becomes transformed into a closed stove, so far as the concealment of the flame and the improvement of the draught are concerned. This is at times very useful with chimneys liable to smoke, particularly when the fire is first lighted, and it is very generally used in Europe, especially in Paris. The blower is composed of one or more leaves of sheet metal (Fig. 60), sliding one over the other in the slots, as shown on the plan. The lowest is supported in the middle by a chain

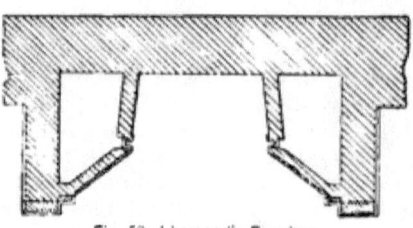

Fig. 59. Lhomond's Fireplace.

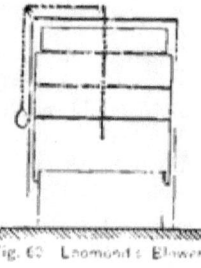

Fig. 60. Lhomond's Blower.

which passes over two pulleys, and is balanced by a weight. The use of this blower is, of course, an effective cure for smoky chimneys, because it may be closed so as entirely to cover the fire; but it is an expensive cure, since it sends a part of the radiant heat up the chimney. It is true that the high conductibility of the metal plate allows heat to pass through it rapidly, but the loss is, nevertheless, very great when closed over non-ventilating fireplaces. Its use is only to be recommended where no better

Fig. 61. Lhomond's Fireplace. Front Elevation.   Fig. 62. Vertical Section.

means of preventing smoke is to be found, or where a powerful draught is required to light the fire rapidly.

A good arrangement of the grate for burning coal is to have the entire grate project beyond the fireplace, so as to utilize the greatest possible amount of radiant heat. A semicircular hood of metal over the fire would then serve to direct the smoke into the chimney. This hood, being a heat conductor, would also transmit a large portion of the rays of heat into the room.

The fireplace of Lhomond, as shown in Figs. 61 and 62, is designed for wood, but by putting a grate in place of the andirons it may be used for coal.

THE MOVABLE GRATE.

Fig. 63 represents the movable grate, invented by Bronzac. The fuel rests on a small carriage, with wheels or casters, which allow of its being brought forward into the room when the fire is once lighted and burning well. The grate, or carriage, consists of a cast-iron box, open in front, and was used with an ordinary fireplace of Lhomond or Rumford. These grates, according to Peclet, well made at first, met with great success; but upon the expiration of the term of the patent right their construction was less careful, and they fell into comparative disuse. At the Universal Exhibition of 1855, an apparatus of the same nature was exhibited. The grate could be brought forward several meters into the room, the smoke then passing into the chimney through a flue formed of sliding tubes, fitting into each other like those of a telescope. As to how far the use of such a device is likely to spread in our modern apartments is a question of which each is best able to judge for himself. But it seems to the writer more suitable for the shop of the tinsmith or the laboratory of the chemist than for an ordinary living-room.

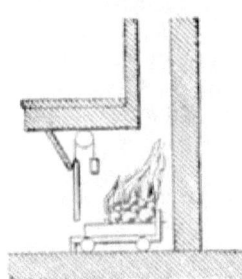

Fig. 63. Bronzac's Movable Grate.

Various other forms of the movable grate have been invented, a common form among which is the hanging-basket grate, now occasionally used, supported by a chain on a swivel bracket projecting from one of the jambs of the fireplace. This form of grate is objectionable on account of the difficulty of holding it firmly while replenishing or poking the fuel. It is sometimes used on account of its oddity or picturesqueness.

FIREPLACES WITH INVERTED SMOKE-FLUE.

In 1745 Franklin invented the famous Pennsylvanian Fireplace (Fig. 64), in which the smoke descends to the bottom of the fireplace before it enters the flue, in order to heat the surfaces of the fresh-air channels enclosed in the fire-back. This fireplace of Franklin's, however, was closed in front, and was objectionable on that account, the fire not being visible. It belongs, therefore, rather to the stove family than to that of the fireplace, as its name implies. It was modified by Desarnod, who opened the front to expose the fire (Fig. 65), and added on each side

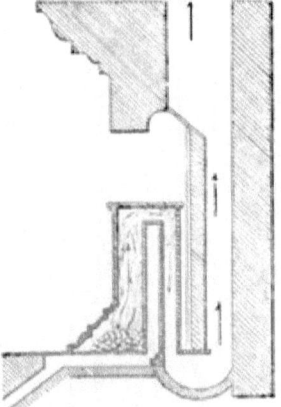

Fig. 64. Franklin's Pennsylvania Fireplace.

three little tubes which entered a larger one, through which the smoke passed and gave out a large part of its heat before entering the chimney. In short, the apparatus consists of a small fireplace inside of a larger one. Above the smaller is the opening through which fresh air enters the room. The system of an inverted smoke-flue was also adopted by Montalembert,

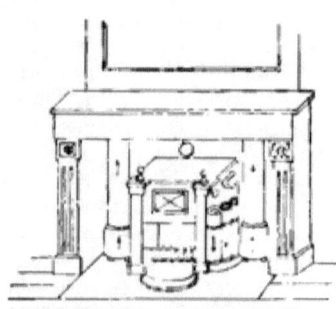

Fig. 65. Desarnod's Fireplace. From Jolly.

who in 1763 invented the fireplace and chimney represented in Fig. 66. It consists of a small chimney inside of a larger one. Upon lighting the fire, the damper at the top of the inside flue is opened, and that on the outside flue closed, by means of cords and tassels, allowing the smoke to rise directly into the chimney. Once the fire is well lighted, the dampers are reversed, and the smoke is forced to follow the course indicated by the arrows. When the walls of these flues are constructed of a good heat-conducting material, the saving by their use may be very great; if constructed of brick and the usual furring put upon the chimney breast the gain is, on the contrary, but slight. Notwithstanding this objection and the complication of the construction, these chimneys became quite popular at the time of their introduction.

The chief difficulty with all these arrangements having the reversed draught is their liability to smoke, and to clog with soot. Where the principle of multiplied circulation is employed to bring the fresh air and smoke flue in contact with each other, the circulation should, if possible, be on the part of the fresh air, and not of the smoke, unless convenient openings can be provided for cleaning out. Another form of fireplace, constructed on the same principle, is that of Douglas Galton, represented in Figs. 67 and 68. In this the fireplace projects entirely into the room. The smoke passes through the large central flue, and is surrounded by fresh-air chambers, which bring the warm air into the room through the openings shown in the section at the top of the stove, following the direction shown by the arrows. The fireplace is constructed of fire-brick,

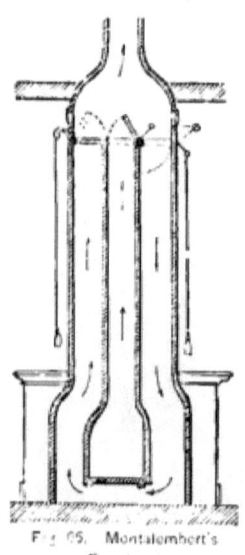

Fig. 66. Montalembert's Fireplace.

Fig. 67. Douglas Galton's Fireplace.

which absorbs a great quantity of heat, and, when once thoroughly warmed through, has the peculiarity of radiating the heat in all directions very rapidly. Soapstone has the same property. The grate and case of the fireplace are made of iron. This apparatus can only be employed with safety where the chimney draught is very regular and powerful, the vertical flue being heated from some external source, as in the Herbert Hospital, Woolwich, England, where, by the side of the upright flue, is placed a spare flue terminating in a fireplace in the basement, which enables the vertical flue to be warmed, so as either to make it draw when the fire is first lighted, or to enable a current to be maintained for ventilating purposes through the fireplace when the fire is not lighted.

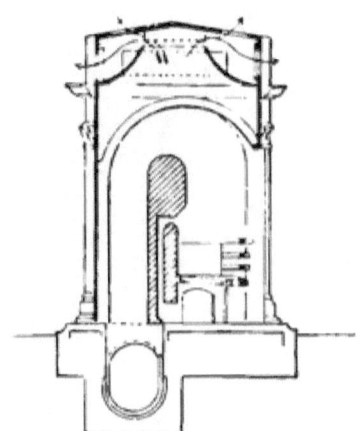

Fig. 68. Douglas Galton's Fireplace.

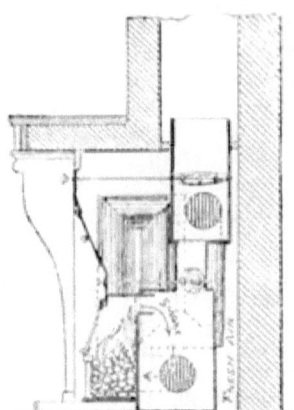

Fig. 69. Fireplace of Desroizilles.

The horizontal flue is swept by pushing a brush along it to force the soot into the vertical flue, whence it can be removed by a special contrivance.

The fireplace of Descroizilles, with smoke-flue constructed on the same principle, is shown in Fig. 69.

In order to diminish the unnecessary entrance of cool air into the chimney-flue above the fire, without at the same time curtailing the view of the flame, Descroizilles closed the upper part of the opening with a curtain of fine metal gauze. This, applied to both wood and coal fires, gave excellent results. Glass and mica slate have been used for the same purpose, but, owing to their frangible nature, have had but a limited use. The apparatus for warming the fresh air shown in the figure is much too complicated ever to become popular, even if it were not objectionable in many other particulars. The whole is constructed of metal. The metal gauze in front of the fire is made to turn on a hinge on its upper side, so that it may be opened or closed at pleasure. The smoke is allowed to pass directly into the chimney when the fire is first lighted; but when the flue has been sufficiently warmed to insure a good draught, the small damper above the fire is closed, and the smoke is compelled to descend, turn to the right and left, rise again, and circulate through the bent pipes, as shown in full and dotted lines, before it finally escapes into the chimney. While the machine is in good order it warms the fresh air economically and effectually, provided it is not attempted to warm too much air. But it is particularly liable to clog with soot, and very difficult to clean out again, it being necessary to take it entirely apart in order to do this. Moreover, the frequent changes in shape and direction of the various parts of the smoke-flue give rise to numerous counteracting eddies, which seriously retard the passage of the smoke; and often to such a degree that, with fireplaces having openings of the ordinary size for burning wood, its use without the gauze blower would be quite out of the question.

Fig. 70 gives a simpler device, but one which is also objectionable on account of back eddies, soot clogging, and smoke, without the advantage of the damper leading into the direct flue to fall back upon when the draught is feeble.

Figs. 71 and 72 represent a ventilating fireplace taken from Peclet's "Traité de la Chaleur." It is composed of a small fireplace of sheet-iron, placed inside of a larger one containing the fresh-air tubes, TT. These tubes are arranged in plan as shown in Fig. 72, in such a manner as to take from the smoke, as it passes between them, as much heat as possible, without obstructing its passage or occupying too much space. The small inside fireplace is distinct from the larger one containing the tubes, so that it can easily be removed when it is desired to clean out the latter. The smoke and hot air of combustion, rising from the fuel, pass over

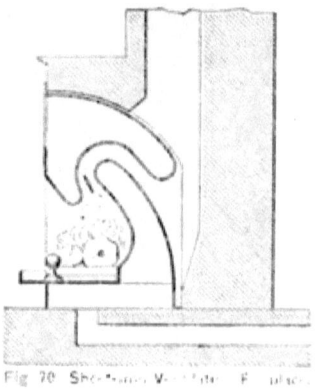

Fig. 70 Sh...... V...... F......

the back of the inside fireplace, descend between the fresh-air tubes, and pass out into the main flue through the large opening at the bottom, F. An opening above, E, furnished with a damper, serves to establish the draught when the fire is lighted. The fresh air circulates through the tubes, and enters warmed into the room through a register just above the fire. The usual blower for diminishing the size of the fireplace opening accompanies the apparatus. This fireplace is simple and easily set in any ordinary chimney opening. It was tested by Peclet, and highly recommended by him.

The reverberatory fireplace, invented by a Mr. John Taylor, an English architect, is represented in Fig. 73. It is constructed of hollow bricks laid round an iron frame in such a manner that the smoke is obliged to pass around and below the fire before ascending the flue. An opening with a damper immediately above the fire allowed the smoke, however, to rise directly into the main flue when the fire was first lighted. The interior of the grate was entirely lined with hollow fire-bricks, and the front part of the grate was provided with openings arranged to correspond with the construction of the air-flues behind, and also to present a highly ornamental appearance. The fresh air warmed in the hot-air flues formed of fire-bricks passed through these openings into the room. This hollow brick interior was heated by the fire resting against the bricks, and by the smoke passing around them. The objections to this fireplace were, that the descending flue as here constructed would be liable to smoke, and would quickly become clogged with soot, to remove which would be difficult, especially in the lower corners, where it would soonest condense. Another serious objection was the liability of the hollow bricks to become destroyed by the action of the fire, and disturb the whole arrangement. This might be partially removed by the substitution of iron for brick; but such a substitution would involve difficulties of other kinds. On the whole the deficiencies were conspicuous enough to prevent its making a permanent impression, and it now appears to have become forgotten.

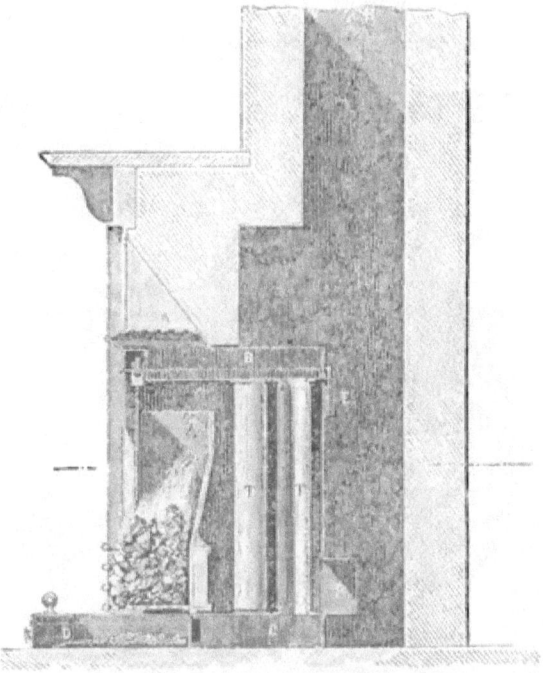

Fig. 16. Ventilating Fireplace.

M. Joly, in his "Traité du Chauffage et de la Ventilation," says, "When we make a careful examination of our open fireplaces as we actually find them, the first thought which strikes us is, 'How absurd they are!'" They are indeed nothing more than excellent producers of dangerous draughts, and it is particularly to them that applies the famous proverb, —

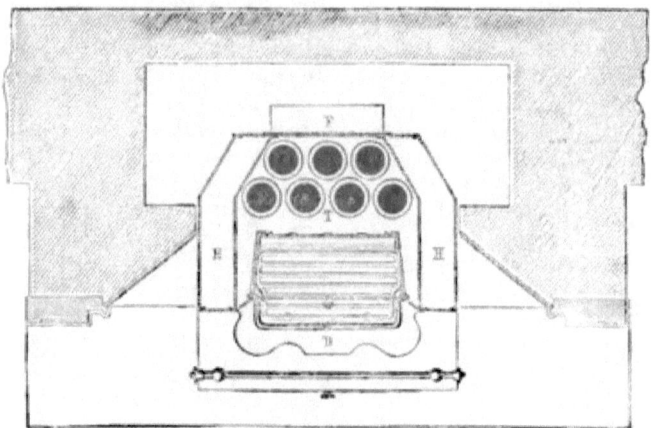

Fig. 72. Plan of Ventilating Fireplace. From Peclet.

Fig. 73. Taylor's Fireplace.

*"Si le vent souffle sur toi au travers d'une fente,
Fais ton testament et mets ordre à ta conscience."*

"The second thought is this: Why not take advantage of the heat at the point where it is most intense, that is, at the top of the fireplace?

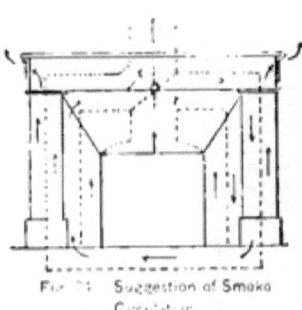

Fig. 74. Suggestion of Smoke Circulation.

Why cause the smoke to enter the main flue at a height of 0 meter .70 from the ground, rather than at the height of 1 meter? Why not utilize first all the radiant heat, and then by means of a damper in the smoke-flue just over the fire (Fig. 74), when the fire is lighted and the draught established, why not, as in the Russian and Swedish stoves, turn the smoke into one of the idle piers under the mantel, converting it into a reversed smoke-flue, to lead the smoke under the hearth to the base of the other pier, through which it again rises to the mantel and returns to its starting-point before entering the flue? Why not bring all this smoke in contact with fresh air introduced from the outside, and entering the room through the fresh-air registers, as shown at the right and left of the mantel? This would be more expensive than our ordinary fireplaces; but does the fuel that one burns cost nothing? Do we derive from it all the advantage of which it is capable?"

VENTILATING STOVE FIREPLACES WITH FRESH-AIR CIRCULATION.

We now come to the iron fireplace with direct or straight smoke-flue and circulating air-flues. Fig. 75 represents the fireplace of M. Leras, professor of physics at the Lyceum of Alençon, France. The fireplace is very shallow, and consequently a great amount of radiant heat is obtained. The fresh air circulates first under the hearth, then behind the back and sides of the fireplace, and finally escapes into the room through the register at the sides of the mantel. The fireplace opening is covered with plates of

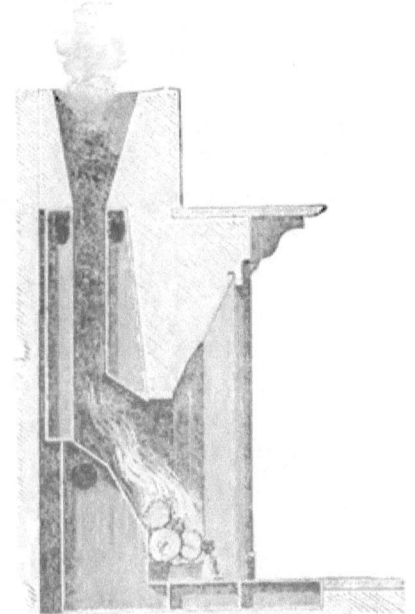

Fig. 75. Fireplace of Leras. From Planat.

*"If through a crack the draught you feel,
Settle your conscience and make your will."*

polished copper, to increase the radiant heat. This fireplace would seem difficult to repair when out of order, and liable to smoke on account of its incorrect form. The chimney-throat just above the fire is too large, and the back of the fireplace retreats above, where it should advance. The upper

Fig. 76. Ventilating Fireplace Vertical Air Tubes

Fig. 77. Vertical Section

part of the flue, shown in the figure, increases in size suddenly in the section where the iron flue enters the chimney. This sudden increase would be unnecessary except as a transition from an oblong to a square flue.

Figs. 76 and 77 represent another device with a better section of the

Fig. 78. Section of Ventilating Fireplace with Horizontal Air Tubes. From Peclet.

Fig. 79. Front Elevation

flue. Under the hearth is a shallow rectangular case of sheet-iron communicating with the external air. Upon the rear part of this box are fixed a number of bent tubes for conducting the air from it to the fresh-air register above the fire. The burnt air passes between the tubes before entering the brick flue, and warms the fresh air in its passage to the room. Fig. 78 gives, in section, a fireplace with the tubes for fresh air horizontal instead of perpendicular. This arrangement is less effective than the preceding, in which a draught of fresh air into the room is produced in the tubes by the height of the column of warm air in them independently of the chimney-draught. With horizontal tubes no such independent draught exists. The apparatus represented in Figs. 79, 80, 81, and 82 consists of a sheet-iron open stove fitted into the opening of a fireplace over a fresh-air inlet situated under the hearth. A register opens into the room from the upper part of the stove, through which the warm air enters. The stove consists of two sheet-iron boxes, one inside of the other, so as to leave a space between them for the circulation of the fresh air. The

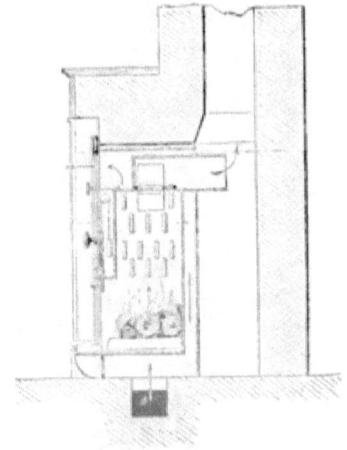

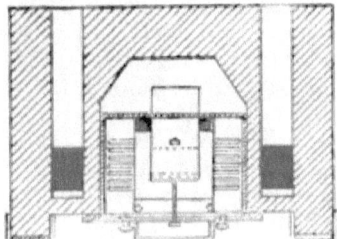

Fig. 81. Horizontal Section.

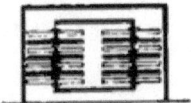

Fig. 80. Vertical Section of Fireplace with Metallic Heat-conducting Plates. From Péclet.

Fig. 82. Section of Plate.

iron smoke-flue is furnished with a damper at its junction with the stove, which is its proper place. The cheeks of the iron case are pierced with small metal plates, which extend into the fire and into the air-spaces between the two cases. The outside air enters through the fresh-air channels, rises, and comes in contact with the ends of the metal plates heated by the flame at the opposite ends. It then enters the room through the register just above the fire. The apparatus, considering its complication, is feeble in heating power. The heating surface added by the plates is too small to justify the outlay; moreover, the spaces between them would quickly get clogged with soot, and to clean them is exceedingly inconvenient.

If these plates were omitted, as shown in Fig. 83, a better form of ventilating fireplace would be obtained.

The fireplace of Fondet is represented in Figs. 84 and 85. It is composed of two horizontal cast-iron cylinders united by a number of small upright prismatic tubes arranged in rows, diagonally opposite and behind each other, in such a way that the smoke can pass between them before entering the chimney-flue, as shown by the arrow in the section. These tubes, which thus form the back of the fireplace, connect with the fresh-air inlet duct at the lower end, and at the upper with the warm-air registers at the right and left of the mantel, as shown in the elevation. The fresh air circulating through them is warmed by the fire, and then thrown into the room through the registers. The soot is removed from the outsides of the small prismatic tubes by means of a thin scraper passed between them.

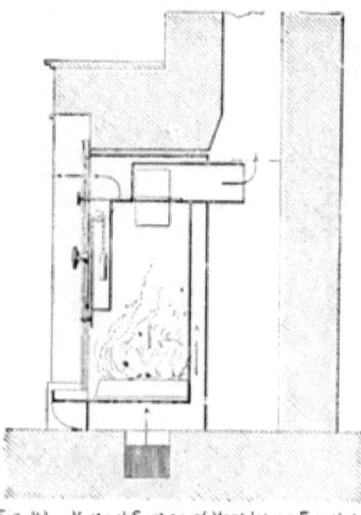

Fig. 83. Vertical Section of Ventilating Fireplace without Plates.

This apparatus is now one of the most extensively used in Paris, and gives the greatest satisfaction. It is, however, open to the objection of obstructing passage into the chimney-flue in a manner which renders the removal of the soot from the latter quite difficult.

To obviate the objection Cordier modified the back so as to render it movable. During the sweeping of the chimney the back can be moved to

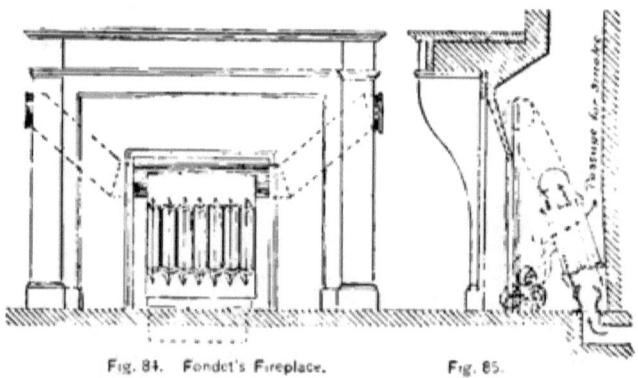

Fig. 84. Fondet's Fireplace.   Fig. 85.

the position shown by the dotted lines in Fig. 86, thus entirely opening the mouth of the chimney. In other respects the operation of this apparatus is like that of Fondet. Fig. 87 shows it in perspective. Fig. 88 shows the movable back, with the collars on the right and left of the upper horizontal cylinder to shut over the ends of the same when in position, for the purpose of keeping out the soot. The upright tubes in the Cordier fireplace are larger than in that of Fondet, and present more heating surface. At the same time they are less easily burned out. To increase their durability, however, the small perforated shield (Fig. 89) is fitted to the front of the tubes to protect them from the immediate contact of the fire and fuel. Fig. 90 shows the fireplace back in profile.

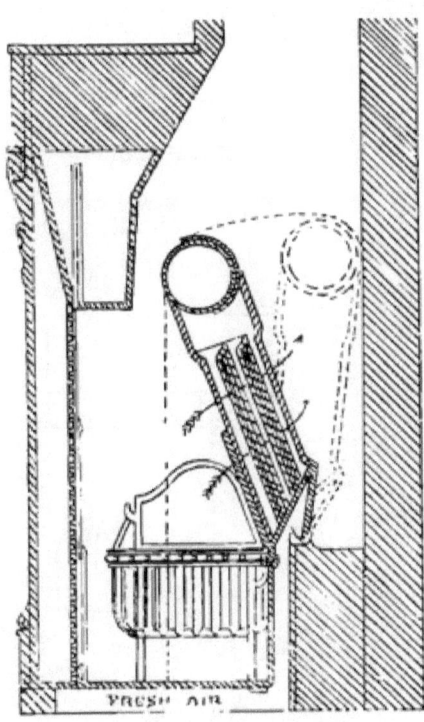

According to M. Bose, a French architect and writer on heating and ventilation, the calorific power of this apparatus is much greater than that of Fondet. He gives the results of some experiments made by the Central Society of Architects, Paris, to show this. The experiments were made in a room, he says, containing about 54 cubic meters of air. At the moment of lighting, the thermometer stood at 17° Centigrade. 9 kilograms of wood were burned, and at the end of 2 hours the thermometer stood at 30°, showing an increase of 13°. A similar experiment, made a few days afterwards in the same room with one of Fondet's better-known fireplaces, gave, in the same time and with the same amount of wood, an increase of only 7° instead of 13°.

In Fig. 87 is shown, behind the mantel, a portion of the smoke-flue made large enough to contain a number of small fresh-air tubes. By this means a still greater amount of heat may be extracted from the smoke before it enters the brick flue. But the upper enlargement with enclosed air-tubes does not form a necessary part of the apparatus. It is objectionable, as well on account of its costliness and complexity, as on account of the difficulty of cleaning or making repairs.

The Lloyd fireplace is represented by Figs. 91, 92, 93, 94, and 95. Two strips of sheet-iron, bent as shown in Fig. 94, are fastened to the back of the fireplace, of which Fig. 92 gives a horizontal section, and make the fresh-air flues shown in Fig. 95. These two side flues are connected above the fireplace with a cross tube square in section (Fig. 94).

The fresh air enters behind the fireplace, circulates below, on each side, and above the stove, and enters the room just over the mantel at the back edge of the shelf, as shown in the vertical section (Fig. 91). This fireplace is to be highly recommended on account of its extreme simplicity. But the radiating surface of its heating flues being small, compared with those of Cordier, Fondet, Joly, Peclet, Descroizilles, and others, it is correspondingly deficient in calorific power. In common with all the above-

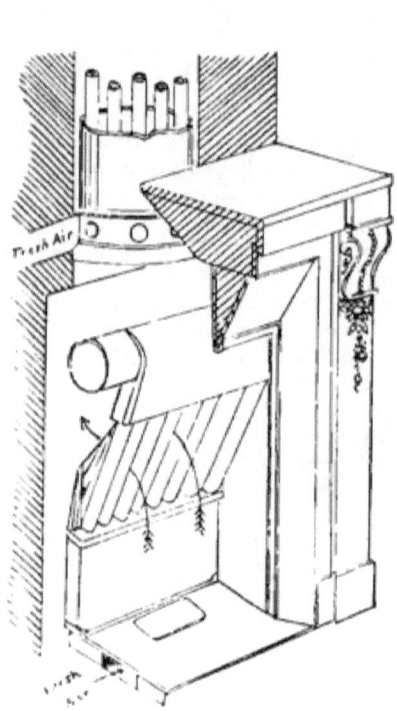

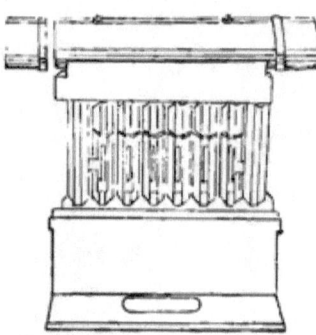

Fig. 88. Back of Cordier's Fireplace.

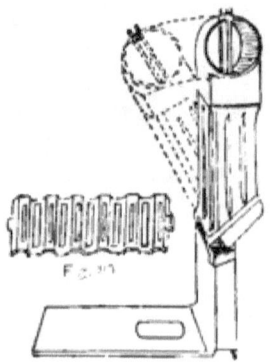

Fig. 87. Perspective View of Cordier's Fireplace.

Fig. 90. Detail of Cordier's Fireplace.

mentioned fireplaces, it is objectionable in bringing the air into immediate contact with highly heated iron about the grate and burning fuel. For the purpose of deriving the utmost advantage from an open fire, the radiant heat of the fuel, which, on account of its preciousness (from a sanitary point of view), might be called "golden" heat as distinguished from the ordinary heat of convection, should be made the most of. To this end the back and sides of the grate or fireplace should be constructed of the best radiating or reflecting material, avoiding the metals. Fire-clay, tiles, or soapstone should be sought. The conducting materials may be used in places comparatively remote from the fire, whereby the waste heat of the smoke may be saved without danger of burning the air. Or, in other words, the conducting materials should be used higher up above the points available for radiation.

Mr. Lloyd placed a strip of metal on the mantel just in front of the warm-air entrance, with the idea that it was necessary in order to deflect the current upwards as it entered, and thus prevent horizontal draughts. Such a deflector is, however, an unnecessary complication. The direction of the air current would be influenced chiefly by its gravity or temperature, and, if warmer than the air of the room, would rise at once to the ceiling; if colder, it would fall to the ground without much regard for the trifling impediment offered by the deflector. This would be as powerless to influence the general direction of the air current as would be a stone at the bottom of a river to counteract the laws of gravity by which its course was determined. The action of this fireplace when first introduced is thus described by Mr. Lloyd : —

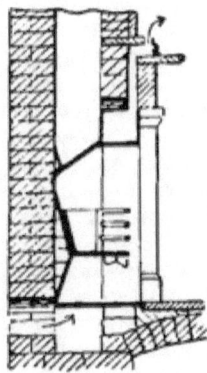

Fig. 91. Lloyd's Tubular Fireplace.

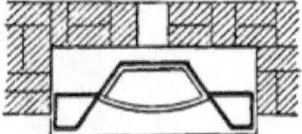

Fig. 92. Lloyd's Tubular Fireplace.

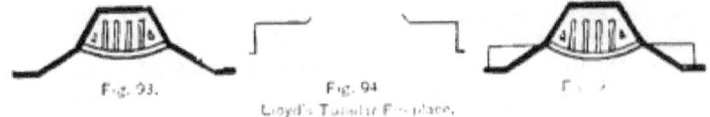

Fig. 93.   Fig. 94.   Fig.
Lloyd's Tubular Fireplace.

"The complete and agreeable change in the character of the air of the room was at once apparent to every one; and instead of the room being barely habitable in cold weather, it was found to be the most comfortable in the house. This stove was fixed at the latter end of December, 1850, and has been in use ever since without the slightest difficulty of management, and with entire satisfaction to the inmates of the house. During the first winter careful observations were made on its action, and the results are in many respects remarkable. Within an hour after the fire is lighted, the air issuing from the air-passages is found to be raised to a comfortable temperature, and it soon attains a heat of 80°, at which it can be maintained during the day with a moderate fire. The highest temperature that has been attained has been 95°, whilst the lowest on cold days, with only a small fire, has been 70°. The result of 20 observations gave the following temperatures: on two occasions the temperature was 95°; the fire was large, and the door of the room was left open so that the draught through the air-tubes was diminished; on 5 occasions the temperature was below 80°, averaging 75°; the remaining 15 gave an average of 80°. The mean temperature of the room at the level of respiration was 64°, while the uniformity was so perfect that thermometers hanging on the three sides of the room rarely exhibited a greater difference than 1°, although two of the sides were external walls. As might be expected, there was no sensible draught from the door and window. On observing the relative temperatures of the inflowing and general air of the room, it appeared that there must be a regular current from the ceiling down to the lower part of the room, and thence to the fire. The inflowing current, being of a temperature nearly approximating to that of the body, was not easily detected by the hand; but on being tried by the flame of a candle it was observed to be very rapid, and to pursue a course nearly perpendicular towards the top of the room, widening as it ascended. It was also noticed that the odor of dinner was imperceptible in a remarkably short time after the meal was concluded. In order to trace the course of the air with some exactitude various expedients were made use of. It was felt to be a matter of great interest to ascertain if possible the direction of air respired by the lungs. The smoke of a cigar, as discharged from the mouth, has probably a temperature about the same as respired air, higher rather than lower, and was therefore assumed to be a satisfactory indicator. On its being repeatedly tried, it was observed that the smoke did not ascend to any great height in the room, but tended to form itself into a filmy cloud at about 3 feet above the floor, at which level it maintained itself steadily, while it was gently wafted along the room to the fireplace. In order to get an abundant supply of visible smoke at a moderate temperature, a fumigator charged with cut brown paper was used. By this means a dense volume of smoke was obtained in a few seconds; and it conducted itself as in the last-mentioned experiment. On discharging smoke into the *inflowing air current*, it was diffused so rapidly that its course could not be traced; but in a short time no smoke was observable in the room. Another experiment was made with a small balloon, charged with carburetted hydrogen gas, and balanced to the specific gravity of the air. On setting it at liberty near the air-opening it was borne rapidly to the ceiling, near which it floated to one of the sides of the room, according to the part of the current in which it was set free; it then invariably descended slowly, and made its way with a gentle motion towards the fire. The air has always felt fresh and agreeable, however many continuous hours the room may have been occupied, or however numerous the occupants. It is difficult to estimate the velocity of the inflowing current; but if it be assumed to be 10 feet per second, there would pass through the air-tubes in 12 minutes as much air as will equal the contents of the room. And as it appears that the air so admitted passes from the room in a continuous horizontal stream, carrying with it up the chimney vitiated air from the lamps or candles, and all vapors rising from the table, it is by no means surprising that the air should always be refreshing and healthful. Since this stove has been fixed, others have elsewhere been fitted up on the same principle, and have been found to exhibit similar satisfactory results."[1]

We give in Figs. 96, 97, 98, 99, 100, 101, plan, sections, and details

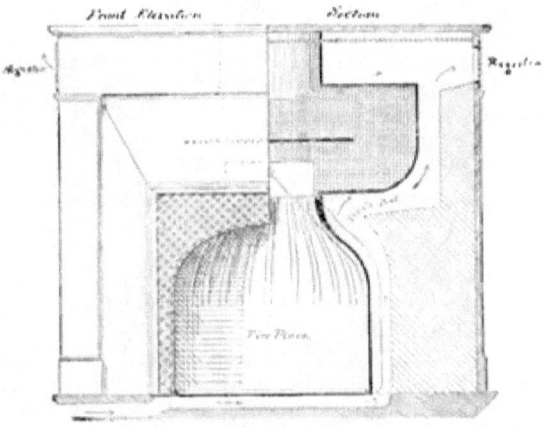

Fig. 96. Joly's Fireplace. From Joly.

of the fireplace of Joly. It is unquestionably one of the best of its kind known. It is easy to set, easy to repair or clean, and easy to manage; simple in construction, effective in action, unobjectionable in appearance, and equally suitable for any kind of fuel.

The fresh air enters under the hearth through a proper duct, and passes into the hot-air chamber behind the cast-iron shell forming the back of the fireplace. Within this shell are placed either andirons or a grate, according as wood or coal is to be burned. A frame and damper at the chimney-throat regulate the size of the opening. The fresh air passes under, behind, around, and above the shell, and enters well heated through the registers at the right and left under the mantel. M. Joly has given ample room for the fresh air, in accordance with the correct principle of supplying an ample quantity of air

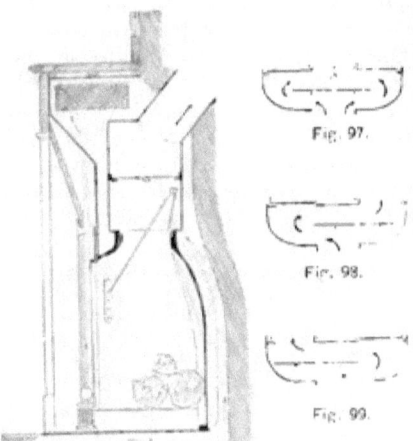

Fig. 97.

Fig. 98.

Fig. 99.

Fig. 100. Section of j...

---

[1] Francis Lloyd's *Practical Remarks on the Warming, Ventilation, and Humidity of Rooms*. London, 1851.

warmed to a moderate degree, rather than a small quantity raised to a very high temperature, unduly tried and perhaps burned.

An ordinary sliding blower is attached to the front face of the fireplace, for the purpose of increasing the draught when desired. In order to utilize the heat of the smoke as far as possible, a drum is placed above, and by an ingenious arrangement of slides the smoke may be made to pass to the right or left at pleasure, or to suit the position of the brick flue, as shown in Figs. 98 and 99; or, again, it may be made to pass on both sides, as is shown in the uppermost cut.

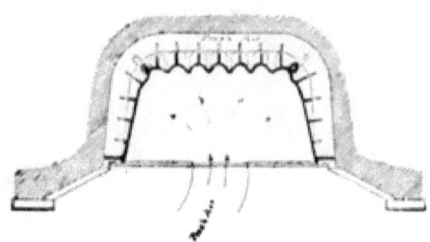

Fig. 101. Horizontal Section of Joly's Fireplace.

Figs. 102, 103, and 104 represent the fire-grate recommended by the English Commission appointed for improving the Sanitary Condition of Barracks and Hospitals. This apparatus, sometimes called the Galton Ventilating Fireplace, though simple, combines the advantages of many of those just described, the heat-radiating ribs or flanges of Joly's fireplace, the splayed sides of Ganger and Rumford, the contracted throat, and at the same time furnishes us with an example of the use of a non-conducting, powerfully radiating material for fire-back and immediate contact with the fuel. The grate is placed as far forward in the room as possible. The hearth is made of plate or cast-iron. The grates are of three sizes, according to the cubic contents of the room to be heated. A grate with a fire-opening of about 40 centimeters is for a room of about 150 cubic meters' capacity; with an opening of 45 centimeters for 250 cubic meters; and with an opening of 55 centimeters for 350 cubic meters. Beyond this, two or more grates are required. Between the fire-clay lump and the iron back of this grate is a half-inch air-space to admit a supply of heated air to the fuel, and secure a more perfect combustion of the smoke. This grate is easily cleaned or repaired, the front being secured by screws, which can be taken out when required, and thus render the interior and air-chambers accessible. In this fireplace fresh air is heated only in the immediate neighborhood of the grate; but Captain Galton, in the appendix to his book on the Construction of Hospitals, recommends extending the available heating surface of the smoke-flue by carrying it through some fresh-air flue. This plan was adopted in the Herbert Hospital, in the manner shown in the preceding

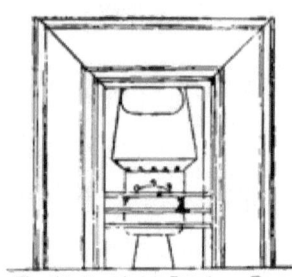

Fig. 102. Ventilating Fireplace. From Douglas Galton.

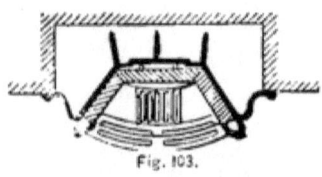

Fig. 103.

Fig. 68, where the fireplace is in the centre of the ward, and the chimney consequently passes under the floor, as shown in section in the figure. The flue is placed in the centre of a square fresh-air flue (also shown in section), which supplies the air to be warmed by the fireplace. By this means a heating surface for the fresh air of about 4 square meters additional to that of the fireplace is obtained. The smoke-flue need not, of course, descend as in the Herbert Hospital. Instead of attempting to warm the fresh air before it has reached the ventilating fireplace, which involves a descending smoke-flue, this air may be first passed behind the fireplace, and then caused to circulate around the smoke-flue. The smoke then passes off without reversion. The manner in which it may be accomplished is shown in Fig. 105, and in this form of chimney we find the true principle of the ventilating fireplace. The radiant heat of the fire is increased by the fire-brick backing, while the heat of the smoke is utilized for a considerable distance up the flue, the fresh air being warmed in a chamber remote from the burning fuel. The fireplace stands well out from the wall. The fresh air enters behind and below the grate, and enters the room near the ceiling well warmed.

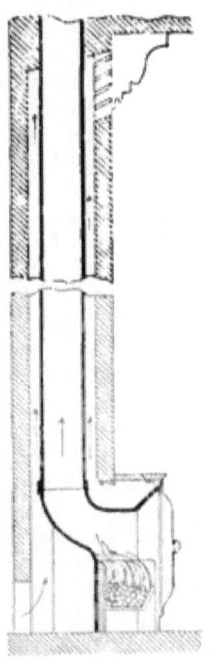

Fig. 105. Double Ventilating Flue.

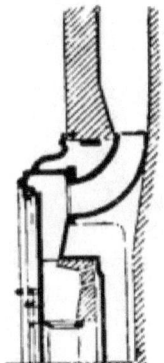

Fig. 104. From Douglas Galton.

Figs. 106 and 107 show the plan of this fireplace, the first designed with a grate to burn coal, and the second with andirons, and recessed deeper, to burn wood. This apparatus is simply a modification by General Morin of that described by Peclet in 1828 (Fig. 108), in which the fresh air passes through a tube, while the smoke surrounds it as it passes up the brick smoke-flue. This system is inferior to that of General Morin, inasmuch as a greater proportion of heat is lost by absorption in the surrounding brick-

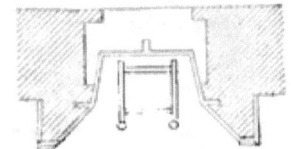

Fig. 107. Morin's Fireplace. From Bose.

work. The ascent of the smoke, moreover, is more difficult on account of the obstructions offered, not only by the roughness of the brickwork, but by the presence of the fresh-air flue; whereas in Morin's chimney the round iron pipe furnishes a smooth passage of a form the most favorable possible for the ascent of smoke.

In 1832 Captain Belmas, in the "Mémorial de l'Officier du Génie," speaks of a chimney similar in principle to that of Peclet. Finally Douglas Galton applied the same principle, very slightly modifying the form, in heating the English barracks.

According to General Morin, these fireplaces were designed to utilize more effectually than the common forms the heat given out by the fuel by introducing a considerable quantity of fresh air, warmed to a moderate degree, to replace that which has passed up the chimney, and also to reduce the amount of cold air entering from the outside through the cracks of the doors and windows. "But while," he says, "the plans at first proposed drew in but a small quantity of fresh air, scarcely equal to one-tenth of that passing out through the chimney, and raised it to temperatures of from 90° to 110° C. (about 200° to 250° F.), and often more, the forms devised by the ingenious Captain Douglas Galton for the fireplaces of English barracks have furnished a very satisfactory solution of the problem, as has been proved by some experiments made with two fireplaces of this kind at the Conservatory of Arts and Trades. Observations show that the amount of air admitted to the room at the ceiling through the fresh-air ducts at 26° C. (about 80° F.) differs but little from that passing off up the chimney, so that the admission of cold air through the doors is almost prevented. This introduction of warm air, in addition to the warmth produced by the ordinary radiation from the fire, increases its heating effect, which becomes as much as 35 per cent. of the heat produced by the fuel; while the common forms of fireplace give but 12 or 14 per cent., and those supplied with Fondet's apparatus but about 20 per cent."[1]

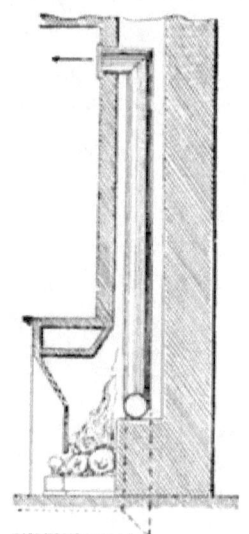

Fig. 103. Douglas Galton's Fireplace.

Nevertheless, the Galton fireplace is but little known, and seldom to be found in actual use. Bose lays its failure to the difficulty of removing it when worn out, and to the unusual amount of space it requires in the chimney-breast. "This kind of chimney-flue," he says, "requires too much room, and cannot be used in our modern constructions, where it becomes frequently necessary to carry up 8 smoke-flues in a wall 4 meters long." The same objections are urged by Joly, who says, "It is always necessary to provide access to these double flues for the purpose of cleaning or repair, and if they are built in the walls the space required for the 25 or 30 flues of an ordinary house would be enormous. On the other

---

[1] *Annales du Conservatoire*, 6e volume, 1896.

hand, what an effect these double envelopes would have in our apartments if concealed behind movable cases subject to expansion and contraction under the influence of the heat? The principle is good for barracks; but why not here simply leave the flues exposed to view?" It may be further objected that the actual saving of heat by the use of such an arrangement is still too limited, although, according to General Morin, it is even greater than with the apparatus of Fondet.

VENTILATING FIREPLACES MANUFACTURED IN THIS COUNTRY.

Figs. 109 and 110 represent in plan and section an excellent form of ventilating fireplace made in this country.

It is similar in principle to the Joly fireplace, but is in some respects

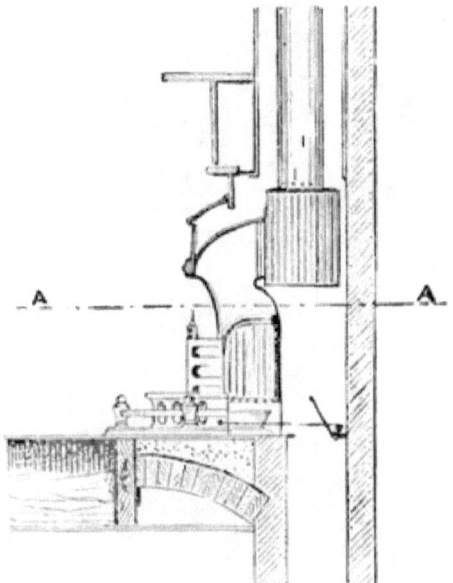
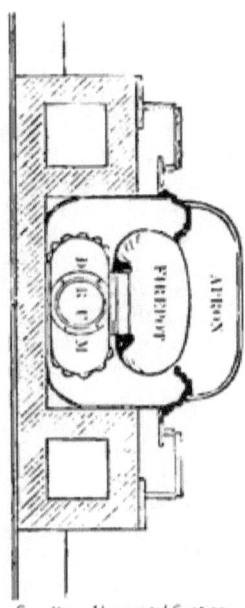

superior to the French example. The back of the grate is lined with fireclay, by which the radiation is increased and the iron protected. Instead of the ribs or gills cast on the outer surface of the Joly grate, for increasing the radiation of the iron in contact with the fresh air, we have here a jacket of corrugated sheet-iron fitting closely around the grate. This is an ingenious substitute for the fixed ribs, and has the advantage of economy and compactness, while it serves at once as a radiator and as a series of hot-air flues conducting the fresh air upwards, and retaining it in close contact with the iron back.

Above is a drum like that of Joly, but better located, inasmuch as it is farther from the flame, and is thrown back, so that, while it allows the fresh air to impinge upon its lower surface as well as upon its sides, it throws the fireplace forward into the room, where its radiation is more effective. The drum is also provided with a corrugated-iron jacket. The air is admitted into the room either through a register, placed in the projecting iron hood just over the grate and under the mantel-piece, and forming part of the portable fireplace, or it may pass up the fresh-air duct, surrounding an iron smoke-flue, to the ceiling, where it may be admitted, as in the Galton fireplaces, through a register near the cornice. It may be used, therefore, either with or without the double smoke-flue, and the warmed fresh air may be conducted into rooms above as well as into that containing the fireplace. Figs. 111 and 112 explain the manner in which this is done.

A novel and useful feature in this fireplace is the sliding blower or blowers of iron, embellished with transparencies of mica slate, so constructed as to slide back into gas-tight pockets. These gas-tight pockets afford, it is claimed, additional security against the leakage of gas into the air-heating chamber. The blowers, one above, in front of the grate, and one below, in front of the ash-pit, may be wholly or partially opened.

Ample space is left behind the fire-back for the introduction of earthen jars or other devices for evaporating water; or a regular furnace evaporating-dish may be used, with ball-cock and supply-pan outside. The cost of this fireplace,

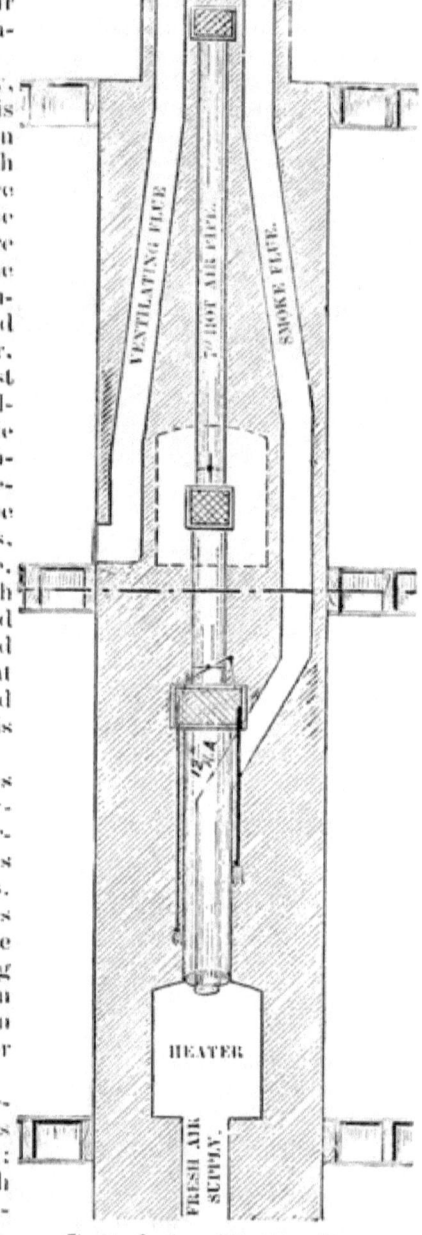

Fig. 111. Smoke and Ventilating Flues

which is called the "Fire on the Hearth" Heater, is advertised at from $15 to $50.[1]

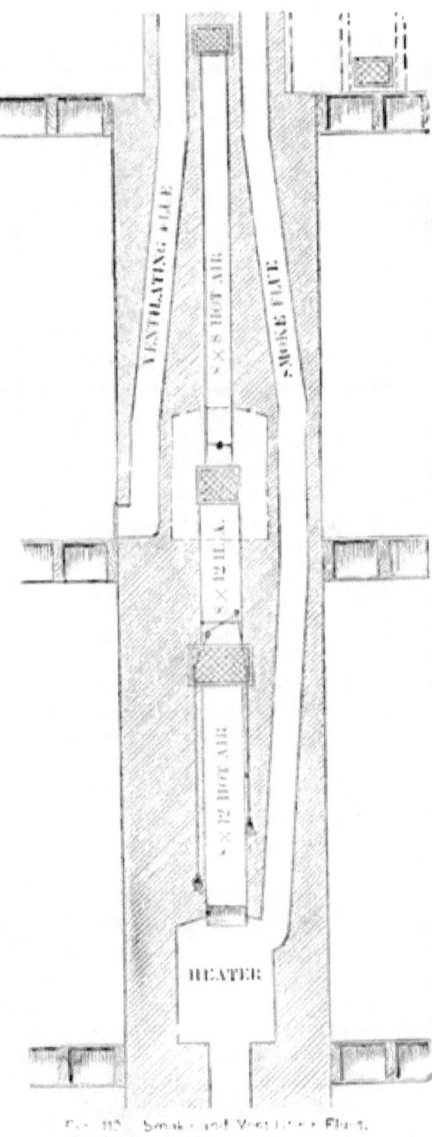

Manufactured by the Open Stove Ventilating Company, New York.

Much of the success of these ventilating fireplaces depends on intelligent setting, and care in following out the directions given by the manufacturers. The fresh-air ducts should have an area equal to that of the smoke-flue, in order that all the air passing up the chimney may be drawn from that source, and not be compelled to enter through doors and window-cracks. The writer has used this fireplace in one of his office rooms during the winter, and made the following practical tests as to its heating and ventilating powers. The room is the same in which the experiments on the old fireplace represented in Figs. 1 and 2 were made, and measured 6 by 6 by 3 meters (about 20 by 20 by 10 feet).

The old fireplace was removed and the ventilating fireplace put in its place. We have seen by our experiments with the ordinary fireplace originally used in the office that the combustion of 3 kilograms of wood served to raise the general temperature of the room but 1° C. Although the outside air stood as high as 13° C. above freezing, it was still 6° below that of the room when the experiment was begun; and, as there was no furnace in the building, the air to supply the draught was obliged to come in unwarmed from the outside, and was sufficiently cold to combat successfully the heat of the fuel, of which we found only 6 per cent. was utilized, the remainder, or 94 per cent., passing away up the chimney to be utterly lost.

EXPERIMENTS WITH THE "FIRE ON THE HEARTH" HEATER.

The first of our experiments with the "Fire on the Hearth" Heater were made on the 1st of January, 1879, when the external air stood at 0° C. At the beginning of the experiment the thermometer in the room stood at 11.25° C.; 4 kilograms of dry pine wood were burned. At the end of half an hour the mercury had risen to 15.50° C., and from thence it began gradually to fall, as the fire went out, until, at the end of an hour, it stood at 15°. The fresh air was conducted to the back of the heater through a brick flue opening to the outer air under the window. It entered the room warmed through two openings just under the mantel, right and left, over the heater.

Table III. (Appendix) gives the result of the test.

This table shows us that 3 kilograms of wood burned in this fireplace raised the temperature of the room 4¼° C., or over 4 times as much as the same amount burned in the ordinary fireplace accomplished.

The heat saved from the back of the fireplace was sufficient to raise the temperature of $2,229.90 + 878.85 = 3,108.75$ cubic meters of air 1° C. Or, since 1 cubic meter of air weighs 1.3 kilograms, 3,109 cubic meters would weigh 4,041.7 kilograms, and the specific heat of air being 0.24, we have $4,041.7 \times 0.24 = 970$ heat units saved. Add about $\frac{3}{100}$ for heat still remaining in the back and sides of the fireplace at the end of the experiment, and we have a total of about 1,000 units of heat saved by this apparatus in every 4 kilograms of wood.

If we assume as before that 1 kilogram of our dry wood yielded 3,590 units of heat in the process of combustion, 4 kilograms would have yielded 14,360 units. Therefore, our 1,000 units saved would be equivalent to 7 per cent. of the whole amount of heat possible to be obtained from the fuel. Add 6 per cent. for that due to direct radiation, and we have 13 per cent. utilized, or over twice as much as was obtained from the ordinary fireplace. With coal the amount of heat utilized would be $7 + 13 = 20$ per cent., or the same as is obtained from the apparatus of Foudet, according to the calculations of General Morin. If, in connection with this heater, the double flue of Belmas or Galton is used, as is recommended by the manufacturers, the saving may be 5 or 10 per cent. greater, making a total of 25 or 30 per cent. In order that the conditions under which this heater was tested might be as nearly as possible the same as those attending the test made on the old fireplace, recorded in Table I., another experiment was made later in the season, when the thermometer of the external air stood at 13° C. The air of the room was raised by the combustion of 3 kilograms of wood from 17° to 21°, or again, 4° C., and in all the experiments the temperature in all parts of the room was very nearly the same. The entrance of cold currents through doors and window-cracks was almost entirely avoided. The movement in the air was imperceptible, yet the ventilation was perfect, and no disagreeable odor was perceptible for any length of time, even after the room had been filled with mechanics and laborers. We see by columns 7 and 8 that there passed into the room a ventilating current of warm air at the rate of over a cubic meter a minute from each of the two registers, making together in the hour over 160 cubic meters. This air was at no time heated above $32°$ C., and averaged about $22°$,—a mild and pleasant temperature.

A test was also made at the top of the chimney to ascertain the temperature of the air as it issued from the mouth. The thermometer rose as high as $82°$, and then began to fall. By Table I. it will be seen that the temperature with the old fireplace rose to $81°$ and $90°$. The difference by this test was, therefore, apparently unimportant, though a careful measurement, with the anemometer and thermometer, of the heat units thrown out would have shown a saving corresponding with that detected below.

Fig. 113. The "Fire on the Hearth" Stove.

Fig. 113 gives a sectional cut of another fireplace manufactured by the same company. This apparatus consists of a double stove, the inner one being used to hold the fuel and carry off the products of combustion, and the space between the inner and the outer serving to warm the fresh air to be introduced into the room. If a blower be used over the fire, the open fireplace is converted into a close stove or furnace, with fresh-air flues, etc. It is unquestionably one of the most satisfactory stoves known in this country, designed for combining health with economy.

THE DIMMICK HEATER.

We now have manufactured in this country another excellent ventilating fireplace, called the Dimmick Heater, of which Figs. 114 and 115 give perspective view and vertical section.

The principle of this heater is the same as in the apparatus represented by Figs. 76 and 77. It has, however, this advantage over the latter, that the upright fresh-air tubes are joined together so as to form an air-tight fire-back, and enter a common hot-air chamber directly over the flame, having its lower side inclined at an angle with the back so as to reflect the heat into the room and throw the flame forward. This arrangement of the tubes and hot-air box gives the fireplace a more desirable section for radiating heat. As for the artistic effect of the exterior, none of the ventilating fireplaces heretofore represented have much to claim, and in the present case it is possible to conceive of a form more pleasing than that represented in our cut. But a slight modification in the treatment of the hood would probably be sufficient to remove all objection on the score of appearance.

The fresh air, after having been heated in the tubes and box, is either conducted immediately into the room through registers opening under the mantel, or it rises in a double flue to the ceiling or to the rooms above, as shown in the section (Fig. 115).

In order to make an accurate test of the heating power of this fireplace, the writer had one placed in the room in which the previous experiments were made, and obtained the following results: —

Fig. 04. — The Dimmick Heater.

EXPERIMENTS WITH THE DIMMICK HEATER.

The heater was set out in the room in front of the mantel, and the fresh air conducted through a brick flue direct from the outside to the iron chamber under the upright tubes. The heated air entered the room through two openings perforated in the upper hot-air box over the fire already described, one at the right, having an area of 40 square centimeters, and one at the left, having an area of 104 square centimeters, and it was assumed that the volume of the fresh air given out by each was in proportion to the size of the opening, while the temperature was the same. The observations were made upon the right-hand opening. In order to protect the thermometer from the direct radiation of the iron, a brick flue was built around this opening and carried outwards horizontally about 8 inches, and thence upwards about a foot, so that a thermometer hung

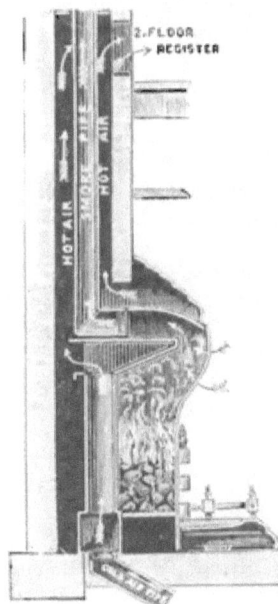

Fig. 35. Section of the Dimmick Heater.

in the upright portion of the flue would indicate with greater accuracy the temperature of the hot-air current and not be greatly influenced by radiation from any outward source.

At the time of the experiment recorded in Table IV., in the Appendix, from 9 to 11 o'clock in the evening of April 11, 1879, the outside air stood at 4° C., and the air in the room at 16°. The anemometer was again tested in a current of air of known velocity, and found to be accurate. The allowance to be made for friction was recalculated, and found to agree with that made in the previous tests.

Three kilograms of dry pine wood were burned, and the amount of ventilation effected and heat saved by the apparatus is shown by Table IV. (Appendix).

This table shows us (column 6) that the heat saved from the back of the fireplace and issuing with the air through the right-hand opening of 40 square centimeters area was sufficient to raise the temperature of 1,180 cubic meters of air 1° C. The other opening, having an area of 104 square centimeters, must therefore have given out heat sufficient to raise $1,180 \times \frac{104}{40} = 3,068$ cubic meters of air 1° C., the two making a total of $3,068 + 1,180 = 4,248$ cubic meters. Since, as before, 1 cubic meter of air weighs 1.3 kilograms, and the specific heat of air is 0.24, we have $4,248 \times 1.3 \times 0.24 = 1,325$ heat units saved by this apparatus in every 3 kilograms of wood.

Assuming that the 3 kilograms of wood here used yielded 10,770 heat units in the process of combustion, our 1,325 units saved would be equivalent to $\frac{1325}{10770} = 12$ per cent. of the whole. Add 6 per cent. for that due to direct radiation, and we have 18 per cent. for the total amount of heat realized from the fuel, or just 3 times as much as was obtained from the ordinary fireplace. With coal the amount of heat utilized would be $12 + 13 = 25$ per cent., or 5 per cent. more than is obtained from the apparatus of Fondet, according to the calculations of General Morin. If, again, in connection with the Dimmick Heater, we use the upright double flue as shown in the sectional cut, the heat realized is increased 5 or 10 per cent., making a total of 30 or 35 per cent. It therefore appears from these experiments that the calorific power of the Dimmick Heater is somewhat greater than that of the "Fire on the Hearth" Heater. But, whereas the latter threw into the room during the combustion of 4 kilograms of wood, as shown by columns 7 and 8 of Table III., $82.05 + 78.85 = 160.90 + (\frac{5}{20} \times 160.9) = 169$ cubic meters of air heated on the average to a mild temperature of 22° C., and at no time exceeding

32° C., the Dimmick Heater supplied only $16.4 + (\frac{1}{25} \times 16.4) = 17$ cubic meters through the right-hand opening, and $17 \times \frac{129}{50} = 44$ cubic meters through the left-hand opening, or a total of 61 cubic meters during the combustion of 3 kilograms of wood. Or for 4 kilograms $61 + \frac{1}{3}(61) = 80$ cubic meters heated during 20 minutes of the time up to 100° C., or the boiling-point of water, and at one time as high as 121° C. By using a fire-clay back in front of the cast-iron tubes, and by either increasing the size of the fresh-air passages or else allowing the fresh air to circulate behind the tubes as well as through them, the heater might be materially improved, and a still greater percentage of saving obtained. This improvement might be made in setting, without altering the castings. The cold-air entrance pipe shown in Fig. 115 should be increased in size, and should receive the air behind as well as under the upright pipes. It should be provided with a simple damper to diminish the supply of cold air at pleasure to correspond with the ventilation required or the amount of fuel burned. The air passing up behind would then serve not only to lower the temperature of the pipes themselves by extracting some of the heat which would otherwise pass off, by absorption, into the brickwork, but also to diminish, by dilution, the heat of the air issuing from their tops, and improve the ventilation of the apartment by introducing into it a larger volume of air heated to a lower temperature. Even as it is, it ranks as one of the best and most powerful ventilating fireplaces of its kind yet known to the public. It is advertised at from $10 to $50, with $10 extra for flue to carry heat to ceiling or to story above.[1]

The Tables III. and IV., although records of single experiments, are representatives of a large number made to verify each other. The tests were made with such care that the results were closely similar where the amounts of fuel burned were the same, and its hygrometric condition the same, i.e., containing about 10 per cent. of water.

Where larger quantities of fuel were burned, the saving of heat would vary in proportion, on account of the varying absorption of heat in the walls of the heaters and in the brickwork. There should also be a slight variation, for the same reason, between the calorific power of the heaters themselves, corresponding to variations in the amounts of fuel consumed, because of the different methods of setting, and of the presence or absence of a fire-back inside the iron case of the stove.

In order to ascertain these differences, as well as to test more fully the accuracy of the results previously obtained, careful experiments were made, on two successive evenings, on the Dimmick Heater, and on the "Fire on the Hearth" Heater. These two heaters may be taken as types of the various kinds of ventilating fireplaces heretofore described, and their calorific power once accurately obtained we have a gauge for the rest.

These may be divided into two classes, the first having hot-air circulation tubes, and the second having a radiating drum above the fire and

---

[1] It can be had of the Dimmick Heater Company, Cincinnati, Ohio.

a smooth or ribbed shell for its fire-box. The Dimmick Heater represents the first, and the "Fire on the Hearth" Heater the second class. The experiments were made under similar conditions with those previously made, but burning in each case 8 kilograms of wood, instead of 3. Most of the experiments herein described having been made after office hours the liability to interruption was avoided and greater accuracy assured.

Great care was taken to protect the thermometers by plates of glazed tile from the direct radiation of surrounding objects likely to affect them. The experiment recorded in Table V. (Appendix) was made on the "Fire on the Hearth" Heater; that in Table VI. on the Dimmick Heater. In the former the size of the left-hand register was slightly enlarged beyond what it had been in the previous experiments, measuring in this 150 square centimeters in area and in the previous only 110 square centimeters. Both heaters were set in the most careful manner, so as to insure the best contact of the fresh air with their heating surfaces, and the observations were taken nearly every minute, although only one in every five minutes is recorded in the accompanying tables, on account of want of space. The calculations were made on the figures for each minute, and the sums of the results obtained for intermediate minutes not here recorded are placed in the tables opposite those given.

By Table V. we find the heat saved by the "Fire on the Hearth" Heater in burning 8 kilograms of wood was sufficient to raise the temperature of 6,797 cubic meters of air $1°$ C. This is equivalent to 2,121 heat units. Assuming that our 8 kilograms of wood, containing about 10 per cent. of water, yielded $8 \times 3,590 = 28,720$ units, the amount saved was again 7 per cent., as in the previous experiments, of which Table III. records one. Add 6 per cent. for radiation, and we have again 13 per cent. utilized where wood is burned, and $7 + 13$, or 20, per cent. where coal is the fuel, and with the upright double flue attachment 25 per cent. or 30 per cent. as before. We see by this table, columns 1 and 10, that, while it took but a little over an hour to burn up the 8 kilograms of wood, the heat remained in the fire-back and brickwork for over $2\frac{1}{2}$ hours after the wood was burnt out, and that, indeed, more heat was given out after the fire had gone out than while it was burning.

By Table VI. we have an equivalent of 2,645 cubic meters raised $1°$ C. for the opening of 40 square centimeters area, and $2,645 \times \frac{130}{50} = 6,877$ cubic meters raised $1°$ C. for the other opening, making a total of 9,522 cubic meters. This is equivalent to 2,974 heat units, making a saving of 13 per cent., or 1 per cent. more than was obtained by the previous experiment, recorded in Table IV.

Fig. 116, redrawn from Johnson's Encyclopædia, represents a ventilating fireplace exhibited in the English Department of the Centennial Exhibition of 1876. It is very similar to the Dimmick Heater in principle, though widely different in the appearance of the exterior and in the manner in which the heated air is introduced into the apartment. These two fireplaces are not provided with set blowers, as is the case with the "Fire on the Hearth" Heater, and with the various forms of the Baltimore Heater.

so called. In the "Fire on the Hearth" Heater a fire may be kept over night by replenishing with fuel before retiring and leaving all blowers wide open and the base draught damper slides closed. If it be desired to put out the fire altogether, the lower sliding-blowers and the base draught damper should be shut and the upper blower slide left wide open. On the other hand the fire may be made to burn out slowly where the chimney draught is strong, by shutting all blowers. There will be sufficient inflow of air through crevices to burn out all fire before morning. Thus the fire is quite under control, and may be regulated to suit any condition by properly adjusting the blowers and the sliding dampers in front of the base of the stove. When these blowers are closed the "Fire on the Hearth" Heater is somewhat similar in exterior appearance to the Baltimore Heater, but more inviting-looking for private houses as having less the appearance of a furnace in the arrangement of the blowers. The Baltimore Heater is said to have been invented about 30 years ago by Latrobe, and was for some time called the "Latrobe Heater." It is now manufactured by different firms under various names, prominent among which are the "New Silver Palace" and the "Baltimorean," made by Bibb & Son, of Baltimore, Md., the "Lawson's Fireplace Furnace," manufactured by Fuller, Warren & Co., of Troy, N.Y., and the "Sunnyside Fireplace Heater," of Stuart, Peterson & Co., Philadelphia.

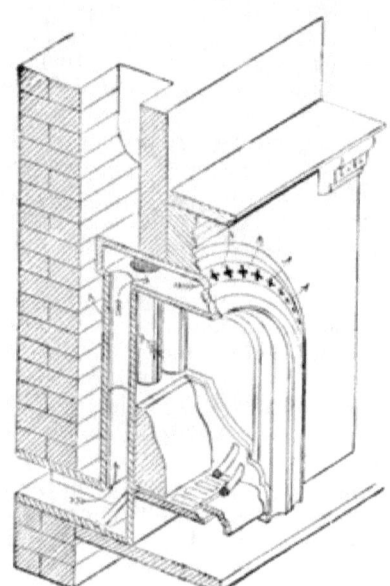

Fig. 116   Ventilating Fireplace.   Redrawn from Johnson's Encyclopædia.

These heaters are really nothing more than small furnaces, set in an ordinary fireplace under a mantel. They have regular swinging furnace doors, provided with transparent mica panels arranged in tiers over each other like the windows of steamboat state-rooms. They have, however, this great advantage over the ordinary furnace, that though they cannot be converted into an open fireplace at pleasure by simply sliding the blowers into side pockets, they nevertheless furnish direct radiation in that part of the house where it is needed and healthful, rather than in the cellar, where it is worse than useless. These heaters are provided with double flues to utilize the heat of the smoke in the manner already shown in Figs. 111, 112, and 115.

Figs. 117 and 118 show a Yankee method of treating the Galton flue in a "tasty" manner. The outer pipe takes the form of "an elegant stove," and is placed in the room in front of the fireplace, which is built for ornament, and "closed up nicely with a screen." With all its tastiness, what a cheerless and uninviting effect is produced, and how false the treat-

ment both artistically and economically! In one sense the design is true,
—the heat is generated by a stove below, and by a stove above it is represented. But in every other sense it is false. The envelope has the form of a heat generator without performing its functions of consuming fuel or producing ventilation; and the fireplace is a sham of the worst kind. Practically this treatment is contrary to the correct principles of heating, inas-

Fig. 117. Stove Radiator

much as, except where a hot-air furnace is used in connection with the apparatus, the ventilation of the room is reduced to a minimum, notwithstanding the deceiving presence of the fireplace, even when unscreened.

Used with a furnace the principle may be employed to advantage; but, without its assistance, this radiator, instead of warming fresh air from the outside on its entrance, as it should, simply creates a feeble current in the neighborhood of the stove itself, without changing the air of the room; and what fresh air will find unwelcomed entrance must squeeze itself in through door and window-cracks, contraband, and do what mischief it can, in revenge for its cold reception, before it is hustled out again through the fireplace opening. Hence no proper ventilating draught is produced by this fireplace, and the imitation stove, hav-

Fig. 113. Stove Radiator.

ing no fire of its own, is even more absolutely hostile to ventilation than the famous anti-ventilating German porcelain stove itself. It is worse than the ordinary stove, because it is necessarily hermetically sealed for the sake of the draught in the range below.

JACKSON'S VENTILATING FIREPLACE.*

We come now to a form of ventilating fireplace which combines to a remarkable extent the desiderata heretofore set forth, and at the same time presents a most pleasing external appearance. In the front elevation (Fig. 121) we see apparently nothing more than the usual open fireplace with a frame decorated in a tasteful manner. The fresh air enters the room through the openworked top of the frame at F. The section (Fig. 119) shows us the manner in which this fresh air is warmed. It enters the lower chamber B B through the register A, where it is partially warmed before it rises to the chamber surrounding the back and sides of the fireplace. Thence it enters the chamber D, where it plays around the short tubes forming the chimney-throat, and passes thence through the perforated frame above described into the apartment. Fig. 122 shows the plan of the grate and the apparatus for shutting off the fresh-air supply. This latter consists simply of a disc of iron rotated by a lever so as to close wholly or in part the mouth of the fresh-air duct shown in section at A. Fig. 120 shows the small smoke-pipes in the chimney-throat with the fresh-air chamber surrounding them.

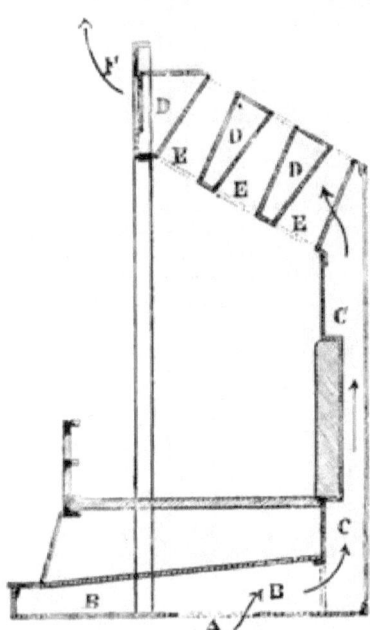

Fig. 119. Jackson's Ventilating Fireplace.

Table VII. (Appendix) shows the heating power of the Jackson Fireplace. Before lighting the fire the anemometer at the register was motionless,

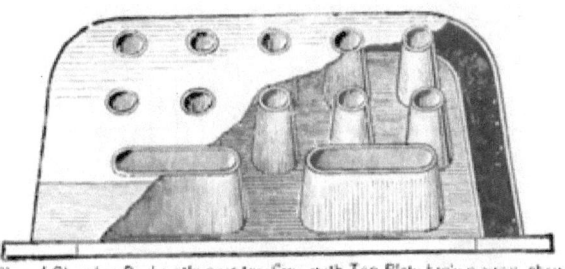

showing that the air was stagnant, and the ventilation nothing, or at least imperceptible, inasmuch as the doors and windows were tightly closed.

---

* See appendix.

The moment the fire was kindled a current of fresh air set in, and in a few moments became powerful enough to blow out the light of a candle

Fig. 121. Front View of Jackson's Ventilating Fireplace.

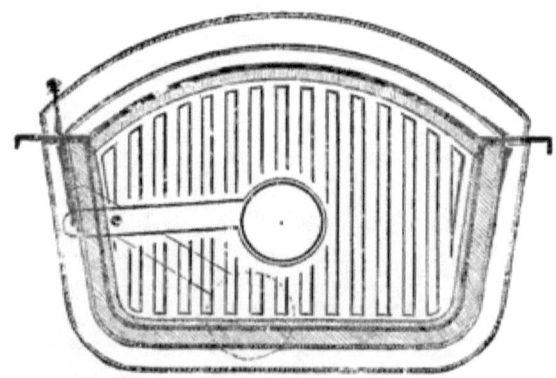

Fig. 122. Plan of Chamber B, directly under the Fire.

held in it, and warm enough to melt the wax. As will be seen by the table, it poured into the room at the rate of 138 meters a minute, heated nearly to the boiling-point of water. Indeed, so great was the heat that the metallic part of the anemometer held in the current soon became too hot to touch, and showed that where hot fires are needed the mantel-shelf used over these fireplaces should be constructed of terra-cotta, marble, or some incombustible material, in order to avoid danger of destruction by the heat.

In order to render the tests more reliable, a wooden box or flue was built around the fresh-air inlet register, to collect the air and conduct it outwards and upwards so that the thermometer placed in the current would be protected from radiation from the fireplace and other external sources. The air thus collected entered the room, of course, in a stronger current than it would otherwise have done.

By the combustion of 3 kilograms of wood enough heat was saved to raise the temperature of 9,674 kilograms of air $1°$ Centigrade (supposing the air at $0°$, $20°$, $40°$, $60°$, $100°$, weighed respectively 1.3, 1.2, 1.1, 1, and 0.9 kilograms per cubic meter). This is equivalent to 2,321 units. The wood used in the experiment contained 9 per cent., by weight, of water. Allowing for perfectly dry wood 4,000 units, our wood would yield $.91 \times 4,000 = 3,640$ units per kilogram, and for 3 kilograms 10,920 units. But to evaporate the .09 of water contained in the wood would render latent $(534 + 75) \times 3 \times .09 = 164$ units of the heat generated. This should therefore be deducted from the 10,920 units, giving an available power of 10,756. In the above equation 534 represents, according to Despretz, the number of units rendered latent in transforming 1 kilog. of water at $100°$ Centigrade to vapor under ordinary atmospheric pressure, and 75 represents the number of units required to raise to the boiling-point the temperature of 1 kilogram of water from $25°$ Centigrade, which was the temperature of the outer air and of our fuel at the beginning of the experiment. The amount saved, 2,321 units, was therefore $\frac{2321}{10756} = 21$ per cent. of the total available heat generated. Add 6 per cent. for that obtained for direct radiation, and we have 27 per cent. utilized. Adding, as before, 5 per cent. where the upright iron flue is added, and we have a grand total of 32 per cent. obtained by the Jackson Fireplace.

Few persons realize the extent to which kiln-dried wood reabsorbs the moisture expelled by the drying. The wood used in the experiment had been kiln-dried, but had again absorbed from the atmosphere 9 per cent. of water. A portion of that used was cut up into small pieces and weighed. It was then redried and weighed again. The drying was conducted in an air bath maintained at a temperature of $150°$ Centigrade. Before drying the sample weighed 36,155 grams, and after drying only 33,169 grams, showing a loss of 2,986 grams, or nearly 9 per cent. of the whole; or, in other words, that the kiln-dried wood used in our experiment had reabsorbed 9 per cent. of water from the atmosphere.

In testing the wood used in the experiments on the Dimmick and Fireplace Heaters, the sample, weighing 22,683 grams, lost, after drying for 20 minutes in air heated to $150°$, 3,097 grams, or 13 per cent. of its weight. A further exposure for 3 hours to the drying heat reduced its weight only 22 ten thousandths of a gram, so that the wood might then be considered practically dry. The sample was then exposed for a week to the air of the house, and again weighed. It was found to have regained the greater part of the water expelled by the drying. It weighed 24.33+ grams, showing a gain of 1.774+ grams, or 7 per cent. of its weight. The rapidity with which kiln-dried wood, when fresh from the kiln and very dry, absorbs moisture from the air was shown in the process of weighing our samples. When placed on the scales, immediately after drying, it was found to gain 2 or 3 ten thousandths of a gram per minute. These experiments on the dryness of wood show how much the calorific power of the material is affected, not only by the method of preparing it, but also by the time it has stood exposed to the air after drying, and even with the condition of the atmosphere at the time of its use. The kiln-dried wood tested showed a variation of 8 per cent. in the amount of moisture it contained after drying. In other words, its available calorific power varied between 1,000 and about 3,600. Hence the importance of knowing the hygrometric condition of our wood before making our experiments. Hence, also, the economy of seeing that the wood we buy for fuel is perfectly dry.

These experiments were made in the laboratory of Mr. W. E. C. Eustis, whose liberality in offering me the free use of a set of scales of unusual delicacy, and other apparatus needed, I take this occasion gratefully to acknowledge.

In another experiment made on the Jackson Fireplace quite a strong breeze was blowing into the fresh-air duct from the outside, so that the anemometer recorded an entering current of 70 meters per minute before the fire was lighted. This outside pressure of course increased the effectiveness of the heater, and the saving amounted to about 1 per cent. more than when the air outside was still. This test was made on the very warm evening of June 25, from 9 to 12 o'clock, the thermometer outside standing at 25° C. (77° F.). In winter, when the difference between the outer air and that of the flue is lower, a greater saving of heat is realized from any of these heaters; but the experiments lose in accuracy, partly on account of the difficulty of measuring the temperature of the inflowing fresh air current at the beginning and end of the experiment. The thermometer is influenced by radiation from the surrounding objects in the room, from which it is, of course, impossible to protect it absolutely. If it were possible, it would indicate a temperature of over 100° below the freezing-point of water, the temperature of celestial space being, according to Pouillet, as low as $-150°$ C. Only an approximate degree of accuracy can, therefore, be expected, and it is greatest when the temperature of the room is nearest that of the inflowing air currents, as is the case in summer.

The Jackson Fireplace is at present manufactured in two sizes only. The price now (1881) of the smaller size, 30 in. wide and 32 in. high, requiring a fireplace opening in brickwork 28 in. wide, 32 in. high, and 15 in. deep, is $85, in brass; $65, all nickel-plated or bronzed; or $55, black.

with nickeled basket. Another size, made for very large rooms, is 39 in. wide, 36 in. high (outside of frame), and requires a fireplace 32 in. wide, 35½ in. high, and 15 in. deep. They are to be obtained of Edwin A. Jackson & Brother, No. 315 East Twenty-eighth street, New York.[1]

Fig. 123.

The manufacturers are prepared to furnish with each grate an ornamental band of metal to diminish the height of the opening at the top after the manner of a narrow blower, for cases where the draught of the chimney is not good. By means of this strip this fireplace may be used with safety even where the chimney-draught is feeble.

With any of the fireplaces mentioned herein a flue, for disposing of the ashes, may be constructed below the grate, as shown in Fig. 123. The flue forms an ash-pit, into which the ashes fall from the grate when shaken or dumped. The ashes are then removed through the door B, in the basement, at the bottom of the flue. A "soufflet" pipe, D, has been provided, through which air may be taken from below to increase the draught, when desired, after the principle of the Winter Fireplace; but the soufflet, in a well-constructed fireplace, is unnecessary, and its use is only to be recommended when better construction is impracticable.

In the fireplace represented in the accompanying cut, Fig. 124, called the "Franklin Reflector," the smoke circulates behind and below the fire, as indicated by the arrows, in order to increase the radiating surface of the heater. But no fresh air is brought in contact with these surfaces, and they are not arranged in the manner best calculated to give out their heat. The reflecting surface over the fuel is intended to perform the double office of reflecting the rays of heat from the fire into the room, and of turning the currents of air from the room upon the fire, thus securing the greatest amount of radiation, and producing a more complete combustion of the fuel, while it also diminishes the amount of cool air entering the chimney-flue. The same objects were accomplished by the fireplace of M. Tonet Chambor, already described in Figs. 42 and 43,

---

[1] Another form, lately perfected, is to be obtained of Wm. H. Jackson & Co., Union Square, New York. See Appendix.

where the precaution was taken to provide openings above the reflector, for the purpose of carrying the smoke directly into the flue when the fire was first lighted. We believe that, with certain modifications hereafter to be suggested, the Franklin Reflector may be made to combine in the form of

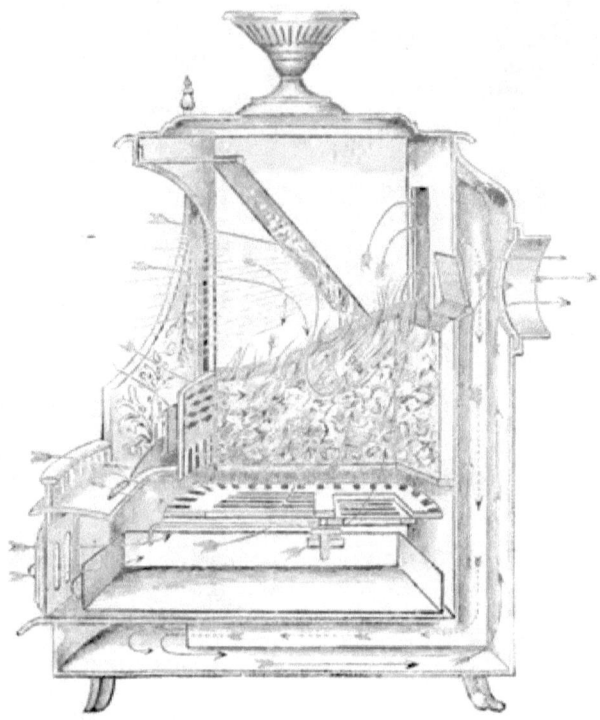

Fig. 124. Franklin Reflector.

a stove most of the advantages possible to be obtained by an open fireplace. It is manufactured by James Spear & Co., of Philadelphia.

To conclude our historical sketch, we have reserved a fireplace described by Peclet in his "Treatise on Heat," and shown in Fig. 125, as the best in principle, and one which, though crude and defective in form, is yet most likely to lead to important results.

The principle of this device is the formation of the chief heating surface above the fireplace, and in the waste space behind the chimney-breast, rather than in the immediate neighborhood of the fire.

The great advantages of the arrangement are (1), the acquirement of ample room in the waste space of the chimney-breast for the proper development of the heating surface; (2), the removal of this surface from immediate contact with the fire, by which it might be overheated to the injury of the fresh air, and finally destroyed; (3), the detachment of the air-heating surfaces from the fireplace proper, which may, therefore, be made of any form or material desired. If the fireplace already exist it may be left untouched, except above, where it has to be connected with the air-heater; (4), the facility with which the heating surface may be reached for cleaning, repair, or renewal without disturbing fireplace or mantel;

Fig. 125. Ventilating Fireplace. From Peclet.

and, finally (5), the simplicity and cheapness of its construction. Notwithstanding its evident advantages, the principle was left undeveloped, and as the apparatus described by Peclet was defective it was abandoned. It was seen that the bends in the smoke-flue and the reversed course of the smoke were liable to injure the draught and corrode the pipe. These difficulties were easiest removed by simply pulling the pipe out straight again, which was accordingly done at once, and all that remained was the original Galton flue. Thus the problem was solved somewhat after the manner of the Gordian knot, and the device was summarily consigned to oblivion. Thus it is that the fireplace of to-day stands in practice nearly as it did at the time of Gauger.

The English, whose national fondness for the old open fireplace ought to have led them to study its utmost development, seem, with their characteristic slowness to adopt new and foreign methods, to have stubbornly refused to follow any other course than that laid out for them by Rumford.

The Germans are satisfied with their porcelain stove.

The French have been so busy working up the Gauger fireplace that they have not yet thought of looking behind the chimney-breast to reflect upon the waste of useful space; and the Americans have been too busy with everything else to give the subject until lately any thought at all.

Fig. 126. The "Country Parson's" Grate.

The fireplace given in Figs. 126 and 127, for instance, just brought out in England with éclat, indicates the tendency in that country. A correspondent of the London *Times* of January 30, 1877, writes of this form of fireplace: it "has excited much attention, for I have received in two days more than two hundred letters on the subject, to which printed replies will be sent in a few days. Many of these letters are from hospitals, public schools, military and other public institutions," etc. Yet they are nothing more than a modification of the Rumford grate, and yield, at the utmost, but from 5 to 15 per cent. of the heat generated by the fuel, while they retain all the radical defects of the ordinary fireplace.

Constructed upon a principle quite the reverse of that of the Franklin Reflector, they are set high, and are in form high, narrow, and shallow, instead of low, broad, and deep. They have the advantage of heating the floor better for being set high, and occasion less dangerous draughts around the feet. Their shape is favorable for the slow combustion of coal, and for radiation; but they are not suitable for burning wood, since their depth is not over $1\frac{1}{2}$ inches from back to front at the base, and $5\frac{1}{2}$ inches at the level of the top bar. The floor of the fire-trough is of fire-brick.

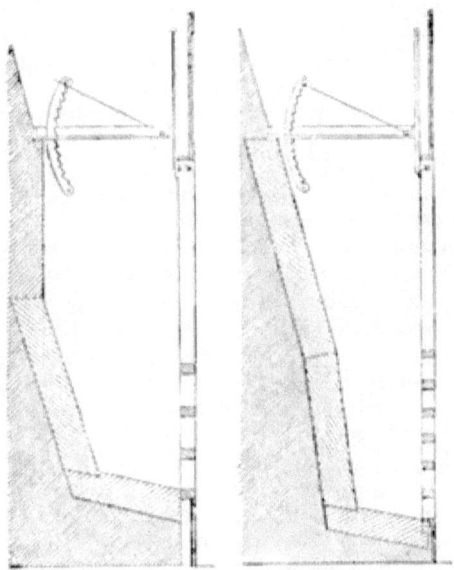

Fig. 127. Sectional Views.

and not of grating, so that air passes into the fire through the front of the grate, and not under it. This causes the coal to burn slowly, and each coal glows on the side toward the room. Coke, with a small admixture of coal, may be burned in them, instead of coal alone.

The Englishman, proud as he is of his careful arrangements for domestic comfort and luxury, is outdone in this most important particular even by the inhabitants of distant Asia. The Persian enjoys his pipe before an open fireplace as much more rational in construction as it is more pleasing in appearance than the comparatively miserable object now receiving the commendation of the civilized Briton. The picture at the end of this chapter shows us a cheerful fire sparkling like a gem in a casket so high and ample that its radiating power is utilized to the best advantage, while the hood and sides serve the purpose of a stove in heating the surrounding air and objects by convection and radiation.

The direct rays of the sun are necessary to the complete development of animal life, and the great difference in the amount of radiation of solar light and heat in the various parts of the globe causes a marked difference in national character. Where the sun cannot be enjoyed, or where its rays are feeble and insufficient, the open fireplace becomes its natural substitute, and so long as our physical natures remain the same, so long will the open fire be cherished as a priceless boon and companion.

It is a provision of nature that there shall be a wide difference between the temperature of our bodies and that of the air about us; and we find that the greater that difference, within certain reasonable limits, the more energetic and vigorous is the action of all our animal functions. Air entering our lungs at a low temperature, near freezing-point, does, as we have said, twice as much work in purifying the blood as the same amount of air entering at the temperature of our bodies, and in winter, with the warm rays of the sun striking us, we feel twice as vigorous as we do in summer, when the air is hot and suffocating.

When a room is warmed by an open fire the walls are warmer than the air, because radiant heat has the remarkable property of passing through air without raising its temperature. Thus the occupant breathes air refreshingly cool, while the walls, being comparatively highly heated, do not absorb his animal heat with inconvenient rapidity. Nevertheless the outside air must be tempered to a certain extent before entering the room to avoid the danger caused by cold currents striking our bodies, and it is the object of the ventilating fireplace to temper this incoming air to the proper degree, without waste of fuel or labor.

We have reviewed the progressive steps already made in this direction up to the present time, and we find the utmost that has been accomplished, to our knowledge, by any form of fireplace, in the way of utilizing to good advantage the heat generated by the fuel, has been a saving of from 30 to 40 per cent., applied rarely to the best advantage in preparing and distributing the fresh air for our use. At its best, it is looked upon as a luxury too expensive for the poor man to enjoy. Under the assumption that the element of wastefulness is a necessary condition of its being, he turns, as his only resort, to the closed stove. The efforts of the inventor are therefore directed to increasing the economy of the heater which is used where the value of economy is best appreciated, to the neglect of the open fireplace which he has been accustomed to look upon as incurable.

It is the duty of those who entertain a contrary opinion, and who have the facilities for putting their views in a practical form, to contribute the results of their investigations to the general fund. Small as may be the value of individual results in themselves, they may yet serve as suggestions from which, in other hands, valuable fruit may spring; and little as we may expect to receive from any single contributor, yet the labor of many working together, in the light of past experience and with the aid of the advanced scientific and mechanical knowledge of the day, may, before long, be sufficient to convert the open fireplace from an expensive, troublesome, and even dangerous luxury enjoyed only by the few, into a source of health, comfort, and economy for all.

Fig. 128. Persian Fireplace.

PLATES.

PLATE VII.

Bed-chamber in a château of the fifteenth century. The chimney breast is overloaded with sculpture, as is also the furniture, and the entire finish of the room, characteristic of the Gothic style in its decadence. From Viollet-le-Duc's "Dictionaire du Mobilier Français." A. Morel & Co., Publishers, Paris.

PLATE VII.

PLATE VIII.

Stone fireplace in the Hotel de Ville of Lyons, France. Seventeenth century. From E. Rouyer, "L'Art Architectural en France." Noblet et Baudry, Publishers, Paris.

PLATE VIII.

PLATE IX.

Fireplace in the style of the French Renaissance. Built in 1567.
From *L'Art pour Tous*. A. Morel & Co., Publishers, Paris.

PLATE IX.

PLATE X.

Fireplace in the Persian drawing-room of the house of M. le Comte Branicki, Paris. From the *Encyclopédie d'Architecture*. A. Morel & Co., Publishers, Paris.

PLATE X.

PLATE XI.

Wooden fireplace in the bed-chamber of Louis XIII., king of France, in the Chateau of Cheverny (near Blois, France). The picture over the mantel represents a scene in the history of Perseus. Conducted by Minerva he petrifies his enemies by showing them the head of Medusa. The small tablet on the facing is made of mosaic on a gold ground. It represents children playing with the head of Medusa. Other scenes in the life of Perseus and Andromeda are painted on the ceiling and over the doors. The walls are covered with magnificent tapestry, of which a part is shown at the right and left of the mantel. *L'Art Architectural en France*. Vol. I. By E. Rouet. Noblet et Baudry, Publishers, Paris.

PLATE XI.

PLATE XII.

Dining-room fireplace designed by Mr. Escalier, architect, Paris. From *Le Moniteur des Architectes* for June, 1880. A. Levy, Publisher, Paris.

PLATE XII.

PLATE XIII.

Fireplace in a bed-chamber in the Château de Tanlay, France. From Sauvageot, "Palais et Châteaux de France." A. Morel & Co., Publishers, Paris.

PLATE XIII.

PLATE XIV.

Fireplace in the castle of Heidelberg.

PLATE XIV.

PLATE XV.

Fireplace in the "Salle des Gardes," at the Château de Cormatin. Seventeenth century. Louis XIII. From *L'Art pour Tous* for 1867, 1868. A. Morel & Co., Publishers, Paris.

PLATE XV.

PLATE XVI.

Stone fireplace at the Museum of the Hôtel de Cluny, Paris. French Renaissance. The fireplace formerly stood in a house built at Troyes in the sixteenth century, and was brought to Paris soon after the foundation of the Museum. From *L'Art pour Tous* for 1869, 1870. A. Morel & Co., Publishers, Paris.

PLATE XVI.

PLATE XVII.

Stone fireplace in a house at Sarlat, France. The sculpture above the mantel is life-size. From E. Rouyer, "L'Art Architectural en France." Noblet et Baudry, Publishers, Paris.

PLATE XVII.

PLATE XVIII.

Fireplace in the "Salle des Gardes," in the "Hôtel D'Alluyer," at Blois, France. House of the Minister Robertet, of Louis XII. and François I. It is built of stone, measures 3^m, 68 in height and 3^m, 24 in width. The arms of Robertet are sculptured over the piers. The main panel is surrounded by a moulding which contains the knotted cordelière of Anne de Bretagne. The field of the panel is decorated with the losanges alternately of France and Bretagne. The shield of France is surmounted by the crown and surrounded by the collar of the order of St. Michel. The birds in the carved cornice are sculptured with the arms of Michelle Saillard, wife of Robertet. From Rouyer, "L'Art Architectural en France." Noblet et Baudry, Publishers, Paris.

PLATE XVIII.

PLATE XIX.

Fireplace in the chamber of the Archbishop, Château de Tanlay, France. From Sauvageot, "Palais et Châteaux de France." A. Morel & Co., Publishers, Paris.

PLATE XIX.

PLATE XX.

Stone fireplace in the Château de Baynac, France. Renaissance style. From E. Rouyer, "L'Art Architectural en France." Noblet et Baudry, Publishers, Paris.

PLATE XX.

PLATE XXI.

Dining-room fireplace in modern English Gothic style. From B. J. Talbert.

PLATE XXI.

PLATE XXII.

Fireplace in the Hôtel de Vogué, at Dijon. Fireplace built in the beginning of the eighteenth century. From Sauvageot, "Palais, Châteaux, etc., de France." A. Morel & Co., Publishers, Paris.

PLATE XXII.

PLATE XXIII.

Fireplace in the smoking-room of the house of M. Le Comte Branicki, Paris. From the "Encyclopedie d'Architecture." A. Morel & Co., Publishers, Paris.

PLATE XXIII.

PLATE XXIV.

Fireplace in the "Salon des Médailles," in the Palace of Versailles; age of Louis XV. From E. Rouyer, "L'Art Architectural en France." Noblet et Bandry, Publishers, Paris.

PLATE XXIV.

PLATE XXV.

Renaissance fireplace.   Exhibited at the Paris Exhibition of 1878.

PLATE XXV.

PLATE XXVI.

Fireplace in a house in the Rue de Berlin, Paris; L. Dupré, architect; A. Millèt, sculptor. The fireplace is built of stone with facings of red marble. The sculpture on the frieze is in bas-relief, in white marble, and represents Winter. The total width is 1^m, 90, and the height to the top of the pediment is 2^m, 40. Its cost was 6,000 francs, made at Paris. From the " Revue Générale de l'Architecture et des Travaux Publics," César Daly. 1872. Vol. xxix. Ducher & Co., Publishers, Paris.

PLATE XXVI.

PLATE XXVII.

Fireplace in the grand drawing-room of the Bishop's palace at Beauvais, France. By Mr. E. Vaudremer, diocesan architect of the city of Paris. From the "Revue Générale de l'Architecture et des Travaux Publics." Ducher & Co., Publishers, Paris.

PLATE XXVII.

PLATE XXVIII.

Fireplace displayed at the Centennial Exhibition of 1876 at Philadelphia, exhibited by Howard & Sons, of London. From Harper's Weekly, of Oct. 14th, 1876, published by Harper & Brothers, New York.

PLATE XXVIII.

PLATE XXIX.
Old fireplace at Morlaix, Bretagne, France.

PLATE XXIX.

PLATE XXX.
Fireplace at San Germano, Italy.

PLATE XXX.

PLATE XXXI.

Fireplace in the National Museum, at Florence, Italy.

PLATE XXXI.

CHAPTER III.

SUGGESTIONS FOR THE IMPROVEMENT OF THE OPEN FIREPLACE.

If we were to see a tribe of savages sitting astride of locomotive steam engines, and, in their ignorance of the application of steam, using them as we do ordinary carriages dragged about by horses, we should be inclined to turn up our civilized noses and smile at the exhibition of simplicity. But if when these savages learned how a single engine, with its strength properly applied, was capable of doing the work of the entire tribe, they should, instead of applying steam to the engines already built, continue to use them only as carriages, and build others to act as motors, we would have before us an example of extravagance and folly only equalled by our own in our method of heating.

We fill our houses with open fires and use them only as radiators, although we know that the heat of a single one, properly applied, would be capable of doing the work of the entire house. Instead of applying furnace pipes to one of the fireplaces already built, we continue to use them only as radiators, and build others down cellar to act only as air-heaters.

If the savage condescended to criticise he would have the right to say, "With all your boasted civilization you are even more barbarous than we, because, while it is true that we lose the motive power of our carriages, we are still able to use the carrying power of our motors. You, however, lose both the smoke heat of your upper furnaces and the radiant heat of your lower ones."

We have shown that open fires as they are now used are incapable, without external aid, of properly heating our buildings. The air supplying the draught must, by some means, be moderately warmed before it enters. It should not be as warm as the walls of the room, nor cold enough to occasion discomfort to the occupants. This preparation of the air is usually effected by a furnace in the cellar, and the result of the combination of furnace and fireplace is, *under proper conditions*, and with all precautions taken against gas,[1] satisfactory except from the one stand-point of economy. With it every desideratum given in our description, at the

---

[1] It is probable that the use of steam for heating this fresh air will become much more general, and that in cities and towns steam pipes, like gas, drain, and water pipes, supplied from a central source, will take the place of furnaces. Any improved form of apparatus for heating air by steam will assist, but can never supplant, the open fireplace.

beginning of these articles, of ideal perfection may with care be obtained, excepting the first and all-important consideration, "that all the heat generated by the combustion of the fuel be utilized in heating and ventilating the house, and that the combustion of the fuel be complete." To satisfy this condition it is evident that the furnace and fireplace must be combined in one apparatus, for it is only in this way that a single fire can do the work of both.

How this combination can best be effected, and what sanitary and pecuniary advantages may result therefrom, it is the object of this chapter to inquire.

In our historical sketch we have shown to what extent and by what steps the work has been advanced up to the present time. It reaches its fullest development in the fireplace described by Peclet, Fig. 125, but excepting in this we find no evidence of an attempt to give the air-heating surfaces an extension in the slightest degree proportionate to the size of the grate or to the amount of fuel consumed, or to adapt the improved methods and forms of the hot-air furnace to the new conditions imposed. The air-heating surfaces are small and insignificant compared with the size of the grate, and are confined in most cases to a very small area in the immediate neighborhood of the fire. In the Dimmick Heater, with a grate surface of about a tenth of a square meter, we have a radiating surface of scarcely a square meter, or about 10 times the grate area. In the Fireplace Heater,[1] the Jackson, Joly, Fondet, Cordier, and other similar heaters, the proportion is the same, or but little greater. Yet in our best modern furnaces it mounts to from 50 to 200 times the grate area.

Sanford's Challenge Furnace (No. 40), for instance, to take an American example, has a heating surface of 70 times the grate surface. According to Bose, the proportion should be 160 or 180 to 1, and, according to Morin, from 108 to 200 to 1, though in American practice it is seldom over 50 to 1, with a heating efficiency of perhaps 60 or 70 per cent. of the total heat produced by the fuel. The Peerless Furnace (No. 16), with a grate area of 0.13 square meter, has an air-heating surface of 6.7 square meters, or 51 times its grate surface. The Chilson (No. 8), the Golden Eagle (No. 8), the McGregor (No. 4), and the Soapstone Furnace (No. 18), have respectively, according to measurements made by the writer, heating surfaces of 40, 56, 31, and 74 times their grate surfaces.

Our ventilating fireplaces, then, should have a much greater air-heating surface than has heretofore been given them, if we would obtain from the fuel the greatest amount of heat possible.

In a furnace all the air which enters the fire-pot is brought into close contact with the fuel by the position of its entrance below the grate. The amount of air entering the smoke-flue is, therefore, but slightly in excess of what is actually required to support combustion, and its temperature

---

[1] The jackets surrounding the heater add considerably to the heating power, but cannot, of course, be included in the estimate of direct heating surface. They correspond to the casing of a furnace, and might be extended *ad libitum*.

is correspondingly high. But with an open fire a greater amount of cold air enters the flue, and its temperature is lowered in proportion. It may therefore, reasonably be asked if this cool air from the room would not so much diminish the heating power of the flue as to render its development into a complete furnace useless.

This first and most important consideration should be carefully looked into before we proceed further, and any conclusions reached by reasoning should be tested by actual experiment.

Theoretically. Wood perfectly dry requires for each kilogram burned, say, 10 cubic meters of air, developing, say, 4,000 units of heat. The temperature of this air as it leaves the fire would therefore theoretically be $\frac{4000}{10\times1.486\times21} = 1.282°$ C., which is about the melting-point of steel. So that a certain quantity of air beyond what is absolutely demanded by combustion is necessary to prevent the destruction of the furnace. Were 20 cubic meters of air instead of 10 used, the temperature of the air would be 641° C., or sufficient to raise iron to a dull red heat. In an open fireplace with a contracted chimney-throat tested by the writer, a little over 35 cubic meters of air per kilogram of wood passed up the flue, and its temperature, as tested by a chemist's thermometer placed in a hole perforated in the flue for the purpose, rose somewhat above 300° C. In another fireplace having a larger throat, much more air entered, and the temperature of the smoke in the flue could not be raised above 200° C. with the same quantity of wood burned 1 kilogram at a time. But with a throat contracted still more than in the first place, a still higher temperature of the smoke was obtainable, showing that by regulating the size of the chimney-throat, any temperature of the smoke may be easily obtained up to 400 or 500 degrees. When hard coal is used for fuel a good draught is necessary in order to produce a combustion of the requisite rapidity to heat the house. When the feed-door of a furnace is left open, this draught may be insufficient where hard coal is used. But where soft coal or wood is used, as is generally the case with open fires, no difficulty is found in obtaining ample heat with the feed-door standing open.

In an open fireplace the chimney-throat corresponds with the feed-door of a furnace, and it is this which regulates the amount of cool air entering the chimney, and not the size of the fireplace itself. When this throat is small, the hot products of combustion will fill it to the exclusion of the cold air from the room, and the temperature of the smoke in the flue will be high independently of the actual size of the fireplace.

It must be borne in mind that the flues of a furnace do not heat the fresh air by *radiation*, but by convection or contact of air. With *radiation* the higher the temperature of the heating surface the greater the proportion of heat given out for each degree's difference between the heated body and the surrounding air. But with *convection*, according to the researches of Dulong, the yield per degree's difference is, for all practical purposes, irrespective of the absolute temperature of the heated body, or of the difference of temperature between the heated body and the air in contact with it. With a *radiant* body at a clear red heat of 1,015° C., the amount of heat transmitted per meter per hour for each degree's difference is about 300 times that transmitted at 100° C., and at a bright white heat of 1,415° C. it rises to 4,604 times that amount! The extreme rapidity with which a body at white heat cools down to orange and cherry-red, etc., indicates that at high temperature the loss of heat is exceedingly great.

With convection, however, the difference in the loss of heat per degree is comparatively slight. Supposing that with the heated body at 0° C. and the air at 15° C., the loss by contact or by radiation were 1, at 250° C. it would be by contact only 1.9, while by radiation it would be as high as 3; at 310°, 510°, 1,015°, and 1,415°, the loss by contact would be 2, 2.3, 2.7, and 2.9 respectively, while by radiation it would be 4, 13, 300, and 4,604 times greater respectively than at 0°.

There is, therefore, with furnaces no corresponding gain of heat in quantity to compensate for the loss in quality by having the heating surfaces raised to a high temperature.

For a given amount of fuel the same number of units of heat will be generated by combustion, whether the combustion be slow or rapid. But where it is rapid the products are carried away more rapidly, and the loss of heat at the top of the chimney is greater.

Berman, treating of furnaces, says: " When only a small quantity of air passes through the stove, the cockle is in danger of being overheated. Mr. Sylvester says, 'The cockle surface should not rise above 280° (F.). Beyond this it has a tendency to injure the materials of which the flues are formed. It is also heated with less economy, since, as has been observed, the smoke will pass away at a higher temperature.' The temperature of the surfaces he recommends is, however, a great deal too high; and much of the prejudice against stoves has arisen from this circumstance. Were the surface never to exceed 130° (F.), although the size of the stove would be increased, the salubrity of the air as well as the economy of the fuel would be increased also."

Theoretically, therefore, the temperature of the smoke in the flue of an ordinary fireplace, with its throat properly contracted, is sufficiently high for our purposes, and may be regulated at pleasure.

To put the matter to practical test, the writer has made numerous experiments, with the following results: —

A furnace of wrought-iron was constructed for the purpose, having a radiating surface above the fire-box of 7.5 square meters, or equal to that of a Magee furnace, No. 24. This was attached to the top of an open fireplace (the Fire-Place Heater), which served as the fire-pot, grate, and ash-pit. The apparatus was tested alternately with the feed-door (sliding bowers) open and shut. In each case 3 kilograms of wood, containing 10 per cent of water, were burned, and it was found that nearly the same amount of heat was obtained from the flues, whether the blower was open or shut, the throat being small and the fire brisk. Sufficient air entered to keep the pipes from becoming red-hot, but not enough to reduce the temperature to too low a point. Therefore, while all danger of burning or injuring the air was avoided, the heat was utilized to the best advantage.

Tables VIII. and IX. (Appendix) give in a condensed form the record of two of the experiments referred to.

In the first of the two experiments here recorded, Table VIII., the doors of the fireplace were tightly closed and strips of paper glued over the cracks and joints of the doors to make them air-tight, the base draught damper under the grate being alone left open. The apparatus then formed an ordinary furnace. The air-box was small, and the register throwing the heated air into the room measured but 15×33 centimeters, or 0.05 square meter, so that the heating surfaces were only partially cooled or utilized. Nevertheless, column 7 shows that enough heat was abstracted by what air was allowed to strike the flues to raise the temperature of 6,415 kilograms of air 1° C. This is equivalent to 1,540 units of heat. A thermometer placed one meter from the fireplace rose (column 9) 59 degrees, showing that a large portion of the radiant heat of the fire passed through the iron doors. The heat saved by contact of air amounted to $\frac{1549}{10938.3} = 14$ per cent. of the whole. Adding 3 per cent. for that obtained by radiation, we have a total saving of 17 per cent. The temperature of the room (column 8) was raised 4 degrees.

In the second experiment, Table IX., the doors were left open, and the apparatus formed an ordinary open fireplace, with a furnace attached to its smoke-flue above. Column 7 shows that 6,120 kilograms of air could have been raised 1° C., which is equivalent to 1,469 units of heat, or 13 per cent. of the whole. A thermometer placed 1 meter from the fireplace rose (column 9) 80 degrees. Adding 6 per cent. for direct radiation, we have a total saving of 19 per cent.

The temperature of the room (column 8) was raised 6 degrees. All the conditions were as nearly as possible the same in both experiments. The supply of fresh air brought to bear on the pipes was limited, but the same in both cases. In other experiments made to test the heating power of the apparatus, where double or triple the supply of air was brought in contact with the heating surfaces, and where a proper arrangement of the fresh-air box and registers was provided, the amount of heat saved was two or three times greater than that here effected.

Having found that there is neither theoretical nor practical difficulty on the score of the entrance of cool air through the chimney-throat in the way of our combination, it remains to see what kind of furnace is best adapted for our peculiar purposes.

According to Bernan, the way in which large buildings or rooms were formerly heated, particularly for manufacturing purposes, where open fires were inadmissible, was by a sort of Dutch stove, formed of a large cast or wrought iron vessel, generally square, and set upon a foundation of brickwork, enclosing the fire; and this apparatus was placed in the room to be heated. But it was found to be dangerous, and a large proportion of the accidental fires which in former times destroyed many factories originated with ill-constructed stoves. The air of the room did not move by the heated surface rapidly enough to carry off the heat as fast as it was produced, and the stove was consequently frequently red-hot. This great heat rendered all the adjacent woodwork very combustible, and when the stove cracked, or a joint opened, or any inflammable substance came in contact with it, a conflagration was inevitable. Moreover, close stoves do not assist essentially in promoting ventilation; for the quantity of air withdrawn from the room is only what is needed to support combustion. Morin estimates the ventilation from these to be less than 7 cubic meters of air for every kilogram of coal consumed. Indeed, the circulation of air they produce in a room is so sluggish that the temperature of the room varies greatly at different heights. "Ruttan — whose observations were made in Canada — states that in a stove-heated basement room, over a cold cellar, he has frequently seen water freeze on the floor when the temperature of the air at the ceiling was $100°$; and has often observed a difference of $4\frac{1}{2}°$ (F.) in the temperature of the air for every foot of height in a stove-heated school-room, 16 feet high, which was exposed on 2 sides to outside air at $0°$."[1] But if a casing is arranged around a stove, with a space left between it and the stove, open below and above, the column of air within the casing will be doubly heated by contact on one side with the stove and on the other with the casing. Being protected from the cooling influence of the surrounding air, it will rise rapidly, and produce a circulation in the room which will equalize its temperature.

The next step was to put the stove in a chamber by itself, adjoining or below the room to be heated. The external air was admitted into this chamber, warmed, and conducted by flues about the building; and the whole formed a hot-air furnace. A large amount of fresh air is brought by the casing in contact with the heating surfaces, and it strikes them forcibly on account of the strong current produced by the hot-air flues. The fresh air is generally taken from the outside, and it is in this respect, as well as in the principle of the circulation produced by the casing, that the furnace is superior to the close stove, while in the loss of the advantage of direct radiation from the sides of the heater it stands inferior to it.

The most important point to be considered in the construction of all basement furnaces alike, is the acquisition of a good chimney draught; because, of whatever material or in whatever manner they may be made, they cannot be rendered absolutely gas-tight. Even though the materials be non-porous, and the joints be tight, the very openings required to admit fuel to the fire or air to the fuel may, under a back pressure, also emit gas. Where these openings are out of sight and immediate control of the occupants, the noxious gases, often imperceptible to the senses, may enter the house without their knowledge; and this is the most prevalent cause of trouble with the hot-air furnace as it is now constructed. It is, therefore, of the first importance with these that the draught of the smoke-flue should exceed in strength that of the hot-air circulation pipes, whose powerful action is shown by the force with which the warm air

---

[1] Johnson's *Universal Cyclopædia*.

issues from the registers. The hot-air flues in a basement furnace being frequently nearly as long as the smoke-flue, and the maximum utilization of the heat of the fuel, or of its smoke, being considered the grand desideratum, these hot-air flues become hotter than the smoke-flue. The column of air in the former being, therefore, lighter than that in the latter, the smoke or gases will rush into the fresh-air flues through any crack or joint connecting the two columns together, or they will enter the house through the feed and draught doors.

The above difficulties might, however, be obviated, and absolute safety against the escape of gas be obtained, together with a complete utilization of the heat of the smoke, by bringing distinct currents of fresh air simultaneously against the heating surfaces of the furnace at various points of these surfaces, properly located with reference to each other, and entirely separated from each other. By this means a good draught might be obtained at all times, and yet the temperature of the smoke-flue be reduced to very nearly that of the outside air.

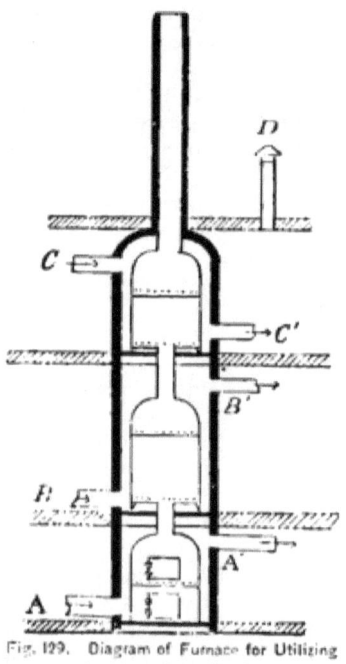

Fig. 129. Diagram of Furnace for Utilizing the Heat of the Smoke.

Let Fig. 129 represent a furnace (simply for illustration) constructed after this principle. The fresh air enters the furnace at A, B, and C, simultaneously, but into heating chambers entirely separated from each other, say at points corresponding with each floor of the house. The hot-air flues start at A', B', and C'. The outer air entering the first chamber might lower the smoke, say, from 300° to 150°, and be itself raised from 0° to 50°. A second current of fresh air at B, entering the second chamber or division of the furnace, might further cool the smoke to 75°, and be itself raised from 0° to 40°; and, finally a third supply at C, entering the third chamber, might, by taking a direction the reverse to that of the smoke, reduce the latter to or very near to 0°, and itself be raised to 40°. The average temperature of the smoke in the chimney would, though entirely cooled at the top, be

$$\frac{300+150}{2} + \frac{150+75}{2} + \frac{75+0}{2} = 225+112.5+37.5 = 125°.$$

This would be much higher, and the velocity correspondingly greater, than that in any fresh-air flue, so that the chimney draught would be good, even if the fresh-air flues were maintained at 40° or 50° throughout their entire length, and this length were equal to that of the smoke-flue. In a furnace constructed in the manner described, however, each compartment of the furnace would have only its own floor to warm, and the air-flues would have little or no perpendicular extension beyond what would be required to create in them the necessary draught. The temperature, therefore, of the fresh-air column would practically be that of the house, say 20°, and its length only the distance from its commencement, at A', B', and C', to the ventilator, D, on the roof, and consequently always less than that of the smoke-flue.

Inasmuch as the diffusion of gases will take place even in opposition to a considerable current of air, no porous material is suitable, under any circumstances, for the construction of a furnace, since the porosity not only permits an escape of gas at all times, but also serves as a connection between the hot-air and smoke columns in cases of back draught. The joints should be made in such a manner that the contraction and expansion of the materials cannot work them loose, however long the furnace be in service.

Where metal is used, its kind or thickness has but little effect, within ordinary limits, upon its heating power; for the quantity of heat which can be conducted through the thickness of metal usually employed is much greater than can be carried away by contact of air. But for greater thicknesses the amount transmitted by small pipes increases with the thickness. A cast-iron pipe 1 decimeter in internal diameter, heated on the inside to 100°, and exposed to the air at 15°, with different thicknesses of metal, would lose heat per meter and per hour as follows: The thickness being nothing, or infinitely small, the loss would be 254 units; for thickness of 2.5, 5, 10, and 15 centimeters the loss would be, respectively, 363, 472, 676, and 848 units, or in the ratios of 1.4, 1.8, 2.6, and 3.3 to 1 respectively. Where stone, brick, or terra-cotta pipes are used, whose conductibilities are much smaller than that of iron, say as 15 and 1 to 250, the variation for great thicknesses is much smaller. The reason of this is that the increase of thickness increases the radiating surface of the exterior, so that while each square meter of such surface gives out less heat than a square meter of the surface of the thin pipe, in the proportion of 0.95, 0.92, 0.89, and 0.85 to 1, for the cast-iron pipe 1 decimeter in diameter, of the thicknesses mentioned above, yet the surfaces are greater in the proportion of 1.5, 2, 3, and 4 to 1. Thus, thickening the heating or radiating flues of a furnace made of good heat-conducting materials increases their effectiveness just as do ribs or spikes cast upon the radiating surface, by increasing its superficial area. Indeed, unless the ribs are properly placed, a simple thickening of the pipe is sometimes even more effective. Thus a threaded pipe, 1 centimeter thick, 18 centimeters in diameter, and 10 meters long, threading 0.5 centimeter deep, standing vertically, was tested by the writer, and found to yield less heat than a smooth pipe 1 centimeter thick, and of the same diameter and height, although the actual radiating surface was twice as great on the threaded as on the smooth pipe. The threading being perpendicular to the direction of the air current, it lost more than half of its effectiveness in heating the air by convection, owing to the fact that the ascending air current struck only the lower outside edge of each thread, while the loss by radiation remained the same, because, though the radiating surface was twice as large, yet half the rays fell upon the surfaces of the threads themselves, and were by them reabsorbed.

MOISTURE IN THE AIR.

It is a mistake to suppose that furnace heat is *necessarily* dry and unhealthy. Where the heating surface is raised to a high temperature, the vegetable and animal matters which are always to be found, to a greater or less degree, floating in the air, and can easily be seen under a ray of sunlight, coming in contact with an overheated surface are roasted or burned, and emit an unpleasant odor. When these surfaces become red-hot they may decompose the air itself, forming, with the iron, acid gases injurious to the health, or gases may pass through the furnace, as already stated; but so far as depriving the air of its moisture is concerned, by which a too rapid evaporation from the skin is induced, causing headache and unpleasant sensations of the nose and throat, the same effect is produced by steam or hot-water pipes and by every other method of heating, when the temperature of the outer air is warmed to the same degree. Cold air, when expanded by heat, has a greater capacity for moisture in proportion to the extent of the expansion. In the open fields this needed moisture is supplied by nature through the agency of rivers and lakes. In our houses, where rivers and lakes do not form themselves naturally about our hot-air furnaces (unless the unskilful plumber has opened for them sources in the drain and water pipes), their places should be supplied by art in the form of evaporating-pans, and the disagreeable sensations arising from dryness will quickly disappear.

SPECIAL FORMS OF CONSTRUCTION.

It is clear that for a given amount of fuel burned, any furnace may, by extending the heating surface, be made to yield the same amount of heat to the fresh air; but the heating surfaces may be ill or well constructed with reference to favoring the draught, economy of space, tightness of joints, facility for cleaning, durability, and cheapness, and upon this depends its value. The various kinds of hot-air furnaces now in use are characterized by the degree of excellence obtained in some one or other of the above desiderata, no one combining all the excellences, so that in searching for the form best adapted to our purpose many must be reviewed. In so doing we find that they divide themselves into two general classes: first, those in which the hot air circulates in flues, while the smoke fills the space surrounding them; and, second, those in which the reverse takes place, the smoke being inside and the fresh air circulating around them.

The heating effect of the latter method is, for the same extent of surface, much greater than that of the former, because when the smoke passes through the flues the heat radiated from the surface warms the inner walls of the surrounding air-chamber, which, in its turn, gives up its heat to the fresh air in contact with it. Thus both surfaces serve in heating the air, and the furnace acts both by radiation and by convection. The effect produced varies but little with the extent of the chamber, because the amount of heat which it receives is constant, and the smaller its surface the higher its temperature. By the former method all rays of heat which do not strike the fresh-air flues are lost. Figs. 130 and 131 represent fur-

Fig. 130. Section of Furnace with Perpendicular Fresh-air Tubes. From Peclet.

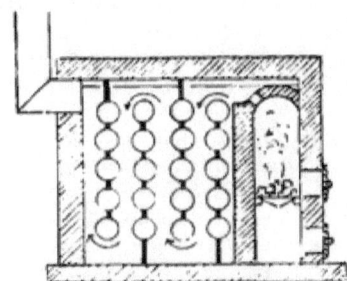

Fig. 131. Section of Furnace with Horizontal Fresh-air Tubes. From Peclet.

naces of this class. In Fig. 130 the smoke flows horizontally across perpendicular fresh-air tubes, and in Fig. 131 the movement of the smoke is perpendicular, and that of the fresh air is horizontal. All the heat received by the masonry of the furnace is lost, since no fresh air is brought in contact with them to carry it off. Abandoning, therefore, this class of furnace, we have only to consider those in which the smoke circulates inside of the flues, and the fresh air surrounds them.

These, again, may be classified into, first, those having simple drums, like the Magee Furnace (Fig. 132), and, second, those having detached tubes, as in the Chilson (Fig. 134). The former has the advantage of simplicity and the minimum of joints for the escape of gas, and the latter of a greater radiating surface. In an ordinary furnace the first consideration is of the greatest importance, because a leakage of dangerous gases may take place without the knowledge of the occupants, in case of downward draughts. Where the furnace is used over an open fireplace,

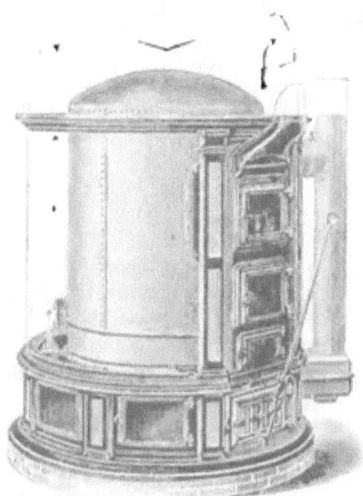

Fig. 132. Magee's Furnace.

leakage may at once be detected by the appearance of the fire, and cured by simply opening the direct smoke-draught, so that here freedom from joints, although important, is of less consequence than an increase of radiating surface.

The movement of the fresh air may take place in the same direction with the smoke or in an opposite direction. When the currents flow in the same direction the smoke will evidently cease to give up its heat when the two gases have the same temperature. But when the currents take place in opposite directions the temperature of the smoke may be lowered to any extent, only limited by that of the outside air. With a basement furnace, as ordinarily constructed, the requirements of the draught are such as to render total extraction of the heat from the smoke undesirable, but where the construction is like that shown in Fig. 129, such a result would be an important desideratum.

Fig. 133. The Peerless Furnace.

In the Peerless Furnace (Fig. 133) we have an illustration of this principle. It is not necessary, however, to have the smoke descend in order to accomplish the work. The smoke may rise direct and the fresh-air current be reversed.

The Chilson Furnace (Fig. 134) is an example of direct smoke-draught.

When the movement of the smoke or fresh air is upwards, if it be divided into separate currents, some means should be adopted to direct the flow equally into each, as otherwise it would follow by preference that which offered the least resistance, and when everything appears to be disposed in a manner perfectly symmetrical the slightest difference determines the movement in one direction or in another. The current will only divide itself equally when the flues have, in the aggregate, a sectional area equal to that of the main pipe, and when the branch flues are themselves equal in area to each other. When, however, the gas flows in a reversed or downward direction, the division will be uniform in the flues without the precaution of making their aggregate sectional area as small as that of the main pipe (Fig. 133).

In the Chilson Furnace (Fig. 134) the means adopted for equalizing the ascent of the smoke in the various upright flues is the tapering of these flues as they ascend. Where they join the horizontal ring above, their aggregate sectional area is but little greater than that of the main flue. This method, however, has the disadvantage of presenting a reheating surface to the ascending air current. A horizontal pipe presents but one side to the ascending air current, and therefore is less effective in heating it than a perpendicular pipe, which may be entirely surrounded by the air. The conical surfaces of the pipes of the Chilson Furnace are open, in a certain degree, to the same objection. If the cones were inverted the fresh air would impinge with much greater force upon their surfaces. But such an inversion would expose them to the danger of clogging by soot. Moreover, the tapering of the flues, whether upward or downward, diminishes their actual superficial area, and consequently their heating power. Some other method should be adopted for regulating the current, not open to these objections. The pipes should be so arranged that they may be easily cleaned, yet so formed that frequent cleaning would be unnecessary.

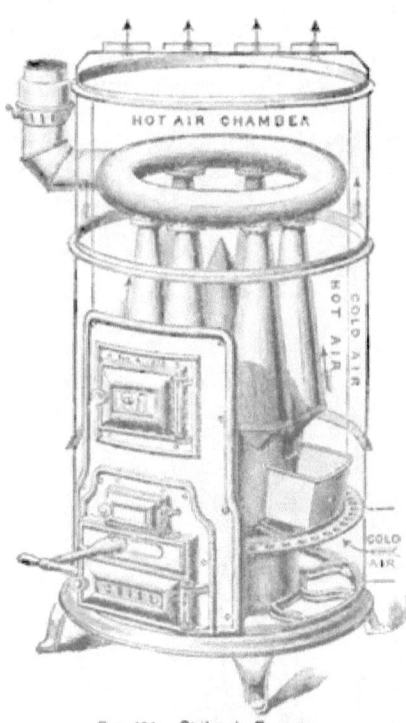

Fig. 124. Chilson's Furnace.

Finally, furnaces may be again subdivided into various classes, according to the material of which they are constructed.

MATERIAL.

It is evident that a porous material is unsuitable for the construction of furnaces, because the noxious gases generated by the burning fuel, especially by anthracite coal, pass through them under a back pressure, or even in cases of a sluggish draught. With an ordinary drum furnace like the Magee or MacGreggor there is almost always an outward pressure from within at the top of the drum even when the draught is good. Under a given pressure the amount of gas passed through a given material will be in direct proportion to its porosity. Cast-iron is said to be permeable to certain gases at high temperatures, and, according to L. Cailletet,[1] to hydrogen gas even when cold. Whether the gases pass through the pores, or through invisible air-holes so minute that they may be classed as pores, is immaterial so far as concerns the furnace-maker. It is sufficient to know that microscopic air-holes are so liable to be present in the castings that the material has been condemned as unsafe

---

[1] "L. Cailletet überzeugte sich dass das Eisen, nicht nur wie Deville und Troost nachgewiesen, im stark erhitzten Zustande, sondern auch bei gewöhnlicher Temperatur von Wasserstoffgas durchdrungen werde." — Wagner's *Jahresbericht*, vol. xiv., p. 51.

and unsuitable for gasholders, compressed-air tubes, and all places where a gas pressure has to be resisted.

In order to test the degree of this permeability under varying pressures, the writer had cast six cylindrical boxes from some of the softer iron used by a foundry-man in making furnace and stove castings.

The boxes, having the section shown in Fig. 135, appeared to be perfect in every particular.

The top or mouth of each piece was threaded after casting so as to receive the end of a piece of gas-pipe 2 meters long threaded to corre-

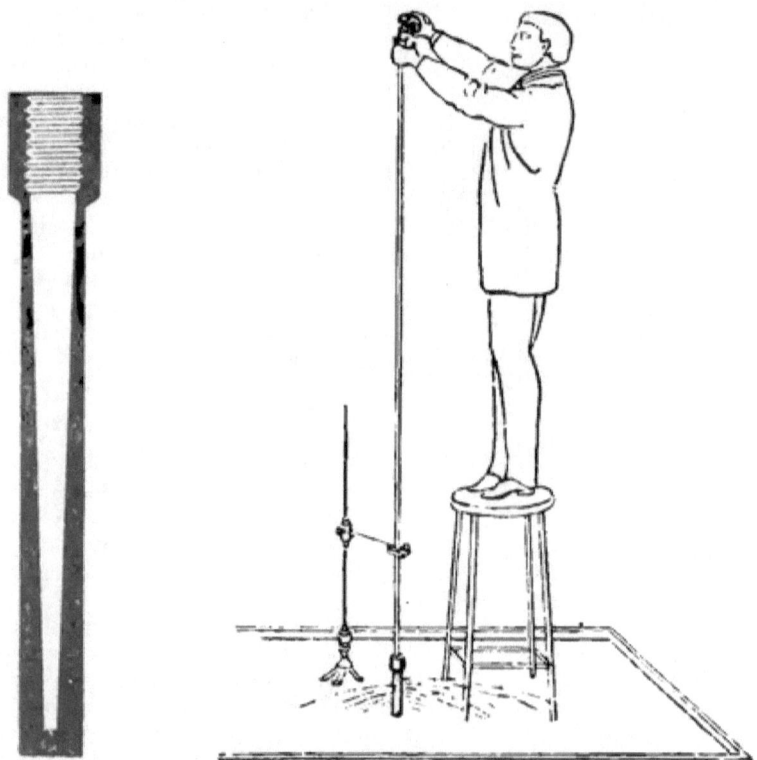

Fig. 135. Cast-iron Cups Tested for Permeability.

Fig. 136. Experiment on the Permeability of Cast-iron.

sponed, making with cement an air-tight joint. (Gas-piping was formerly frequently made of cast-iron, but its permeability to gas under pressure was too great, and it was abandoned in favor of wrought-iron.) Clean mercury was then poured into the gas-pipe, and the pressure in atmospheres on the casting was known by the height of the mercury column (Fig. 136). It was found that under pressures varying from 1 to 3 atmospheres, the first 3 of the 6 castings tested allowed the mercury to pass through the pores or air-holes in minute jets, as shown in Fig. 136, projecting it, when the pressure was greatest, a distance of more than a meter from the vessel. Yet the feeblest pressure was sufficient to cause it to escape from the largest openings. The other 3 castings resisted the test. A greater pressure than 3 atmospheres could not be applied with the materials at command. The mercury became much dirtied, after the first 3 experiments, by impurities in the gas-pipe and castings, so that it is possible that the amalgam thereby formed filled the pores in the last 3 castings and itself prevented the passage of the pure mercury.

This experiment was suggested by the experience of Professor Wolcott Gibbs, of Harvard University, from whom I have the following: He was filling a cast-iron pot with mercury, and had poured into it about 50 kilograms of the metal when it was observed suddenly to shoot out in fine streams in all directions through the pores of the vessel. Professor Gibbs described the iron which he used to be perfect so far as the eye could detect. The boxes in which mercury is put up for the market have to be made of wrought-iron.

The 6 castings tested as above described were 15 centimeters long each, and nearly 2 centimeters in diameter. The metal was 2 millimeters thick at the threaded end under the shoulder, and about 5 millimeters thick at the other end. The object of this gradation of thickness was to discover what effect the thickness of the casting had upon its permeability. It happened that the mercury escaped in all cases at points near the middle of the cylinders, where the metal was of medium thickness. But inasmuch as it did not flow from all parts of the castings with equal freedom, but rather from particular localities in each, it would appear that it could hardly have passed through *pores*, as the term is commonly accepted, but rather through minute accidental pin-holes between the granules or crystals of the materials, not to be avoided in casting. In this case iron of a hard, close texture would be open to these imperfections as well as soft iron, though not to so great a degree on account of the smaller size of the crystals. These openings may be partially closed by filing the surface of the casting. A file was passed over one of the castings tested while the mercury was escaping under the pressure. A number of the jets were obliterated, only the stronger ones remaining. For this reason samples to be tested should not be turned or filed, but subjected to the pressure in the rough state as they come from the foundry. It is also in this state that they appear in furnaces, for the sake of which the tests are made.

Hammering is still more effective than filing, and in wrought-iron the pores and air-holes are completely closed.

Thus every part, as large as the small samples tested, of every casting used in a furnace is liable to come out riddled, like them, with minute holes invisible to the eye, yet large enough to allow of the escape of gas under pressure. This outward pressure exists more or less frequently in every hot-air furnace now known. In the ordinary dome furnace it is constant in ordinary use, as previously said. Furnace men will differ in regard to this and will say that it is impossible, thinking that a powerful upward chimney-draught would overcome any slight upward tendency given by the height of the dome above the lower opening into the smoke-flue.

Others will be as positive the other way. But the practical furnace man is unfortunately not the authority to consult on these matters. He is commonly ignorant of the scientific principles which should govern the construction or regulate the use of a furnace, and generally unwilling to see the virtue of any arrangement not found in his own.

To ascertain the truth, the writer was obliged to have a hole bored in the top of the dome of his own furnace, which is a wrought-iron MacGreggor furnace No. 4, one which is to be recommended. It is similar to the Magee shown in Fig. 132. The opening was 5 millimeters in diameter and threaded to take a brass tube, as shown in Fig. 137.

A manometer was attached to the tube and the pressure of the gas from within or without accurately measured in millimeters of a water column. It was found that there was *a constant outward pressure* of from 1 to 8 millimeters, according as the check-draught door was from 1 to 5 centimeters open. Or, roughly speaking, a pressure of about 1 millimeter for every centimeter of opening. No valve was used in the smoke-flue. The same pressure outwards occurred when the feed-door was open.

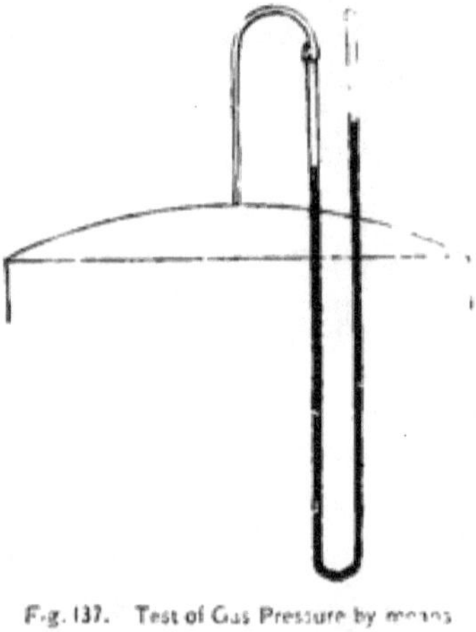

There was never an inward pressure except when the draught up the smoke-flue was too powerful to be left with safety.

From these experiments, therefore, the necessary inference is that cast-iron furnaces afford no adequate security against the escape of gas. Even if tested under pressure before use, a precaution which no furnace dealer or maker would venture to take, even if it were practicable,[1] they would still be unsafe for the following reason: a casting of iron when examined in section, Fig. 138, will be found to be densest at the surface, and more and more open or larger in grain approaching the centre. In a section of soft Scotch pig-iron the granules at the centre appear as large as those in the centre of our figure.

Fig. 137. Test of Gas Pressure by means of a Manometer.

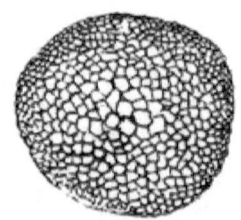

Fig. 138. Section of Pig-iron.

---

[1] The only test made by furnace men is a "careful" ocular inspection. This is evidently equivalent to no test at all, the air-holes being microscopic; a test would involve either setting up the furnace complete and applying atmospheric pressure, or else a special test of each particular casting, both of which are too difficult to be applied in practice.

while the outer portions are very much finer. Outside of all a coating of silicate forms a thin skin comparatively impervious, so that a furnace, which when new would resist every test, might prove to be quite useless as soon as the thin outer coatings were destroyed by heat and rust.

With wrought-iron these objections do not hold. The gas-pipe used in the experiment illustrated in Fig. 136 was of wrought-iron. As was to be expected, no mercury passed through it under the greatest pressure then applied.

Wrought-iron is, however, more quickly burnt out than cast-iron. But the difference is not important, especially where fire-clay linings are used and proper care is taken in its management.

What will happen to iron in a *red-hot* condition seems to me to be entirely of minor importance. The matter is almost wholly dependent upon the *quality of the castings used.*

To obtain castings which, in the *cold* state, will allow no gas to pass through under greater or less pressure, either when new or after a little use, I believe to be difficult, if not impossible, as furnaces are now made, and at best always a matter of chance.

Most basement furnaces are now so constructed that it is never necessary to raise them to a red heat to obtain the best results, and, in practice, this high temperature is seldom seen except under careless management.

The experiments of Deville and Troost (who were bound, as scientific and conscientious investigators, to select with care perfect castings for their test) show that a very small quantity, about *one-half a cubic centimeter*, of carbonic oxide was found at the surface of the iron when heated to redness for *every million cubic centimeters* of air passed over the stove. Of this small quantity, part was generated by the fuel within and permeated the iron, and part was formed on the surface by the decomposition of the constituents of the air coming in contact with it. These experiments, and the report of General Morin to the French Academy, have given rise, for the last ten years, to endless heated discussions as to the danger of iron in this condition, — discussions as fiery when prompted by pecuniary interests as the iron itself under consideration, and having as little to do with the practical question as red-hot iron has to do with properly made modern hot-air furnaces in general. Since these famous experiments the iron has cooled off to a moderate temperature, but the discussions glow as fiercely as ever.

The fire-pot, now much thicker than the iron of the stove tested by Deville and Troost, is, in a proper furnace, also protected by fire-clay (practically to prevent the iron from burning out, but nominally to allay the fears of the worried and excited public). The radiating surfaces remain as thin as before, but are no longer heated to redness.

We pass somewhat blindly from one extreme to another. The opponents to the theory of "red-hot" permeability, and the dealers in cast-iron furnaces generally, are convinced that the French Academy was mistaken, and that it is practically impossible for gases to pass through red-hot iron. In defence of their position they march out a small army of "distinguished" chemists, physicians, professors, and doctors of philosophy, who advertise liberally in behalf of the cast-iron furnace men that "cast-iron is no more permeable than wrought-iron;" that "any scientific chemist of experience must consider the exposition made in favor of wrought-iron much in the same light as a 'mare's nest;'" that "the result of analyses shows that carbonic oxide *has never passed through the metal at any time;*" that they cannot after three months' trial, working night and day, get the smallest particle of gas through the iron; that one has "never known such a thing as these gases passing through either cast or plate iron when used for heating purposes," etc.

Fig. 139 represents the Reynolds Wrought-Iron Furnace, one of the most perfect hot-air furnaces now known. The doors are circular in form, with bevelled edges, turned to fit with the greatest nicety, so that they are

Fig. 139. The Reynolds Furnace.

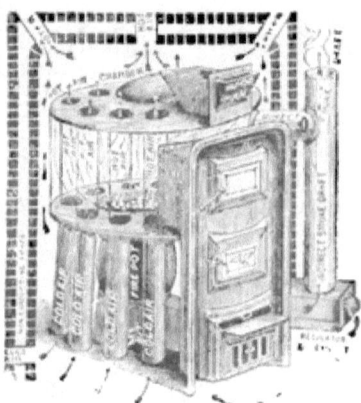
Fig. 140. Dunklee's Golden Eagle Furnace.

nearly air-tight as movable metal furnace joints can be made, and no check-draught door in the smoke-flue is necessary. This is a most important advantage, inasmuch as if no check-draught or damper be required in the smoke-flue, the pressure may be kept continually inwards or at least neutral at every part of the furnace. The radiating surfaces are well placed and large in extent.

Fig. 140 represents Dunklee's Golden Eagle Furnace. In it hot air passes as well inside of the tubes as outside of the drum (not shown in the drawing), enclosing them and the smoke chamber, thus exemplifying both principles of circulation previously described. The tubes are of wrought-iron, and it is claimed that the greater expansion of wrought over cast-iron tightens the joints when the furnace is lighted and lessens the liability of leakage. The furnace has a large radiating surface and is a powerful heater.

In Chubbuck's Cast-Iron Furnace (Fig. 141) we have illustrated the principle of an increase of the heating surface by means of projections on the fire-pot, and in the Gothic Furnace (Fig. 142) by corrugations on the upper and lower radiating surfaces.

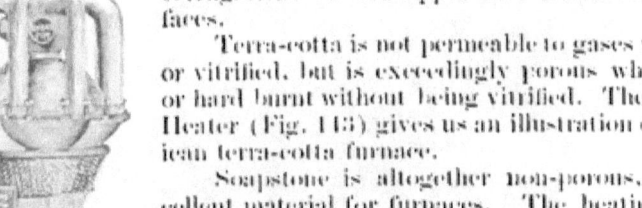

Fig. 141. Chubbuck's Furnace.

Terra-cotta is not permeable to gases when glazed or vitrified, but is exceedingly porous when partially or hard burnt without being vitrified. The Crary Clay Heater (Fig. 143) gives us an illustration of an American terra-cotta furnace.

Soapstone is altogether non-porous, and an excellent material for furnaces. The heating power of the furnace shown in Fig. 144, made by the Boston Soapstone Company, has proved to be much greater than would naturally be expected of material having so low a heat-conducting power.

The advantages claimed for the soapstone furnace are that it is absolutely impermeable to gases;[1] uniformity of heat is easily maintained; the

[1] A piece of soapstone tested with other substances by the writer under a moderate pressure proved impermeable to air.

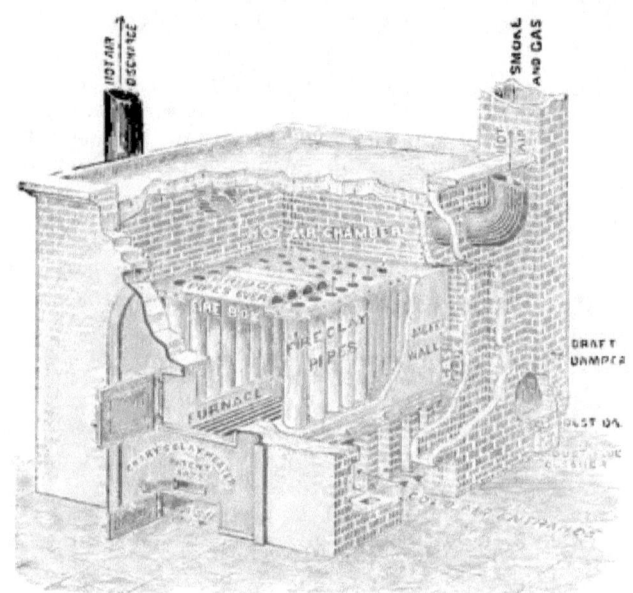

Fig. 143. Crary's Clay Heater.

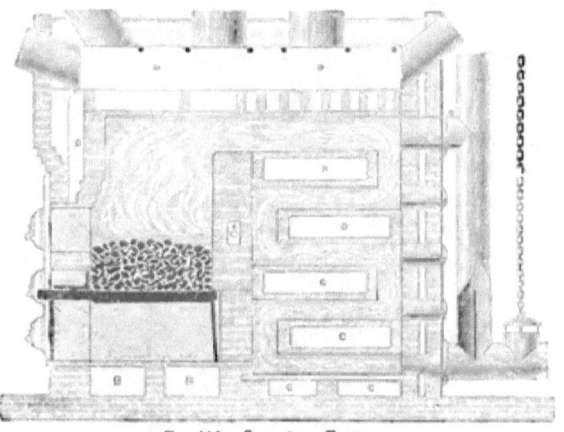

Fig. 144. Soapstone Furnace.

amount of soapstone forming the radiating surface of a single furnace (from 2 to 6 tons) furnishes such a reservoir of heat that sudden changes of temperature in the house are impossible; great durability, tightness of joints, owing to the slight change of the parts by expansion and contraction under changes of temperature, and the similarity of these changes to those of the cements used in the joints; and complete and even combustion of the fuel, owing to the slow heat-conducting power of soapstone and to a special arrangement within the furnace for supplying warmed air to the fire. A soapstone furnace tested for 5 years by the writer, in a house built by him at the West End of Boston, has proved itself a safe, pleasant, and (after the first cost) economical heater.

The disadvantage of the soapstone furnace is that the large amount of radiating surface required involves considerable expense and occupies somewhat more space than an ordinary iron furnace.

A leakage of gas, then, in hot-air furnaces may result, first, from porosity of the material; second, from looseness of the joints; or, third, from cracks at the feed and ash-pit doors. The first and second difficulties may be obviated by using wrought-iron, terra-cotta, or soapstone. The third may be to a certain extent, though not absolutely, avoided by adopting the ground and bevelled joints used in the Reynolds "Air-Tight" furnace.

Where a cast-iron furnace is already set, or where it is inconvenient to adopt either of the two courses recommended, the furnace should be so run that there is a constant inward pressure from without. The pressure may be easily measured by attaching to the highest part of the heating surface a manometer, as already described. In fact, no drum furnace is complete without this attachment. The manometer may consist of 2 simple quarter-inch glass tubes 1 foot long each, united at the bottom by a bend or by a rubber tube, half filled with water, and attached to the furnace by a brass tube screwed into the drum. The whole need not cost over 75 cents, not including the labor of attaching it to the furnace.

To insure a constant inward pressure it will be necessary to keep the temperature of the smoke-flue quite high, and, unless some principle like that illustrated by Fig. 129 be adopted, a great loss of heat will be sustained. The principle, under a modified form, varying with the circumstances, as will hereafter be described, may be applied to any furnace.

Though the escape of gases may be due largely to the permeability of the materials, yet imperfect joints form a source of leakage equally, if not more, important. As above remarked in describing the experiments on the permeability of cast-iron, a small amount of the mercury passed through the iron under the feeblest pressure. Only a fraction of an atmospheric pressure was necessary to drive it through the largest pores, and in the experiment of Professor Gibbs no pressure at all was used above that of the mercury in the vessel itself tested. The holes were too small to be visible to the naked eye, and would therefore escape detection under the ocular examination of the inspector. Yet with the aid of a microscope many could be seen, and would consequently allow water to work through under a pressure of a few millimeters head, or sufficient to overcome its attraction. This proved, by experiment, to be the fact. In the case of gases, friction would only retard their movement, while attraction might prevent altogether the passage of liquids.

As the only certain cure for escape of gas through the pores of the material is to discard porous materials altogether, so the only cure for escape through joints would be to discard joints altogether. This being impossible, the next best thing is to choose a furnace in which the number of joints is at a minimum, and to run the furnace in such a manner that the outward pressure shall always be at a minimum. Whether or not this may be done without loss of heat will hereafter be seen. Furnace-makers will claim that the peculiar kind of cement they use, or their peculiar method of hammering the joints, will prevent leakage and stand fire. The writer visited a furnace advertised by the makers to be absolutely gas-tight. The joints were numerous. In some joints cast-iron was connected with wrought. Pipes of cast-iron were set into wrought-iron plates,—an arrangement the reverse of that used in the Dunklee furnace. To this the writer particularly objected, and inquired of the makers if they could warrant the furnace to stand test at these points. The method of working these joints was, they claimed, *peculiar*. No cement was used, and so great was the care bestowed on each joint that the leakage was a sheer impossibility. A fine new furnace was exhibited to show the excellence of the workmanship. The writer still objected, until challenged by the makers to give proof of any of the numerous furnaces put up by the company having ever leaked gas. Without taking the time to visit any or all of the 500 or more gentlemen whose letters of recommendation adorned the descriptive circular of the firm, the writer expressed himself satisfied if the fine new sample furnace then on exhibition would itself stand the test. With the assurance that he was at liberty to make any reasonable test he pleased, he ordered the furnace to be turned over and water poured into all the joints. To the complete astonishment of the proprietors and of the careful workmen standing around, the water which was poured in poured out again through nearly every one of the score of careful joints, until the furnace seemed to dissolve, and float away in its own tears.

The way in which an escape of gases in furnaces may be caused by the pressure of the wind is very clearly expressed by Dr. Lincoln.[1] But it must be borne in mind that the wind is not the only cause of reversed pressure. Dr. Lincoln says: " In the case of hot-air furnaces it is very desirable to make the seams actually impervious to gas. This cannot be done with the ordinary materials,—cast-iron, putty, and red-lead. The unequal contraction and dilatation of the pieces of casting inevitably crack the putty or cement, a matter of small moment provided we were sure of a constant atmospheric pressure inward. But we cannot be sure that such a pressure will continue under all circumstances; and the manner in which the direction of the pressure may be reversed is easy to understand. For

---

[1] " The Atmosphere," by D. F. Lincoln, M.D., in Buck's *Hygiene and Public Health*.

the iron wall of the furnace represents a diaphragm between two boxes, from each of which a powerful current ascends. One of these boxes is the stove itself, discharging into the chimney; the other is the hot-air box or reservoir, discharging through pipes, registers, halls, and stairways, — all of which taken together may form a kind of rival chimney drawing upon the hot-air box with a force nearly or quite equal to that of the actual chimney. Then the direction of the wind may be such as to favor the exit of air from the box by the duct intended to admit it, and if, under these circumstances, a puff of wind strikes the chimney unfavorably, it is not strange if the pressure should be for the time reversed, and gas escape into the box. In point of fact this not rarely happens in furnaces of cast-iron. A suitable material for avoiding this exists in wrought-iron, which can be made perfectly tight by overlapping, riveting, and hammering the edges. Stone furnaces can be made tight also." The furnace room should be ventilated to carry off accidental leakages or puffs of gas when the feed-door is open. The cold-air box should be made of brick or stone and made perfectly tight, with a clean-out door favorably placed, and the fresh air should be taken from a spot where it is most likely to be pure. It is best to take it from an enclosed spot as little affected by winds as possible. If no such chamber exists, or can conveniently be made, it should be taken in separate ducts from both windward and leeward sides of the house, and proper regulating valves supplied in the ducts, to be operated, if possible, from the parlor or sitting-room by means of wires and cranks. Strictly speaking, the fresh-air box should be large enough to supply all the flues, allowing one-sixth for expansion after heating, so that the longer hot-air flues shall not draw air from the shorter ones, as sometimes happens.

The amount of water evaporated in a furnace to give the air the desired moisture depends upon individual taste and temperament, upon locality and climate, and cannot be definitely specified. The supply should, however, be automatic. The ball-cock used should be of a kind least liable to get out of order, and should be protected from dust.

It is worth while here to remark, as a consideration of some little importance in finishing a house, and one frequently overlooked by owners and architects, that the evaporating pan should be emptied, and the water pipe temporarily plugged up on the furnace side, while the inside finish of kiln-dried stock is being put on. Otherwise the evaporating water will rapidly reënter the wood before it is in place, cracks will result as the house grows old, and the advantages of kiln-drying will be partially nullified.

FRESH AIR IN OUR DWELLINGS.

In attempting to combine in one apparatus the open fireplace and the modern furnace, the first question governing the form of the apparatus which must be answered is, How much space should be allowed for the circulation of fresh air about the radiating or heating surfaces?

Deprived of food we can live on for weeks, but deprived of air we die in three minutes. Nature has, in the construction of our bodies devoted half the space in the main trunk to the machinery for the supply and distribution of fresh air. The working of this machinery heaves the entire frame, giving it the only regular and constant motion apparent, and producing the only regular and constant sound audible to our senses. It occupies the central position in the body, and has in its service the two most prominent features in the place of honor, the face, — that is, the nose and the mouth. Yet in our artificial habitations the machinery devoted to ventilation, if allowed a place at all, is treated with contempt, and crowded into whatever chance space may be left for it after the work of building is done. Its inlets and outlets are disguised or hidden as things of which we should be ashamed, rather than treated after the example set us by nature, as the leading decorative features of the edifice.

In the process of breathing, the blood is exposed to the action of atmospheric air, during which exposure it undergoes certain changes. "The blood from the right side of the heart, when it enters the lungs, is of a dark red color. It is then dispersed in a state of most minute subdivision through the ultimate vessels of the lungs, and in these vessels is brought into contact with the atmospheric air, when it becomes of a bright red color. In other words, the blood changes in the lungs its *venous* appearance, and assumes the character of *arterial* blood. The blood, thus arterialized, returns to the left side of the heart, from whence it is propelled through the arteries of the body. In the minute terminations of the arteries the blood again loses its florid hue, and, reassuming its dark red color, is returned through the veins to the right side of the heart, to be exposed as before to the influence of the atmospheric air, and undergo the same succession of changes." (Pron.)

"The water given off by the lungs is not pure water, such as is liberated in the process of distillation or evaporation, but is contaminated with the most offensive animal effluvia. M. Leblanc states that the odor of the air at the top of the ventilator of a crowded room is of so noxious a character that it is dangerous to be exposed to it even for a short time. If this air be passed through pure water, the water soon exhibits all the phenomena of putrefactive fermentation. The water of respiration, thus loaded with animal impurities, condenses on the inner walls of buildings, and trickles down in fetid streams. In the close and confined dwellings of the poor this vapor condenses on the walls, the ceiling, and the furniture, and gives that permanently loathsome odor which must be familiar to all who take sufficient interest in the poor of large towns ever to enter their dwellings. Take up a chair, and it is clammy to the touch, and the hand retains the ill odor.

"How much disease and misery arises from this cause it would be difficult to state with any approach to accuracy, because the causes of misery are very complicated. In the evidence taken before the House of Commons, on the health of towns, in the year 1840, the medical witnesses stated that scrofulous diseases were the result of bad ventilation, and that in the case of silk-weavers, who pass their lives in a more close and confined air than almost any other class of persons, their children are peculiarly subject to scrofula and softening of the bones. Dr. Arnott stated that an individual, the offspring of persons successively living in bad air, will have a constitution decidedly different from that of a man who is born of a race that has inhabited the country for a long time; that the race would, to a certain extent, continue degenerating. Defective ventilation deadens the mental and bodily energies; it leaves its mark upon the person so that we can distinguish the inhabitants of a town from those of the country. This witness, in alluding to the want of knowledge among all classes on the subject of ventilation, states that he had heard at the Zoölogical Gardens of a class of animals where fifty out of sixty were killed in a month from putting them into a house which had no opening in it but a few inches in the floor. 'It was like putting them under an extinguisher; and this was supposed to be done on scientific principles.'" (Tomlinson.)

"One of the most obvious effects of an insufficient supply of air is the discomfort occasioned in those who are not habituated to the deprivation. This discomfort is an evidence of positive injury, and may increase till headache, prostration of strength, gastric disorders, and fainting occur. Closeness of air, not producing such marked symptoms, may cause dyspepsia and impairment of the general nutrition,— symptoms which are now recognized as related to the development of phthisis." (Lincoln.)

The amount of pure air required for comfort, as judged of by different persons through their senses alone, varies with individuals, and with the same individual at different times; and this to such an extent that their judgment cannot be relied upon. An atmosphere which may seem to one perfectly pure and agreeable may to another, with a more sensitive nose, be extremely nauseous. "It is curious," says Lange, in his work on ventilation,[1] "that the peasant — whose custom of living in the air of the open fields would make it seem most incredible — should be often the very one to insist upon an atmosphere in-doors actually *dense*. In winter the entire household, as well as a part of the stock of domestic animals, live together in a single small room, where all the cooking is done and the peasant smokes his far from savory pipe. He seems to feel himself quite at ease, only when, as the saying goes, *he can cut the air with a knife*.'"

It is necessary, therefore, to refer to a more competent judge than our sense of smell in investigating the purity of the air we breathe.

The air of an ordinary living-room is altered by the occupants in two ways. First, by *a change in its constituents*, the oxygen being slightly diminished, while the carbonic acid and moisture are considerably increased; and, second, by an *addition of matter* in the form of organic exhalations whose chemical composition and proportions are still unknown.

The chief constituents of air are nitrogen, which forms its largest part

---

[1] *Zur Frage der Ventilation, mit Beschreibung des minimetrischen Apparates zur Bestimmung der Luftverunreinigung.* Zurich, 1877.

oxygen, and carbonic acid. The former need not be considered in connection with ventilation. The air of a dwelling-room contains no more nitrogen than that of the open fields.

The relatively small abstraction of oxygen renders the consideration of this component also unimportant. The carbonic acid, though not the injurious element of the air of our houses, impoverished by ordinary respiration, furnishes the best means now known of measuring its impurity. Pettenkofer found that he could remain for hours in air containing 10 parts per 1,000 of carbonic acid without inconvenience. Forster states that he experienced no trace of difficulty in breathing during a stay of 10 minutes in air containing 10 parts in 1,000. Hirt says that workmen in mines do not suffer as long as the proportion of carbonic acid does not exceed 7 parts per 1,000. In our dwellings such high proportions of carbonic acid are obtained only in exceptional cases.

The harmful element of air consists in the *organic impurities* coming from respiration, as well as in the carbonic oxide of combustion, and the organic impurities are particularly injurious when they are left to decompose. These impurities are generally found to exist in direct proportion to the amount of carbonic acid present, so that the latter serves, in default of a more direct method of measurement, to determine the amount of the hurtful ingredients.

As for carbonic oxide, it is a highly poisonous and dangerous gas. 1 part in 100 of air being sufficient to destroy animal life. "The chemist Chenot, having accidentally inhaled a single breath of [this] gas, fell on his back to the ground as if struck by lightning; his eyes were rolled in their sockets, and his extremities drawn up. In a quarter of an hour external sensation returned, with a feeling of cold and suffocation. A heavy sweat covered his whole body, while a peculiar hyperæsthesia of the brain existed.

"Carbonic oxide is known to be often present in minute quantities in the air of inhabited rooms, proceeding from defects in furnaces or stoves, and to some extent from the imperfect combustion of illuminating material. Being a frequent ingredient of illuminating gas, it may enter a room through a leak or through the sides of flexible tubes. It has been found in tobacco-smoke. Many people suffer from small amounts; the effects commonly attributed to its action in ordinary life are giddiness, headache, and prostration of strength. It exists in the smoke of a glowing candle-wick. Death occasionally results from the careless use of braziers containing charcoal, so commonly used in Southern Europe; King Alfonso very nearly lost his life from this cause, a few years ago, in Spain. The danger of closing the chimney-draught of a stove arises chiefly from the probability that quantities of this gas will be thrown back into the room. The fuel (anthracite, wood, coke, charcoal, soft coal), which burns readily and without carbonic oxide while abundant fresh air is supplied, gives rise, when the draught is checked, to the half-oxidized product (CO instead of CO_2). In no case can we say that a given fire produces no carbonic oxide. For example, in a bed of live coals 10 inches deep, we know that it exists in abundance in the central layers, where oxygen is deficient in amount, and that it issues in quantities from the upper layer, where, again meeting with air, it becomes further oxidized or burnt, making a blue or yellowish flame, characteristic of the perfect combustion of anthracite and charcoal, and forming carbonic acid."

"Air may, so far as its effect upon health is concerned, be considered pure and good which contains not more than 6 or 7 parts in 10,000 of carbonic acid. A good rule, is that it should contain under 1 part in 1,000. To attain an absolute purity would be impossible, even with the strongest ventilating currents, both because the outer air is itself not absolutely pure, containing from 2 to 7 parts of carbonic acid in the 10,000, according to the locality; and because the organic product of respiration clings to the walls, ceilings, and furniture so pertinaciously that it may be said to give to every place its peculiar and characteristic odor. Boston Public Garden showed, in May, by four analyses, 3 parts in 10,000." (Storer.)

A SIMPLE TEST TO ASCERTAIN THE PURITY OF THE AIR.

Lange[1] gives a simple method of measuring the amount of carbonic acid in the air. It depends upon the fact that carbonic acid in lime or baryta water produces a precipitate of carbonate of lime or baryta which shows itself by clouding the previously clear solution. To make the test he used 6 glass bottles of different capacities.

No. 1, of 150 cubic centimeters capacity.
" 2, " 350 " " "
" 3, " 300 " " "
" 4, " 250 " " "
" 5, " 200 " " "
" 6, " 150 " " "

When these are quite dry and clean some clear fresh limewater is made, 15 cubic centimeters of the solution measured out, and poured into the smallest of the bottles, containing the air of the room to be tested. The bottle is stopped up and thoroughly shaken. If no cloudiness results therefrom the same experiment is tried with bottle No. 5, and so on, until a distinct cloudiness is discernible. A cloudiness obtained with the sixth bottle indicates at least 16 parts of carbonic acid in 10,000 of the air, an impurity altogether inadmissible, so that no smaller bottle need be used. The fifth shows 12 in 10,000, the fourth about 10 in 10,000, the third 8 in 10,000, or a satisfactory condition of the air. The third shows 7 in 10,000, the second 6 in 10,000, an unusually pure in-door atmosphere; the first indicates from 4 to 5, certainly under 6, in 10,000, a condition rarely obtained except in the open air. In order to distinguish with greater ease and certainty when the cloudiness is sufficiently strong, small pieces

---

[1] Lange, *Ueber Natürliche Ventilation und die Porosität von Baumaterialien.* Stuttgart, 1877.

of white paper with a cross marked on each in pencil may be pasted on the outside of the bottles below the water level, with the cross-mark turned inwards. When this cross-mark can no longer be seen through the solution it may be assumed that the cloudiness is sufficient.

From the experiments of Eresmann[1] it is found that from the consumption of 1,000 liters (about 35 cubic feet) 684 liters of carbonic acid are produced. A burner consuming 140 liters per hour (an ordinary 5-foot burner) generates in this time 92.8 liters of carbonic acid, about equal to that produced by 4 grown-up persons, and in respect to organic substances it corrupts the air as much as 5 grown-up persons.

According to Pettenkofer, a strong workman, weighing 75 kilograms, and 28 years old, produces hourly 22.6 liters of carbonic acid by day while at rest, and 36.3 when at work. A "feeble tailor," weighing 53 kilograms, and 26 years old, produces 16.8 liters while at rest during the day, and 12.7 during the night.

Scharling's[2] observations give the following table:—

	Age.	Weight in Kilos.	Hourly Production of Carbonic Acid in Liters.
Boy	9¼	22.00	10.3
Girl	10	23.00	9.7
Youth	16	57.75	17.4
Maiden	17	55.75	12.9
Man	28	82.00	18.6
Woman	35	65.50	17.0

AMOUNT OF FRESH AIR REQUIRED PER HEAD PER MINUTE.

To calculate the amount of fresh air required per minute by each occupant of a room we will assume the number of respirations per minute to be 17 (average obtained by the writer from 5 different persons at rest). At each breath the volume of air respired amounts to about one-half liter, and contains, say, 43 parts of carbonic acid to 1,000 of air. If we suppose the outside air to contain 0.5 parts per 1,000, and we wish the limit of impurity in the room to be 0.7 parts per 1,000, then each half liter of outside air introduced will add a volume containing 0.7 — 0.5 = 0.2 parts in 1,000 less carbonic acid than is required. The half liter respired contains 43 parts, and as this breath cannot be removed instantly (unless each occupant breathes through a tube communicating directly with a ventilating flue), it must be diluted with as many volumes of the incoming air

---

[1] "Untersuchungen über die Verunreinigung der Luft durch künstliche Beleuchtung und über die Vertheilung der Kohlensäure in geschlossenen Räumen." *Zeitschrift für Biologie*, vol. xii.

[2] C. G. Lehmann, *Handbuch der physiologischen Chemie.* Leipzig, 1854.

as are sufficient to raise it to the required purity; *i.e.*, $\frac{47}{2\cdot18}$ = 216 volumes of one-half liter each for each respiration. For 17 respirations we have 3,672 half-liters = 1,837 liters, or 1.8 cubic meters. General Morin gives for hospitals from 1 to 2.5 cubic meters per head per minute; for theatres from 0.7 to 0.8 per minute; for assembly rooms, long sittings, 1.0 per minute; for short sittings, 0.5 per minute; schools for grown-up pupils, from 0.4 to 0.5; schools for children, from 0.2 to 0.3. A simple rule is to allow *for each individual 1 cubic meter and for each unventilated gas-burner 3 cubic meters per minute*.

ALLOWANCE TO BE MADE FOR NATURAL VENTILATION, OR VENTILATION THROUGH THE PORES AND FISSURES IN THE BUILDING MATERIALS.

The supply of this quantity of air is, in ordinary buildings, partly obtained by *natural ventilation*, though to what extent is at present unknown, as the matter has been but little studied. It is extremely important, therefore, to investigate the subject, and to ascertain, if possible, what allowance should be made in our calculations for this air supply, and either to regulate its quantity at pleasure or to repress it altogether.

Natural ventilation is directly dependent upon the permeability of the building materials and upon the amount of air pressure upon the surfaces of the external walls.

Many of us have observed, especially in unfinished houses, while standing near a bare brick wall on the windward side of the house, that a strong breeze passes easily through the brickwork and produces a perceptible draught in the interior. This pressure is dependent upon three considerations, which are given by Lange as follows: —

1. The difference of temperature between the air within and without the place to be ventilated.
2. The diffusive tendency of the two masses of air separated by the walls of the house.
3. The strength and direction of the wind.

Lange shows that the difference of temperature has but little influence upon the amount of natural ventilation compared with that produced by the wind. It is impossible by any experiments which can be made on an actual building to determine accurately the part played by the temperature alone as distinct from the wind and diffusive tendency of gases. But experiments may be made to advantage on a small scale and with apparatus especially designed for the purpose.

Lange gives, by calculation from such experiments, the pressure on the outer walls of a house 20 meters high, at a barometric pressure of 718 millimeters, the inside temperature being 27.3° C, and the outside temperature 0° C., 1.414 *kilograms per square meter of the exposed surface*. The amount of ventilation resulting from this pressure depends upon the nature of the building materials used, and may be easily calculated when the latter is known.

As for the second consideration, the diffusive power of gases, its influence upon the ventilation of a house through the outer walls is, owing to the small difference in the mechanical mixtures of the air within and without, and to the consequent diminutive pressure against the walls either way, *too small to be appreciable*, and it may therefore be ignored.

By far the most important agent in natural ventilation is the wind.

The following table, calculated from Péclet and Smeaton,[1] shows the pressure of a direct wind per square meter.

TABLE X.

Velocity in Meters per Second.	Velocity in Kilometers per Hour.	Remarks.	Pressure in Kilograms per Square Meter.
0.5	1.8	Breeze hardly felt.	.03
1.	3.6	Breeze sensible.	.2
2.	7.2	Moderate or pleasant wind.	.5
5.5	19.8	Quite strong wind.	1.5
10.	36.	High wind.	20.
20.	72.	Very high wind.	56.
22.5	81.	Storm.	73.
27.	97.2	Severe storm.	105.
36.	129.6	Hurricane.	186.
45.	162.0	Hurricane which uproots trees and overthrows houses.	290.

For an average velocity of the wind of 27 kilometers an hour we should have a pressure of one-half kilogram per square meter. A wind stronger than 36 kilometers an hour would be exceptional, and is not to be reckoned upon. This would give us, according to the table, 22 kilograms per square meter. But in all cases it is necessary for the wind to strike the surface at right angles in order to exert upon it a pressure corresponding to that shown in the table. In consideration of the great variety of force and direction of the wind, it cannot be counted upon as a reliable source of ventilation, our table showing a pressure varying all the way from 0.03 kilograms to 290 kilograms per square meter.

It remains now to ascertain the effect of this pressure in transmitting air through the walls of our buildings. The air may be forced through the wall in two ways, namely, either through the accidental cracks at joints, or through the pores of the materials themselves.

No arguments are needed to show that the ventilation coming from the former is so uncertain in its amount and so disagreeable and dangerous in its character, that every precaution should be taken to reduce it to a minimum. By the use of good cements, packing, and rubber mouldings,

---

[1] *Fortschritte der Physik.*

it may be reduced to so minute an amount as to be practically inappreciable.

Porous building materials have the advantage of greater capacity for warmth. The conductibility decreases as the porosity increases, and what air passes through the walls of a building is warmed in its passage. But inasmuch as the loss of heat in radiation from the outer walls into space is the same for an equal difference of temperature between these walls and the objects receiving the rays, such a transmission of cold air through them must cool them to an extent nearly corresponding to its amount, and deprive them largely of their healthful action in radiating heat upon the bodies of the occupants. The greatest desideratum in heating is to have the walls and floor of a room as warm as possible, leaving the breathing air comparatively cool; and anything tending to destroy this effect should be avoided as far as possible.

Experiments have been made by Pettenkofer, Schultze, Märcker, Lange, and others on various buildings, to determine the quantity of air passing through the walls in a given time, under a given pressure. Pettenkofer found that the amount of air which passed through the walls of his study, per hour, was 0.245 cubic meters per square meter of wall-surface for a difference of 1° C. between the external and the internal temperatures. But these experiments give no reliable or accurate data for practice. The only way to obtain correct results is to make the tests on a simple scale with small pieces of material under a known pressure.

The principal building materials used in different countries differ greatly in their permeability to air. In Germany they appear to be in general more porous than in this country, so that, perhaps, for this reason the need of artificial ventilation is less directly felt with the Germans than with us.

Of all building materials none differs more widely in the matter of porosity than baked clay or terra-cotta, the material most extensively used. In the form of certain kinds of fire-brick its porosity resembles almost that of a sponge, while in the form of vitrified or glazed tile it is absolutely non-porous. A piece of semi-vitrified terra-cotta, used in a furnace constructed by the writer, was tested by him, and found to permit only 9 cubic centimeters of air to pass through per hour, under a pressure of 10 centimeters of a water column which is equivalent to a pressure of 10 grams per square centimeter. The piece was 30 millimeters thick, and presented a surface of 35 square centimeters to the pressure. For a surface of 1 square meter the amount of air forced through would have been 2.6 liters per hour, under the same pressure of 10 grams per square centimeter.

Other pieces, in the form of brick, were tested by Dr. Henry P. Bowditch, with the following results: —

Four Taunton bricks allowed the air to pass at the rate of about 62, 160, 106, and 795 liters respectively, per hour, for the same surface (1 square meter), same thickness (3 centimeters), and same pressure (10 grams per square centimeter). North Bridgewater bricks gave 66 and 132 liters; a New York brick, 330 liters; New Jersey bricks, 24 and 53 liters;

a Philadelphia face brick, 891 liters; a hard Eastern brick, 165 liters; and a Danvers face brick, 234 liters. Ohio sandstone gave 990 liters.

The apparatus used for our tests is represented in Fig. 145. Air was compressed in a gas-holder shown at the left of the table, and conducted by a rubber tube to two bent glass tubes containing, the one chloride of calcium and the other sulphuric acid, in passing through which it was thoroughly dried. The pressure was measured by a water manometer, and the piece of material to be tested was held between two cups of iron securely connected with the rubber tube in such a way that the compressed air could enter freely one exposed side of the sample and escape at the

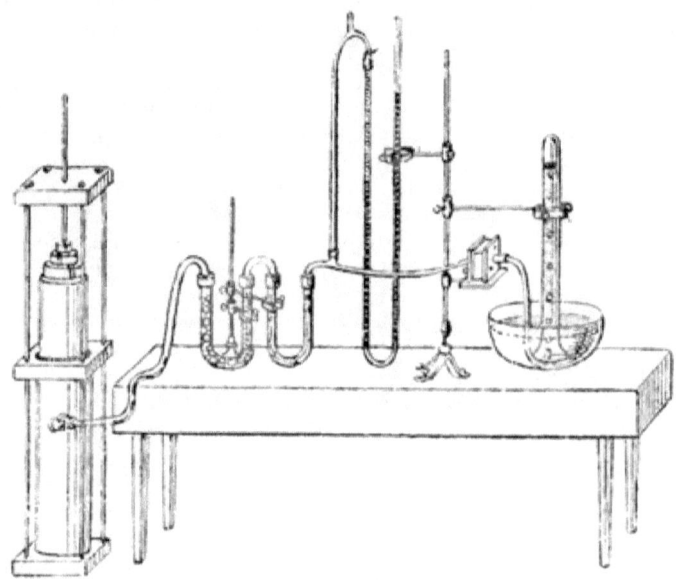

Fig. 145. Apparatus for Testing the Porosity of Building Materials.

opposite side. The four remaining sides were covered with an air-proof cement composed of wax and rosin to prevent the escape of air at any other points than that covered by the cup and tube opposite the one delivering the fresh air, and the whole was kept under water during the test, so that any escape of air might at once be detected by bubbles. The air thus pressed through the material to be tested was finally delivered into a graduated glass vessel inverted over a basin of water, and measured. The same apparatus was used for testing the soapstone before referred to.

The apparatus used by Lange in making his more extended tests in Germany was similar to that above described, except that he measured the volume of air before instead of after passing it through the material to be tested. This method was less exact because some of the air measured might not be actually transmitted through the material, owing to leakage.

The observations of Schürman[1] and Lange show that the amount of air passing through porous materials of homogeneous structure under constant pressure is inversely proportional to the thickness of the pieces tested.

Lange gives the following table showing the permeability of various materials under a constant pressure of 10 grams per square centimeter, and the amount of air in liters or cubic decimeters passing through them per hour, per square meter of surface, the pieces tested being 30 millimeters thick.

According to Lange and Märcker, burning increases the porosity of brick up to the point of vitrification, when it becomes non-porous. The different kinds of bricks vary greatly in porosity. Mortar is exceedingly porous, but after remaining some time immersed in water it becomes less so. We see by the table that Portland cement transmits 192 liters per square meter, under the slight pressure of 10 grams to the square centimeter, or about the hundredth part of one atmospheric pressure. It cannot, therefore, as in the form of concrete for basement cellars, be considered by any means as air or damp proof.

TABLE XI.

Materials Tested.	Amount transmitted in Liters.	Its Permeability is represented by
Green sandstone (Bavarian)	68	0.130
" Swiss	126	0.118
Limestone (calcareous tufa)	28,728	7.980
ARTIFICIAL STONES.		
Brick, sandal brick of Osnabruck	1,398	0.383
" lightly burnt hand-made (Munich)	312	0.087
" hard-burnt " "	732	0.203
" machine-made, "	474	0.132
CEMENTS.		
Mortar	3,264	0.907
Beton	930	0.258
Portland cement	192	0.437
Plaster (gyps.) cast	116	0.011
WOODS.		
Oak	24	0.007
Pine	3,636	1.010

[1] Jahresbericht der chem. Centralstelle für öffentliche Gesundheitspflege in Dresden.

The different woods vary greatly, pine being more porous even than mortar, and oak less porous than the densest brick. Tufaceous limestone was found to be the most porous substance tested.

The different kinds of bricks and sandstones vary greatly. Ten different kinds of sandstone given by Lange varied between 0.3664 and 0.009 cubic meters of air transmitted under the same pressure in the same time, the French sandstone tested transmitting 40 times as much air as the German (Sollingsandstein), which was the least porous.

Lange found that a coat of water-glass (silicate of soda or potash) diminished the porosity, and the more so the longer it stood, until after a certain time it rendered it entirely non-porous. Oil paint acted in the same way as long as it was new. Water-color with glue size (Leim farbe) diminished greatly the permeability, more than half, and the more the stronger the sizing. Lime water-color (Kalk farbe) diminished it the least. Papering diminished the porosity more or less according to the nature of the paper and the thickness of the paste used in hanging it. The diminution of the permeability varied for different tests between 18 and 75 per cent.

Dampness, due to rain on brickwork, etc., diminished the permeability according to the degree of the moistening, in some cases rendering a porous material absolutely non-porous, as in the case of Beton and Portland cement.

Knowing, then, the permeability of our building materials and the pressure of the wind, it is easy to calculate the natural ventilation in any given case. Suppose, for instance, we have a room 6 meters square and 4 meters high, with one exposed side, and that the exposed side contains a window 1 meter wide and 2 meters high. The walls are 40 centimeters thick, 30 of which are brick, 4 air-space, 6 furring and plaster, and present a surface of 24 square meters to the outer air. Take out 2 meters for glass surface, because glass is non-permeable, and we have 22 square meters of brickwork exposed. We have found that 1 square meter of hard Eastern brick, 3 centimeters thick, will admit 465 liters of air under a pressure of 10 grams per square centimeter. We have, by our table, for plaster 446 and for laths 3,636. But supposing their permeability and that of the mortar to be the same with the brick, we have, for our 40 centimeters thickness of wall, $\frac{465 \times 3 \times 22}{45} = 250$ liters of air transmitted under the pressure of 10 grams per square centimeter, or 100 kilograms per square meter.

This pressure is, by the table, equivalent to that of a severe storm bearing directly upon the house.

For a moderate wind the pressure would be about 250 times less, and we should have a ventilation of only 1 liter per hour. For a Philadelphia face-brick wall we should have about 5 liters per hour, up to 500 liters, or half a cubic meter, in case of a severe storm. For a gentle breeze, direct, it would be about 2 liters per hour, and at right angles with the wall, say, 1 liter again per hour. If the wall were papered on the inside or painted in distemper, these figures would be reduced, say one-half, and if oil paint were used the ventilation would be reduced to nothing.

Where the walls are built of the limestone given in Lange's table as transmitting 28.728 liters per hour, the ventilation in a high wind would amount to $\frac{28.728 \times 3 \times 22}{13} = 47.388$ liters = 17.4 cubic meters per hour, or 0.8 cubic meters per minute, an amount quite sufficient for a single occupant. Thus we see that the ventilation, left to the natural permeability of the material, would vary with every material and with every change of the wind, being greatest when the wind was highest and the exterior air was coldest, or, in other words, when least desired. It is therefore in the highest degree unreliable. Such a form of air-supply is objectionable, too, in most cases, on account of its cooling action upon the surrounding walls. We have seen that (calculating from Lange's figures) a building material may admit air enough to supply one person for every 22 square meters of wall-surface exposed directly to the wind.

The matter assumes, then, considerable importance, and demands of the heating and ventilating engineer careful study. Indeed, it is easy to obtain bricks and stones so porous that a candle may be blown out by a slight effort of the breath through pieces many centimeters in thickness. The experiment may easily be performed by any one by attaching rubber tubes to opposite sides of the sample to be tested, and covering the remaining sides with wax in the manner described.

While, therefore, it may for many reasons be desirable to employ porous materials for building, these materials should be carefully coated with non-permeable substances, either outside or inside, or both, and every precaution possible should be taken to prevent the entrance through them of the outer air, though I am aware that this conclusion is exactly the reverse of that held by Lange and others.

If there were cases where no other sufficient fresh-air supply *could* be obtained than through the pores of the building materials, natural ventilation might be recommended. As it is, there are, unfortunately, many buildings in which no other sufficient supply *is* provided, and natural ventilation then becomes, in spite of us, a great good; but as our question here is with well and not ill ventilated buildings, accuracy and success in our arrangements require us to know its greatest extent and provide against it.

THE POSITION OF THE FRESH-AIR INLET.

The walls of our building having been made impermeable to air, and all cracks or accidental openings having been carefully closed, our fresh-air supply may be accurately calculated and controlled, and the heating surfaces over which it is conducted may be utilized to the best advantage.

The size of our heating surface having been determined by the amount of fresh air required to be warmed, and this amount again by the maximum number of persons and gas-burners to be supplied, it only remains to fix upon the best point or points in the room for the fresh-air delivery. Here we enter a long-contested battle-field. Whatever means be employed to warm the air before its introduction, it should enter and be distributed in such a way as to serve all without inconveniencing any. As a general rule, and *always* where an open fireplace is used, the entrance should be *at or near the ceiling*,[1] whatever system of heating or cooling the fresh-air supply be adopted, and whether, upon entering, it be cooler or warmer than the air already in the room. If it enter warmer, it will rise at once to the ceiling, even if it be first introduced at the floor, so that there is no advantage, in the way of heating the floor, by having the hot-air registers in or near it. This may be easily verified by burning some damp straw in the fresh-air box or flues of a furnace and observing the course taken by the warm air, thus rendered visible, as it issues from a floor register. It will be found to shoot upwards in a round column to the ceiling as represented in Fig. 146, more or less rapidly according as its temperature ex-

Fig. 146. Movement of Hot Air from Furnace Flues.

ceeds more or less that of the surrounding air. Outside of this column the air will be no warmer at or near the floor than if no register there existed, until the heated air at the top descends in regular strata to the bottom. In fact, one of the best places to draw off the colder and fouler air from such a room would be through an opening placed directly by the side of this hot-air supply register in the floor. If, on the contrary, the fresh air introduced be cooler than that already in the room, it will, if it enter at the floor, escape at once at the fireplace opening or at any other foul-air exhaust-flue which may be placed near the floor, without rising to the level of the heads of the occupants, and be lost. But if the entering air be cooler than the air of the room it will greatly inconvenience those who may be seated near the inlets, where these inlets are at the bottom of the room, especially in large rooms, as in public halls, school-houses, and theatres; whereas, if the supply registers be at the top, and exhaust registers at the bottom, no such inconvenience will be felt. No opening for extracting the products of respiration should be allowed above the level of the heads of the persons occupying the room. If this rule be ignored, the fresh air will not reach the occupants, and no ventilation will be for them

---

[1] As an exception to this rule may be given the case of a theatre or public-audience hall in which the entrances for fresh air are very numerous or under each seat. In this case the exhaust registers may be in the side walls and even near the ceiling. An excellent example of this may be had in the finely ventilated Madison Square Theatre, of New York, a model worthy of study.

effected. Fig. 117 shows what would be the result in a bedroom where the exhaust register was placed above the head of the sleeper. The warm-air supply register is here represented in the floor. If it were in the ceil-

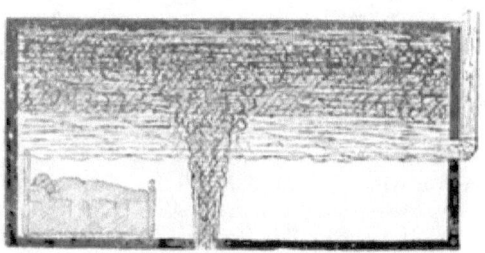

Fig. 147. Exhaust Register placed too high.

ing the results would be the same. The hot air first forms itself along the ceiling in an even horizontal stratum, just as oil lies on the surface of a body of a heavier fluid, such as water. As more hot air enters, the first descends and gives place to it. The lower, cooler, and heavier strata fall; they seek their own level, just as would strata of light and heavy liquids. Air does not follow so docilely and obligingly the paths laid out for it by the would-be ventilators, when they explain their patent arrangements by little arrows meandering about snake-like in pursuit of a "draught" or heated exhaust flue. It does not "head" directly to the exhaust register, even if the so-called "draught" in it be ever so strong. The lower strata only flow out at these exhaust openings just as the lower strata of water in a bucket would flow out of a hole bored in the side near the bottom. We must always bear in mind that it is not the lighter column of air in the chimney *pulling* up the heavier air in the room, but rather the heavy air in the room pushing up the lighter column in the chimney. There is no suction such as the word "draught" would imply, but a simple uplifting, by the cooler masses of air outside of the house and within the room, of the lighter strata or column in the exhaust flue. The word "draught" is a misnomer, and is responsible for much of the confusion existing upon the subject. With an exhaust opening placed as shown in Fig. 117, or, worse still, at the ceiling, where these openings are usually put (though, fortunately, they are seldom operative on account of the want of motive power), the supply of fresh air might be enormous, and yet the sleeper suffer from want of it.

Where a room is heated by a stove, and no fresh air is introduced, this stratification of the air is broken up, as shown in Fig. 148, and the motion becomes more complicated. The currents may be illustrated by heating with electricity, or otherwise, a piece of metal at the bottom of a glass box filled with water containing some coloring matter, and throwing the reflection of the water by means of a lens and calcium-light upon a screen.

These all seem like facts simple and reasonable enough. Why, then, such a diversity of opinion regarding the location of ventilating openings? It is because in ordinary buildings the question of the disposal of the products of respiration is complicated with those of the gas-burners, while the two should be kept entirely distinct, and a separate and opposite system of ventilation provided for each. To carry off the products of gas combustion openings above the head are necessary. When these openings are placed in the ceiling, as is customary in this country, the upper pure and warm strata of air are impoverished by the products of gas combustion, and it is assumed that the only cure is to *draw it all off as fast as it is generated.* The products of respiration do not rise at once to the ceiling, as do those of illumination. The breath is directed downwards by the form of the nostrils, and it becomes so quickly mixed with the surrounding air, that before it has time to rise again to any considerable height it has attained the general temperature, and follows the general movement of the latter, whatever that movement may be. Were the heat and impurities of gas combustion carried off at their source, and not allowed to affect the gen-

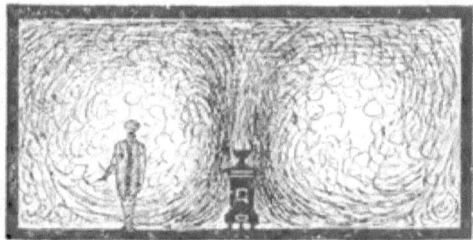

Fig. 149. Movement of Air About a Stove.

eral atmosphere of the room, our problem would be at once simplified. The fresh, warm air at the top of the room would be kept pure until it descended to the level of the occupants, when it would perform its office and pass off through the exhaust registers below.

As a general rule, then, the exhaust openings should be near the floor for buildings heated as is customary at the present day. As an exception to this rule may be mentioned the case of bedrooms in which the fresh-air supply is obtained in winter through the open window, and no warm air is introduced. In this case, the air may enter at a temperature at or near the freezing-point. The purest air will then be at the bottom. The breath and exhalations from the skin will rise to the ceiling, and an exhaust register there placed will be serviceable. It is well, however, even in such rooms, to have an exhaust opening below, as well as above, for use where it is found desirable to warm the pure air before its introduction, as in cases of sickness, or during the daytime, when window ventilation would prove inconvenient.

The exhaust openings would also be in place at the bottom of the room, were the system adopted of supplying air partially warmed, say, at 10° or 15° C. (50° or 60° F.), to rooms heated to a higher temperature by hot pipes or flues behind or beneath the walls and floors. The pure air would then constantly fall below the respired air, and the movement of the strata would be the reverse of that now obtained. Such a system of heating would be the most agreeable and salubrious possible; but heretofore its costliness has stood in the way of its general introduction. The cost being equal, that system which approaches most nearly the desideratum mentioned must be accounted best.

ACCIDENTAL CRACKS.

Under Pressure, however slight, such as that of the air of a furnace flue of little height, air will escape at a thousand minute openings in a room having a number of doors and windows, however carefully the woodwork be fitted, even if no exhaust flue be provided. The aggregate of all these small openings will furnish an outlet if an ample supply be provided under pressure; and where the walls are porous the pores themselves will form an outlet. On the other hand, these same minute openings will, under slight pressure inwards, such as is occasioned by burning a fire in an ordinary open fireplace where no fresh-air supply flues are provided, admit the outer air in quantities larger than is generally supposed. Mr. L. W. Leeds, in his excellent book on ventilation, well says, "In the good old days of open wood-fires, when, as in our childhood, the real chimney-corner was the family sitting-room, so to speak, or at least for the children, then, with all the listing of doors, calking of windows, and filling up of key-holes, there was certain to be an abundance of fresh air that will force its way into the room in spite of all efforts to keep it out. But with the introduction of anthracite coal and air-tight stoves, and, still worse, steam-pipes, placed in a room for heating by direct radiation, the stopping of all draughts, that were before so annoying, became a matter of easy accomplishment. The results thereof have been perfectly frightful; persons have thus unconsciously been smothered to death by the thousands and tens of thousands."

In order to test the influence of a slight pressure in forcing air through the pores and accidental fissures of an ordinary living-room, the writer made the following experiment: A room about 5 meters square and 3.60 meters high, containing 5 windows on 3 sides, 2 doors, and a fireplace, with walls and ceilings plastered, and floors of soft pine, was taken for experiment, in a city corner house, now being built by the writer. A flue 10 meters long, from a basement furnace, furnished the rooms with hot air. The windows and doors were first made as tight as possible with rubber mouldings. The fireplace was then closed by drawing the damper and pasting paper over the cracks. The brick back and jambs were oiled to render them impervious. All the wood-work was thoroughly oiled and shellacked. A good fire was lighted in the furnace, and the register opened into the room, all doors and windows being closed and locked, and the key-holes stopped up. The hot air entered almost as rapidly with the doors closed as when they stood open, and it continued to enter at the rate of 2.5 cubic meters per minute without diminution as long as the experiment was continued. The thermometer stood at $2°$ C. outside. The entering hot air ranged from $40°$ to $55°$ C. The day was March 3, 1880. Other experiments gave the same results. The pressure of the hot air from the register was sufficient only to raise a single piece of cardboard from the register. A portion of the air must have passed through the pores of the materials, and the rest through cracks and fissures which escaped detection. On the 5th of March a coat of oil paint was applied to the walls and ceilings. This diminished the escape of air only about 5 per cent. On the 19th of March 4 coats of oil paint had been put on the walls and ceilings, and 3 coats on the floor, to render them absolutely impervious to air. The escape of air was diminished only about 10 per cent.

On the 25th of March all the window-sashes were carefully examined, and all visible cracks at the joints, at the pulleys, cord fastenings, etc., carefully calked and puttied, and the entire room examined, and putty used freely wherever even a suspicion of a crack could be found. The result of all this was a diminution at the utmost of but 20 per cent. in the escape of the air, or, in other words, in the entrance of air through the register. Each experiment was continued during more than an hour. The air entered as freely at the end as at the beginning of the hour, when a volume of air, more than equal to the entire capacity of the room, had entered it through the register, with no visible outlet.

Nevertheless numerous microscopic outlets must have remained, especially around the window-sashes, through which the air escaped in this large quantity under the slight pressure applied. In order to render the room completely air-tight, therefore, it would be necessary to surround the windows, doors, mantel, and base-board entirely with a thick coating of some absolutely impermeable substance like tar or putty, or to paste over them large sheets of oil-cloth or paper. The room would then, and then only, be hermetically sealed, and the hot air from the furnace would cease to enter as soon as it reached its limit of compressibility under the pressure applied.

VENTILATION OF GAS-BURNERS.

Where an open fireplace is used the foul-air exhaust is of necessity at the bottom of the room. The supply must therefore of necessity be from the top downwards; for, as we have shown, if the air enter cold it would otherwise pass off through the fireplace opening without ventilating the room, and if it enter hot it would rise at once to the ceiling, wherever the inlet might be located. To serve for both, as for summer or winter use, as well as to avoid discharging directly upon the occupants, it must be at the ceiling. To prevent contamination of this air by the gas-burners, it is necessary that the products of combustion should be removed at once upon their generation *at the level of the burners*, by ventilating ducts connected with each burner. It is urged in objection to this, that the appearance of the ventilating ducts would be unsightly, and that no one would

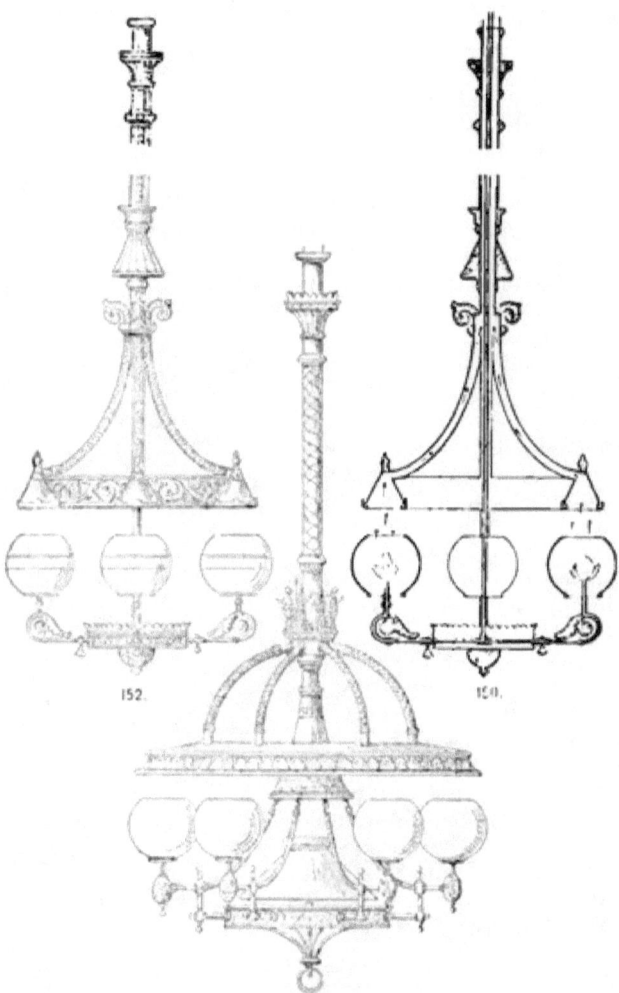

Fig 149 Ventilating Gasoliers.

consent to have so clumsy a contrivance in his house. But the space occupied by the ventilating flues need be no greater than that ordinarily taken up in the designs of gas-fixtures by meaningless scrolls and hollow casings applied solely for the purpose of increasing the apparent weight and size of the pipe and improving its contour.

Figs. 149 to 157 represent ventilating chandeliers designed by the writer. The first two are for the Adams Nervine Hospital, now being built by him at Jamaica Plain. Fig. 149 is for the dining-room, having 8 globes surrounding a central reflector. A section of this chandelier is given in Fig. 151. A bell is formed over the central burner, from which ascends the main ventilating flue enclosing the gas supply pipe. Another bell encircles this, and carries off the gas products from the 8 globe burners; 8 branch flues, 1 over each burner, connect this bell with the main ventilating flue. The branch flues are double, as protection against heat. The diameter of the inner branch flues is 3 centimeters each, the outer coverings are 4 centimeters, that of the main flue 8 centimeters. It is important that the flues should be just large enough to carry off the products of gas combustion, and no more; otherwise the pure warm air of the room will be carried off with it and wasted. The lower rim of each bell is provided with a small gutter to catch the return water of condensation. Figs. 150 and 152 give the parlor chandelier, where each bell is separate from the rest. In this 6 burners are used. The flues are of the same size as in the dining-room chandelier. Both of these designs are kept very simple, in accordance with the instructions of the building committee. Fig. 153 gives a somewhat more elaborate design for a small chandelier with 2 burners and a reflector.

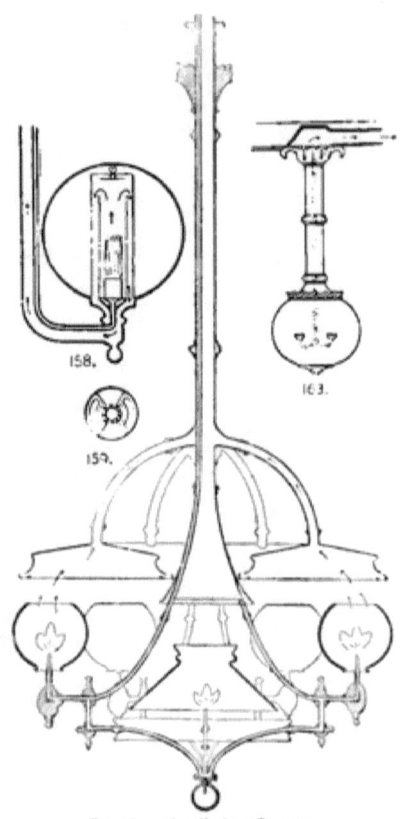

Fig. 151. Ventilating Gasoliers.

This is shown in section in Fig. 154. Fig. 155 gives the bell in detail, with the condensation gutter.[1]

---

[1] The construction of these ventilating chandeliers is attended with no mechanical difficulty other than is due to its novelty. But the size and form of the ventilating tubes; the precautions necessary to protect them from discoloration under heat; the proper arrangement of the bells so that the products of combustion shall be carried off without obscuring the light; and withal the necessity for carrying out the design in an artistic manner, — require considerable experience and taste on the part of the manufacturer. The bell over the burners in the chandelier shown in Figs. 149 and 151 has its upper surface constructed of glass set in ribs of metal radiating from the inner to the outer circle. The object of this is to prevent a dark shadow ring being formed on the ceiling. Over each burner a small metallic funnel carries the gas products to the ventilating flues. These ventilating chandeliers are manufactured by Messrs. Shreve, Crump, & Low, of Boston, under patent rights consigned them by the writer.

130   THE OPEN FIREPLACE.

Figs. 156 and 157 give a view and section of a hall pendant. These designs are intended to be executed in brass, fire-gilt. The bells are to

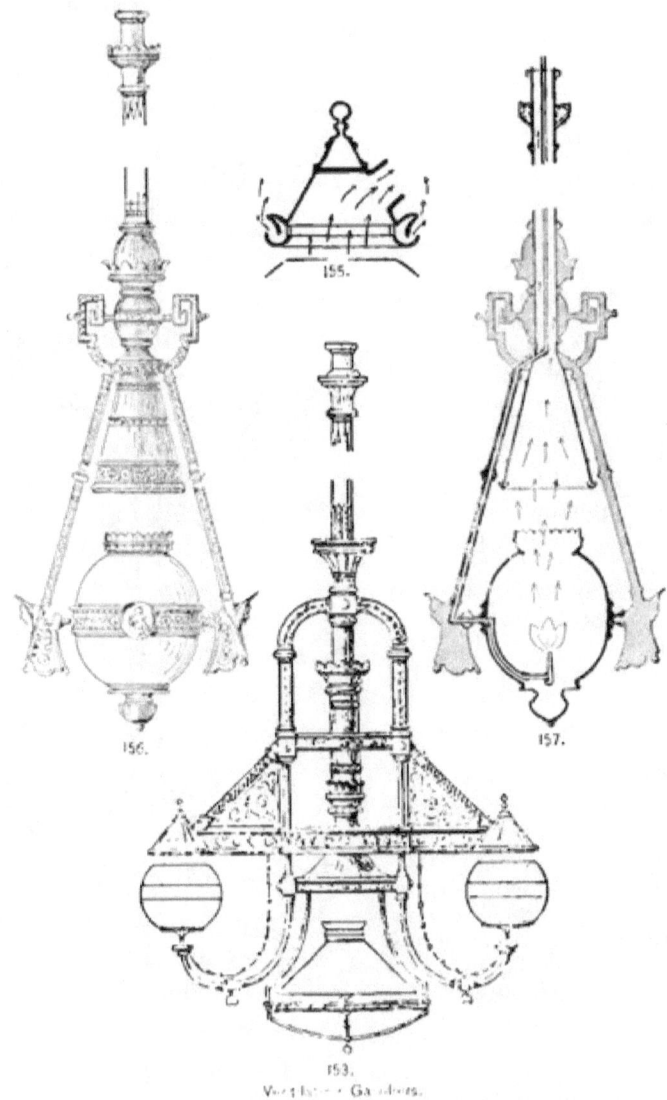

have an inner lining of sheet-iron, with an air-space between it and the brass-work, for the free passage of cool air, to prevent the brass-work from becoming discolored by heat; or the bells may be made of annealed glass.

Figs. 158 and 159 represent an old form of ventilating burner, invented by Faraday in 1840, applying the descending draught and the argand burner with chimney and globe. The glass-holder is made to carry a second chimney larger than the first, and closed at the top with a double cover of mica. The air to supply the burner enters below the flame, through the two triangular spaces of the holder shown in Fig. 159, feeds the flame as it rises in the inside chimney, and then passes down between the two chimneys, and escapes through the exhaust flue attached to the bottom of the outer chimney and holder, as shown by the arrows. The usual form of globe may be used over the whole, or a special form of globe constructed for the purpose, with the top closed, may be adopted as in the figure. If the exhaust tube connects with a cold flue, it is necessary to heat the ascending part in order to produce an initial draught. Fig. 160 represents the same device under a somewhat modified form. The fresh air has free access to the inner chimney from below, and returns after supporting the combustion through 4 branches uniting into one exhaust tube, connected with the space between the two chimneys. The plan of these 4 branch exhaust tubes is given in Fig. 161, and the plan of the main exhaust tube below, with the envelope surrounding it for ornament, is given in Fig. 162.

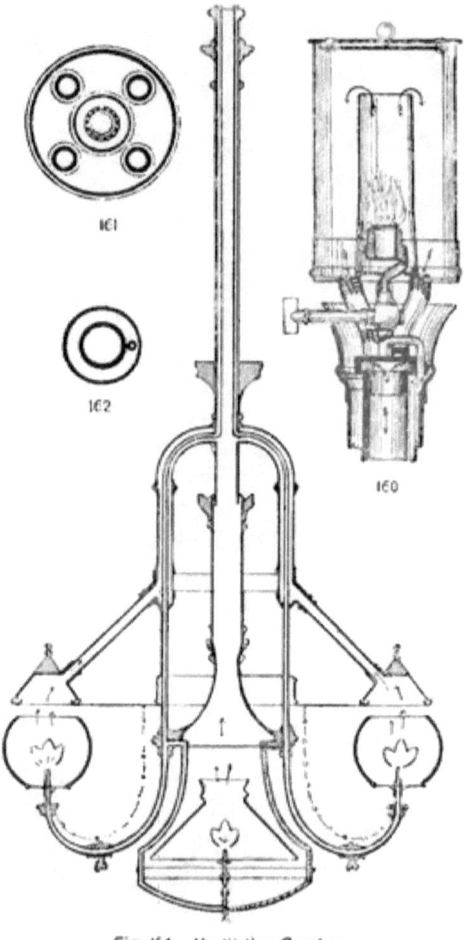

Fig. 154. Ventilating Gasoliers.

This system has been applied in France to the foot-lights of theatres. It has the advantage of lessening the chances of fire catching the dresses of the actors, as well as of maintaining the purity of the air of the stage, — a consideration of peculiar importance for actors and singers, the products of gas combustion being particularly injurious to the throat and lungs.

Another form of ventilating gas-burner, now much used in England, is shown in Fig. 163. The air enters below the globe, and passes out above and also at the ceiling. This exhaust at the ceiling should be closed, for the reasons already given, only the lower opening being used. Fig. 164 gives an arrangement for supplying fresh air to the room in addition to the offices performed by the fixture represented by Fig. 163. Figs.

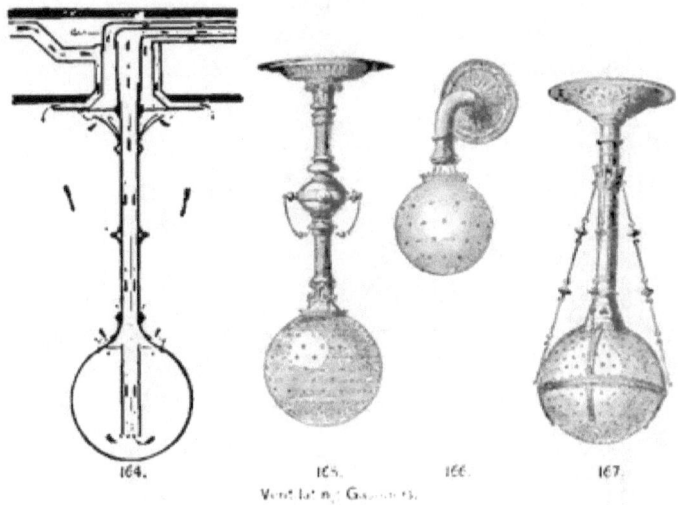

164.   165.   166.   167.
Ventilating Gas Jets.

165, 166, and 167 give various forms of the same device. In London at the present time ventilating chandeliers are used very largely in public buildings. These were originally made in the form of a vast bell or hood, covering the entire chandelier or crown of lights. But by this arrangement a strong shadow was cast on the ceiling by the cover. The inconvenience was remedied by using mica slate, instead of opaque material, in the construction of the bell, the sheets of mica being supported in an open-work metallic frame.

For the single burners of the Adams Hospital, the writer has had constructed a form of ventilator shown in Fig. 168. A little bell is placed over the burner, and connected by means of a small tube, about 5 centimeters in diameter, with a larger flue, 10 centimeters in diameter, descending to the floor. The large flue is provided with a damper near the floor, by means of which the ventilation produced by the heat of the burner may be controlled. The bell and small pipe are double, to prevent injury by heat.

Another form, represented in Fig. 169, he has designed for and used in a private dwelling-house, now nearly completed, on Dartmouth street, Boston. In this, a glass globe is used over the burner, and the hood is brought down to the globe, and may be bent down so as to come in contact with it, or it may be slightly raised so as to leave a very small space above the globe for the admission of air. The effect of this arrangement is quite pleasing. The surface of the globe may be ground, cut, or colored to represent the petals of a hanging flower, the ventilating tube being the stem. The gas in this case is lighted by electricity. Still another and simpler form is given in Fig. 170. This he adopted to ventilate a number

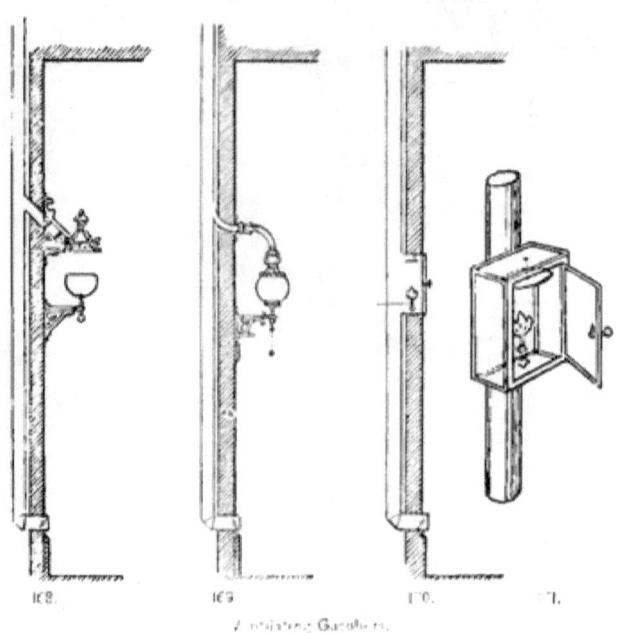

of bath and toilet rooms, in a house built in Salem in 1879. It consists of a square glass box, Fig. 171, connected with the main ventilating flue in each room to be ventilated, and holding the burner. The supply of air in this case comes entirely from the lower opening. To avoid flickering, the box must be brought forward in such a manner that the current of air passes by without striking the flame.

"The existence of sulphur compounds in burning gas is to be regretted as a nearly unavoidable evil; the only remedy seems to be the discharge of the products of combustion through chimneys or flues." (Lincoln.)

According to E. S. Wood, "The sulphurous and sulphuric acids which are produced in burning may injure delicate structures, such as books, gilding, silk, etc., that may be exposed to the air of a room in which gas is burned. Where large quantities of impure gas are burned, it causes a rapid destruction of textile fabrics, with a very acid condition of them. This was especially noticed in the large public libraries of London, many years ago; the covers of many of the books in the Athenaeum Club-house, the College of Surgeons, and elsewhere, becoming destroyed by the sulphuric acid from the burning gas. The amount of this acid was so great that it could be easily tasted by applying the exposed portions of the books to the tongue."

It is well known that the products of combustion of gas are highly injurious, and sometimes fatal, to flowers and plants. These rapidly fade in crowded ball-rooms; and plants growing in our houses for ornament become sickly and feeble where they are not protected from the corrosive influence of the acid gases.

"Nearly all of the sulphur is converted into sulphuric acid, which is a vapor readily condensed on the walls and other objects contained in a room. Gas not unfrequently contains 50 grains of sulphur per 100 cubic feet, which in burning gives rise to 90 grains of sulphuric acid; and this is the amount which would be produced by five 4-foot burners during 5 hours." (Lincoln.)

But, besides carbonic and sulphuric acid gases, we have the dreaded carbonic oxide gas, which escapes into the room in considerable quantities (Parkes) whenever gas is partly burnt. This often happens with the varying pressure in the mains.

The Faraday Gas-Ventilator (Figs. 158–161) is said to be open to the objection that the draught is liable to be irregular and the chimney to become blackened with smoke. Though with careful construction and management both of these objections might be obviated, yet where the chance of this is great other forms should be adopted. For the footlights of theatres a ventilator constructed as in Figs. 172–176 might be practicable. In this the footlight-screen and ventilator are combined. Fig. 172 gives a side view of the device and Fig. 173 a vertical section, showing in both cases a section of the large horizontal ventilating-flue connecting the several branch ventilators together, and passing along at the foot of the lights, partially screening them from the audience. Fig. 174 gives a view as seen from the stage, and Fig. 175 as seen from the auditorium. In both cases a side view of the main flue is given. A horizontal section is shown in Fig. 176. The main flue should, of course, be large enough to carry off the products of combustion from the entire circuit of lights. Each branch-ventilator should be quite small, — only enough, and no more than enough, to serve for its own burner. A gas-jet burning in the perpendicular portion of the main flue would create sufficient initiatory draught therein, and should be lighted with or before the footlights.

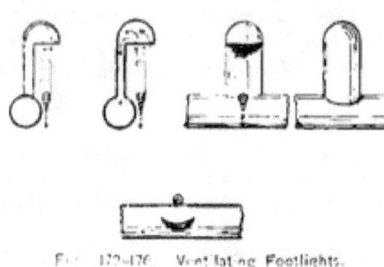

Figs. 172–176. Ventilating Footlights.

The fatigue experienced at and after a late evening party is largely due to the impurity of the air of the ball-room. A dozen unventilated gas-burners exhaust the atmosphere as much as would 40 or 50 guests. The result is general discomfort and often evident permanent injury to the health. Were the host aware of the extent to which the enjoyment of his entertainment — not to say the health of his guests — is impaired by these causes, which a fractional part of the cost of the feast could have removed, he would have provided pure air for the lungs of his friends, even if to do so it had been necessary for him to buy simpler food for their stomachs and reduce his band of fiddlers. The body is covered with little vent tubes, many hundreds in every square inch, called perspiration-tubes, — the aggregate length of which is over 2¼ miles, — for the escape of vapor and fatty matter from the skin. This vapor arises constantly from all parts of the body, carrying with it the decayed organic matter thrown off in large quantities every day from the pores, and mingles with the breath, itself loaded with the impurities which it is its very office to remove from the blood. Nearly 2 pounds of this vapor are given off daily from the skin of an adult, and another pound from the lungs. What if, instead of compelling our guests to feed their lungs upon these exhalations from the skin and nostrils of their friends, both healthy and diseased, while they were allowed fresh viands for eating, we should reverse the treatment, and compel them to eat in rotation one and the same dish, each devouring the morsels that another had masticated and returned again for the enjoyment of the rest! The idea is to us disgusting. But we need to be disgusted to induce us to improve our condition, and the idea would hardly appear more revolting to us than that of consuming the fœtid breath of our neighbors, had not habit rendered us peculiarly callous to the latter. Yet how delicate the structure of our lungs, and how careful should be our treatment of them! The extent of the respiratory surface in the lungs of an average adult is calculated, by Lieberkühn,[1] at 1,400 square feet, and the number of air-cells of which it is composed is estimated, by some, at 600,000,000. Through this wonderfully complex structure the air of our crowded ball-rooms is pumped 20 times a minute, loaded with its dust and impurities, although it is here that the blood should be aërated for purification! "There are," says Leeds, "on an average, about 72 pulsations of the heart every minute, and 2 ounces of blood are passed through the lungs at each pulsation, or from 65 to 70 gallons every hour, and from 40 to 60 barrels per day. . . We thus see the very large amounts of blood and air that circulate through the lungs, and can easily imagine of how much greater importance the proper supply of air is to the maintenance of good health than the supply of food, because, while we eat less than 2 pounds daily, we breathe 15 times that amount, or about 30 pounds. Fifty barrels of blood are forced through the hundreds of millions of air-cells of the lungs for the purpose of obtaining the purification of fresh air. Yet we give it foul. An atmosphere 40

---

[1] Simon's Chemistry of Man. Philadelphia, 1846.

miles in height has been provided by Nature, to ensure us an ample supply for this blood purification; and at the same time we have been provided with a breathing apparatus evidently designed to prevent inhalation of the same breath twice. Yet we shut our friends up for entertainment in boxes so arranged that it is impossible for them to obtain a single breath of air that has not been breathed over and over again, perhaps a hundred times and by a hundred different persons. The impurities of the blood have then to be carried back again from the lungs to all parts of the system, and diseases of all forms follow. When the delicate air-cells become choked, consumption begins. Unfortunately we do not always observe in crowded rooms the gradual deterioration of the atmosphere, because the senses become benumbed and accustomed to it; but enter suddenly from the outer air, and the foulness appears at once.

In the room described as allowing 2 cubic meters of air to pass by way of invisible cracks, there were 5 windows, having north, south, and west exposure, and 2 doors, to say nothing of a fireplace and 5 other openings for gas-ventilation, etc. When the experiments were made, all the furnace registers throughout the house were shut, excepting the one in this room, so that the maximum of hot-air pressure might be obtained at this point. The amount of air forced through the chamber was, nevertheless, only 1.5 cubic meters per minute. Were the number of openings reduced one-half, leaving a number more usually found in rooms of the size of this, the ventilation under the same pressure would have been 0.75 cubic meter, — hardly sufficient for one person. Had there been but 2 openings, say 1 window and 1 door, a condition not infrequent, we should have had only about 0.4 meter of fresh air per minute, and the air of the room would very soon become foul, even without the consumption of gas and under the pressure of the hot-air column. Were the pressure removed, the air of the room would have been nearly stagnant.

In heating and ventilating a room provision should be made for the maximum number of persons it is likely at any time to contain, and for each burner contained in it, supposing all to be in use. A parlor, for instance, in which an entertainment for 50 guests is provided, and 10 unventilated gas-burners are used, should have foul-air exhaust openings and fresh-air supply sufficient to change the air at the rate of 100 cubic meters a minute, or, if the gas-burners are ventilated, at the rate of 50 cubic meters per minute, assuming that the room is connected with others equally filled with guests and burners. Supposing we allow the air to travel through the openings at the rate of 100 meters a minute, these openings, both exhaust and supply, should each be at least a meter square in the aggregate, and the arrangements for changing the air should be such that the air is *actually* and not merely *apparently* changed at the rate established, and this without extraordinary expense or inconvenience. There are few rooms to be found with even an approximation to such ventilation. It is nevertheless possible, and the manner in which it has been accomplished by the writer will next be described.

THE FURNACE VENTILATING FIREPLACE.

Fig. 179 gives a plan of the parlor floor of the writer's house, now being built in Boston, after his drawings and specifications. Fig. 181 represents a portion of the fireplace side of the front parlor, a room about 7 meters square and 4 meters high, — large enough to seat 25 guests com-

Fig. 181. Improved Parlor Ventilating Fireplace.

fortably. In it there are 10 gas-burners. These were unwillingly left unventilated, because of associations attaching to the chandeliers long used by the family. Provision has therefore been made for changing the air, on special occasions, at the rate of 65 cubic meters per minute through exhaust openings placed both at the ceiling and at the floor. The use of the unventilated gas-burners is a serious blemish in the system of ventilation employed. But as this unfortunately is a condition at present usually

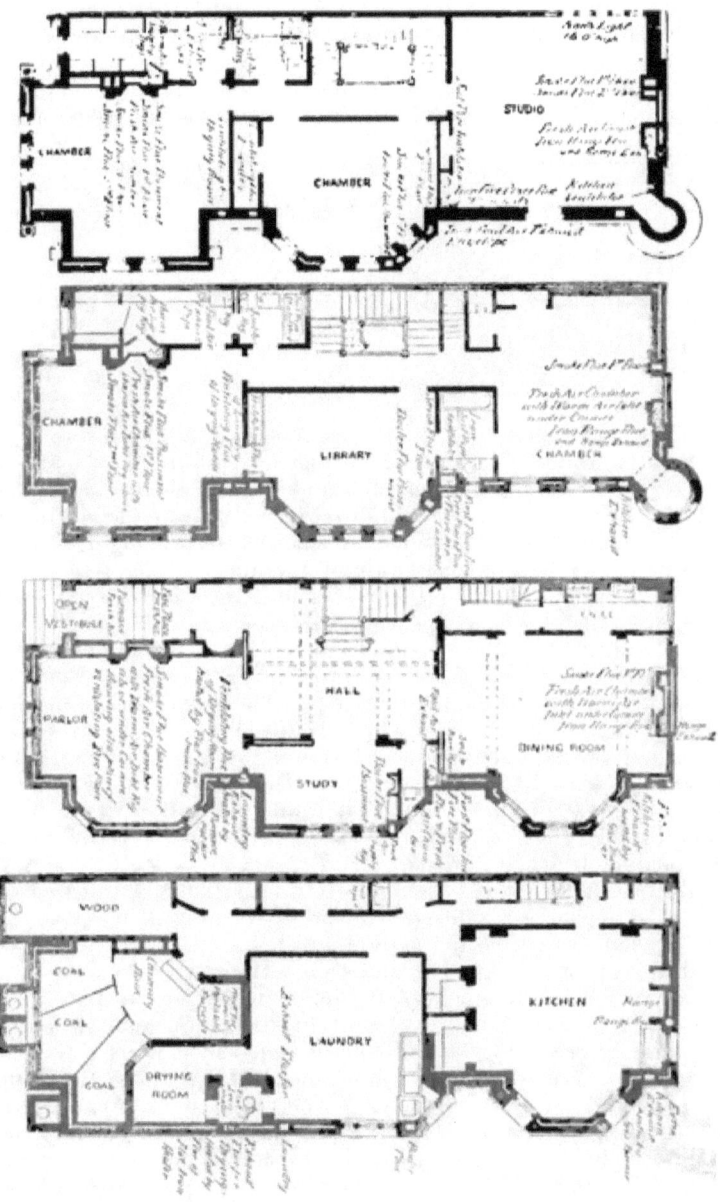

encountered by the sanitarian, who would find few persons willing to alter their fixtures for the sake of pure air, it is important to know the best way to meet it.

The plan of the fireplace in this room is shown in Fig. 182. The back is constructed of a slab of soapstone, faced on the room side with

Fig. 182. Horizontal Section of Pure Ventilating Fireplace.

ornamental unglazed tiles. The sides are built of fire-brick, faced with glazed tiles, which reflect the light and heat of the flames and add to the effect of the fire. Behind the back and sides of the fireplace is a fresh-air space, into which pure air is admitted directly from the outside through a register opening from the open vestibule, as shown in Figs. 178 and 185, the latter being the front elevation of the house. The register is placed a meter up from the floor of the vestibule, which is tiled up to the ceiling and open to the outer air, the front door being further in. The purity of the fresh air at all times is thus ensured. Its supply is regulated by a simple valve near the register, operated from the parlor by a cord at the right-hand side of the chimney-breast. The valve is nothing more than a plate of ¼-inch iron or brass, which is lifted when the cord is pulled from within, and opens the register, closing it again wholly or partially when the cord is released. The valve should fit tightly, so that when no fire is burning no cold air shall enter. It would be well to have 2 valves, one outside of the other, with an air-space between, to cut off the air supply more completely when desired.

The fresh air is first moderately warmed by coming in contact with the heated back and sides of the fireplace, and then rises into a large fresh-air chamber above the mantel and behind the chimney-breast, represented in section in Figs. 184 and 185. Here it strikes the hot walls of an enlargement of the smoke-flue, similar in purpose to that described by Péclet (Fig. 125), though different in size, form, and principle of construction. After having been further warmed by contact with this furnace-attachment or heat-distributor in the smoke-flue, it enters the room through an ornamental cut-brass register in the chimney-breast, near the ceiling (Fig. 184), or it may be allowed to pass into the second-story room above through a valve in the ceiling of the fresh-air chamber, shown at the top of Fig. 184, operated by a cord and tassel at the left-hand side of the chimney-breast. The air of the room, instead of the outer air, may be warmed against the smoke-flue if desired. For this purpose a register,

140   THE OPEN FIREPLACE.

Fig. 183. Front Elevation of House on Dartmouth Street

Fig. 187. Ventilation Chim

with valves, should always be provided, in the lower part of the chimney-breast, to admit the air of the room. The furnace, or "distributor," is in this case made of carefully baked terra-cotta, especially prepared with a view to resisting the strongest heat, and the most sudden changes of temperature, without cracking. As a test, before making one of these radia-

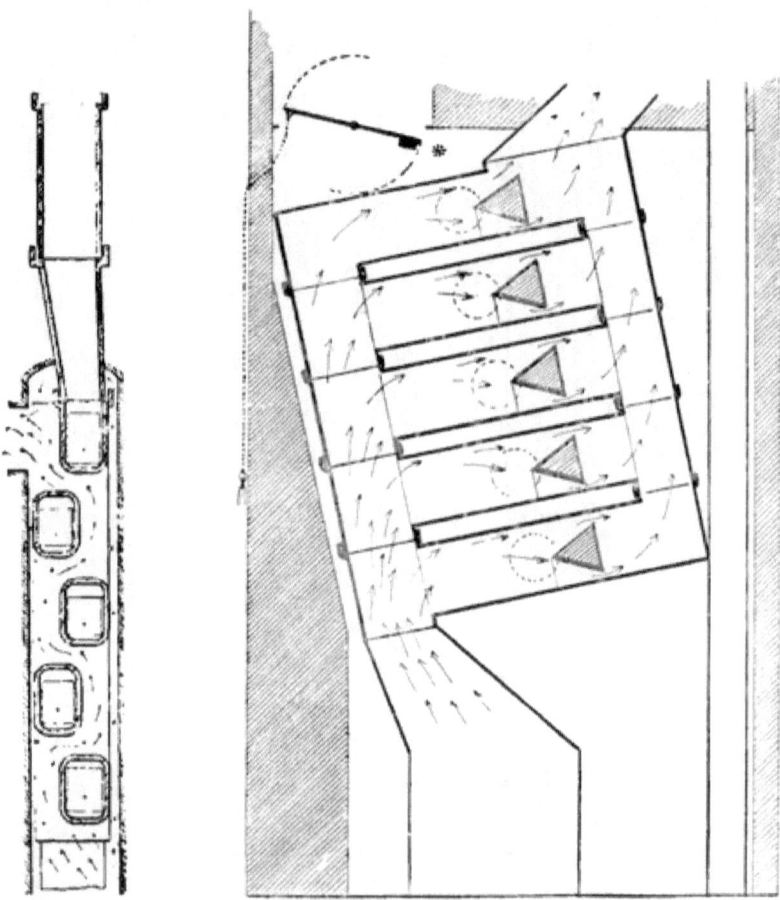

Fig. 185. Vertical Section of Terra-Cotta Distributor.

Fig. 184. Vertical Section of Terra-Cotta Distributor.

tors, the writer had a piece of terra-cotta, of the kind to be used, heated to different degrees of heat, including red-heat. Cold water dashed upon the sample raised to these temperatures produced no apparent injurious effect. On the other hand, if the clay is not of the proper kind, and properly baked, a strong flame may quickly crack it when it is surrounded with cold air. Fig. 186 gives this distributor in perspective, somewhat modified in form, to show another way of arranging the dampers. The name "distributor" is given it, in preference to "radiator," as expressing more accurately its office,—the heat is not obtained from it by radiation, except in a slight degree, but by convection, and "convector" would therefore be a more appropriate term. But any hot flue would in this sense be a heat "convector" as well as this. Its most characteristic function is to break up and spread out the current of smoke, and *distribute* its heat over a large surface, that it may be more readily taken up by the fresh air brought in contact therewith.

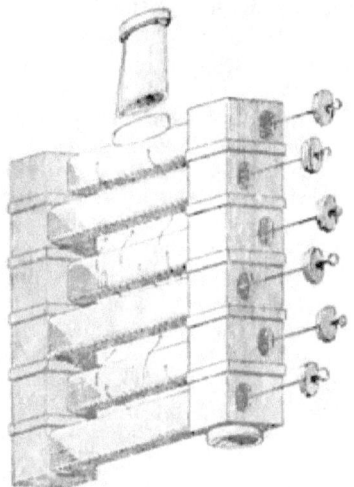

Fig. 186. Terra-Cotta Distributor, for Ventilating Fireplace. Perspective View.

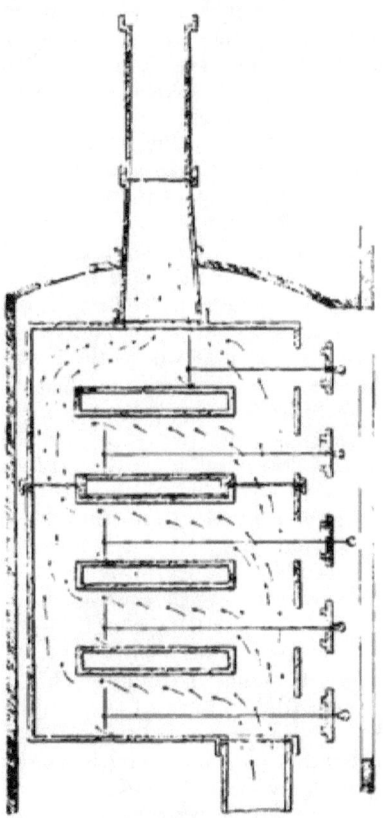

Fig. 186 A. Section.

The movement of the smoke and of the fresh air are clearly represented in the sections by arrows. By referring to Fig. 144 of the soapstone furnace, it will be seen that the general principle of circulation is somewhat similar in the two devices. The column of smoke is subdivided and brought efficiently in contact with a large heating-surface, without encountering sufficient resistance dangerously to obstruct its passage. The fresh air strikes almost every part of the heating-surface, without in its turn encountering serious resistance. By referring again to the Chilson furnace (Fig. 134), we see how the smoke is distributed equally among the six upright flues by a contraction of these flues at the top. To avoid the danger of clogging with soot, as well as the loss of heating-surface that would be involved by a diminution of the flues, the principle of an *interior*, instead of an exterior cone, in the form of a movable cone-shaped damper, has been adopted, so placed in each flue that, while it diminishes the opening, it leaves the heating-surface undiminished. By this means, on the one hand, clogging is avoided, and cleaning facilitated, and, on the other, a greater heating-surface is presented to the rising fresh air, at less cost and in a more effective manner. The retreating surfaces of the cone, which appear rather to shun than to court the contact of the air, are avoided. Parallel surfaces are substituted, and these may be perpendicular, or they may be placed at an inclination, as in Fig. 184, and so arranged diagonally over each other (as in Fig. 185) that the fresh air is forced to embrace every part. To ascertain if this contact took place *actually*, and not merely theoretically, an opening in the fresh-air chamber enclosing the heater was made in such a manner that the movement of the current of air could be seen by the aid of a little smoke mixed with it. The air was found to circulate about the pipes exactly as expected, and as indicated by the arrows. The connecting pipes should never be placed horizontally, unless the draught in the chimney is powerful, but either at an inclination or perpendicularly, as in Fig. 187, because in these positions very little obstruction is offered to the passage of the smoke. *The dampers should always be placed as far from the throat of the fireplace as possible*, in order to give the smoke opportunity to rise as far as possible, and fill the pipes before meeting with the least obstruction.

If these precautions be observed, such a distributor may be used in the same flue at each story of a building of any number of stories, without destroying the draught, for the slight obstruction occasioned by each distributor is more than offset by the improvement of the draught made by each additional story added in the height of the chimney.

In the chimney of the fireplace in question two distributors were used. These appear to have no injurious effect whatever upon the draught, although flat dampers are used in them instead of the cone-shaped ones recommended and shown in the drawings.

The fresh warm air having entered the room as described, at the ceiling, descends as it cools, and gives place to that which follows, until it reaches the fireplace opening below, through which it finally escapes. In this way, for every-day use, the draught of the fireplace is supplied entirely with fresh air, previously warmed against the smoke-flue, and the amount of air changed is, on these occasions, dependent upon the size of the smoke-flue, the inlet registers being as large as desired. For special occasions, however, when the room is full, and a much greater change of air is needed, the ventilators are caused to act in a manner quite different. The cold-air supply register at the back of the fireplace is closed. The damper at the top of the fresh-air chamber (Fig. 184, top) is opened, and the warm-air supply register at the top of the room becomes a foul-air exhaust-flue, to assist the fireplace smoke-flue in carrying off the extra quantity of heat and foul air generated by the gas-lights and guests, to the corresponding chambers above. Thence it enters a large exhaust-flue provided for it at the top of the house, and is removed. Fig. 187 shows the chimney-stack, with this exhaust-flue at the top. This system may be adopted always in summer.

Where the rooms above are, as is customary, used for cloak-rooms or dressing-rooms during an entertainment, the open fireplaces in them may be made to assist in the ventilation of the occupied room below, as follows: The registers in the chimney-breasts at the tops of these rooms are left open. That part of the foul air which does not escape through the damper at the top of the air-chamber containing the distributor enters the room through these registers, and is carried off through the open fireplaces, just as does the fresh air in the room below. At the close of the entertainment these rooms may be thoroughly aired by opening the windows. Such use of the upper rooms is, of course, not to be recommended; but where, for the sake of economy, the exhaust-flue at the top of the house is omitted, recourse may be had to this method. The removal of the foul air being thus provided for, the fresh air is supplied on festal occasions as follows: Open fires on these occasions in the occupied rooms are not often used. Their heat would be too unevenly distributed, and would prove insupportable to those nearest them. Moreover but a comparatively small amount of artificial heat is required. Each guest is an open fireplace to the rest, generating about as much heat as an ordinary candle. Each gas-burner forms another open fire, and radiates its heat in every direction. All that is necessary is to take the chill off of the large volume of fresh air introduced, so that, with ample ventilation, no unpleasant draughts are felt. For this purpose a small furnace, with a very large fresh-air box, is placed in the basement. It stands in this case under the parlor, and the fresh air is taken directly from the open vestibule through large cut brass registers, similar to that already described for the open fireplace. Thin cut brass is used in preference to the ordinary enamelled iron, because it does not show the dust as this does. A volume of air as large as is required, and slightly warmed, is thus distributed over the ground floor occupied by the guests. The doors of the entertainment rooms are usually left open so that, if desired, the supply of fresh air comes from the entire house (excepting those rooms which receive and serve as passages for the foul air and are therefore closed off), instead of from a single register, though the latter should be large enough to do the work for each room alone. Should then the weather be moderate, the windows in the upper stories may be opened wide, or, if it be cold, partially opened, and the general temperature of the house lowered as the heat below increases, or regulated at pleasure. No window in the entertainment-rooms need ever be raised, as is now customary generally at supper-time, much to the annoyance and distress of many of the guests.

What, now, is the motive power, which, when the fireplace is not in use, produces in the exhaust-flues a draught of the required velocity, powerful, reliable, steady, and yet easily controlled?

At one end of the house this motive power is furnished by the furnace smoke-flue when a furnace is used, or by a gas-jet in the air-chamber when it is not; at the other end, by the range smoke-flue, which, if desirable, may be aided by a gas-jet in the fresh-air chamber.

In Figs. 184 and 187 the sheet-iron furnace-flue will be seen at the right of the distributor. The iron is 1 millimeter thick and extends up to the ceiling of the third story. The flue at this point becomes an ordinary 8-inch by 12-inch (20 by 30 cm.) brick flue. The parlor fireplace flue and distributors are also constructed of heavy sheet-iron pipe 1 mm. thick and 25 cm. (10 inches) in diameter, but the iron ascends only to the ceiling of the third story, where, like the furnace-flue, it enters a brick flue (in this case 30 cm. square).

No iron flue should ever run to the top of a chimney, for two reasons; first, because of the condensation of the water of combustion, which requires an absorbent material, like brickwork, to take it up before it falls back into the pipe to rust it and make a disagreeable dripping sound; and, second, because of the unnecessary expense of so doing.

This iron furnace-flue, coming in close contact with the fireplace flue, heats it to such an extent that a powerful ventilating draught is maintained in the latter at all times. The furnace-flue also heats the air in the fresh-air chamber, and produces another powerful ventilating draught through the upper register. The velocity at this point may also be increased almost without limit by a lighted gas-jet placed just under the damper opening from the top of the air-chamber into the space above (Fig. 184, top, gas-jet represented by asterisk). This gas is lighted and extinguished in the writer's house by electrical apparatus, — the safest, most economical, and most convenient method; but where electricity is not used, the gas may be lighted with a match or gas-torch, through the brass register at the top of the room.

These two openings, then, — the register above and the fireplace smoke-flue below, — are capable, combined, of carrying off the foul air of the parlor at the rate of 60 or 70 cubic meters a minute, without inconvenience to a single guest. By enlarging the registers and flues, any desired increase of ventilation might have been provided for at but slightly increased cost. Experiments made in the same air-chamber and under similar conditions on two distributors of the same size, one made of terra-cotta and one of iron, showed the yield of heat per hour to be considerably greater for the iron than for the terra-cotta. Nevertheless, the latter raised the air to as high a temperature as was desirable, and, in consideration of its greater durability, may in some cases be preferred to the latter. But, all things considered, stout sheet-iron is much the best material for our purpose, since our object is generally to extract from the smoke the maximum amount of heat at the least cost and in the smallest space. The cost of manufacture in terra-cotta is greater than in iron when the number required is small, but less when it is large.

The form of the iron distributor is seen in Figs. 188 and 189. The connecting-pipes are all perpendicular. Five of these pipes are 15 cm. (6 inches) in diameter, and stand 10 cm. (4 inches) apart from each other; a sixth is 25 cm. in diameter. But it is best to make all the upright pipes as large as the largest (increasing the dampers in proportion), and the heating surface will be so much greater. It is found most economical to make the upper and lower horizontal pipes rectangular in section and the connecting pipes circular. Round pipes are cheaper than square, but the

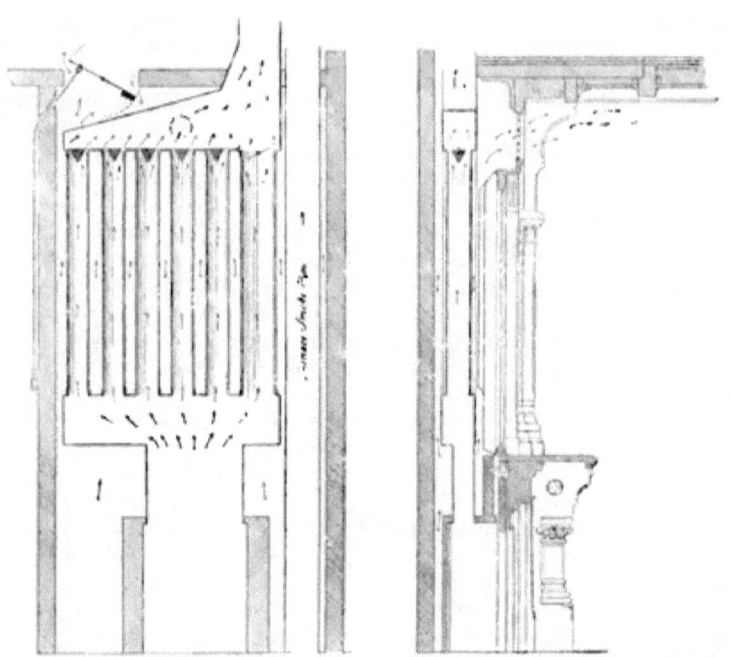

Fig. 188. Vertical Section of Iron "Distributor." Fig. 189. Vertical Section of Iron "Distributor."

upper and lower pipes are made square to simplify the connection and facilitate the riveting. The perpendicular pipes require no clean-out holes when iron is used, because a smart rap on the pipe is sufficient to cause the caked soot to fall to the bottom. The upper horizontal pipe has a round clean-out hole in the centre of the accessible side. The hole is covered with an ordinary tight-fitting sheet-iron cover. The entire distributor should be encased in a metal box like the outer galvanized iron envelope of a portable furnace.

When these distributors are used in a smoke-flue, their size, of course, depends upon the amount of available space behind the chimney-breast. In general, no increase in the size of the breast beyond what is customary is necessary. In the lower stories, where fireplaces are most used, and where the distributor is most desirable, only a single smoke-flue is usually to be found behind the chimney-breast in addition to that of the fireplace in question, namely, the furnace-flue at one end of the house and the range-flue at the other. Nevertheless, on these stories chimney-breasts are usually boxed out to a width of two or more meters to give them an agreeable proportion, and to allow room for the mantelpiece and shelf, so that a space of one or two meters in width is generally utterly wasted. The distributor is built to just occupy this waste space; though, if more room is desired, its width can usually be increased without injury to the appearance of the room. The projection of the breast into the room is not increased over what is customary. In order to permit of ready access to, or of complete removal of, the distributor at any time without injury to the surroundings or to itself, an opening is left in the front or side of the chimney-breast sufficiently large to allow of its removal and replacement in a single piece, together with its metallic envelope; the masonry above being supported by a brick arch, corbel, iron beam (as shown in Fig. 189), or by a heavy piece of flagging which may serve at the same time for the hearth of the fireplace above. The use of the flagging has the advantage of doing away with the need of the trimmer-arch and its header, and of leaving room for the safe passage of the ventilating pipe of the gas-chandeliers, the thickness of the flagging requiring seldom to be as great as the depth of the joists. The joists, usually mortised into the header, may be hung with irons to the outer edge of the flagging, which may be strengthened if desired, where the span is great, by an iron beam. In consideration of this advantage of allowing safe passage for gas-ventilators, and of dispensing with the brick trimmer-arch, and of the saving of tiles, face-brick, or marble, where the smoothed surface of the flagging is allowed to serve as the hearth for the fireplace above, the use of flagging does not necessarily add to the expense of the building, provided the plans are carefully and understandingly drawn before the work is begun. These openings in the masonry of the chimney-breast are then covered by hinged panels, which may be made as ornamental as circumstances and the skill of the architect will allow. When the distributor is not encased in a special metallic box the backs of the panels should, of course, be tinned, with proper air-space behind the tinning to avoid injury from heat radiation. With these precautions this arrangement of the smoke-flue renders it as much safer than the ordinary flue as a double flue is safer than a single one, and justifies lowering the rates of insurance on houses containing them. When the side instead of the front of the chimney-breast contains the door, its decoration becomes, of course, comparatively unimportant, merely a moulding being required to cover the joints of the hinged panel. But openings of the requisite size are rarely practicable at the side, for the reason that the projection of the chimney-breast is insufficient, the flues usually retreating into the main wall.

Instead of the conical dampers shown in Fig. 188, when the draught is good, a simple sheet of iron of nearly the length and width of the horizontal pipe and containing a series of holes cut in it corresponding to the flues below, may be placed over the openings of the upright pipes to regulate the passage of the smoke. The position of the damper over the perpendicular flues regulates the amount of opening in each.

In Fig. 181 the fireplace opening is shown closed with doors of soapstone decorated with incised carving. The writer has not, however, tried these doors, on account of the difficulty of constructing them. They form no necessary part of the apparatus, and are offered merely as suggestions. They are here divided into 3 panels: the lower 2 slide to the right and left, in slots shown in Fig. 182; the upper panel rises like a window-sash, and when open takes the position shown in Fig. 189. It is hung by chains running over pulleys, and balanced by weights, after the principle of the "Lhomond" blower, shown in Figs. 60, 61, 62, 83, and others. The object of this arrangement of doors is twofold. It allows the fire either to be enclosed at night, for safety, by shutting all 3 doors, or it allows it to be increased in activity by opening the lower 2 doors, and using the upper one after the manner of the "Lhomond" blower. These doors are designed to be made of soapstone in order to render them more air-tight than is possible with metal under great changes of temperature. The edges are tongued and grooved to fit nicely into each other when closed. Elastic strips of thin brass might be fastened to the facings to increase the tightness by bearing against the soapstone doors, but it is not probable that the advantage thereby gained would justify the extra outlay, inasmuch as even with them a sufficient degree of tightness could not probably be attained to arrest combustion and keep the cinders alive over night. Were this possible, these dampers would be of the greatest value. As it is, their chief object is security against fire.

In Fig. 190 we have the same device in another form. The panels are in this case made of mica-slate set in a sculptured soapstone frame. The mica-slate becomes blackened by smoke in the course of time, but it may be readily cleaned or replaced by new. The effect of the fire behind them is very pleasing. The drawing is taken from the writer's dining-room, except that the soapstone blowers have not been constructed. Inasmuch as the dining-room fireplace is rarely used, the smoke-flue is left simple. The lower part is, however, made of terra-cotta drain-pipe, which passes through the air-chamber in a straight line to the floor of the room above, and then enters an ordinary brick flue. It thus forms a Galton flue. The free space in the chimney-breast by the side of this flue is occupied by an iron distributor like that shown in Figs. 188 and 189, connected with the smoke-flue of the kitchen-range below. In the chamber above the same flue passes through another similar iron distributor, so that a large enough proportion of the range heat is saved to heat and ventilate both rooms without injury to the draught.

It may be sometimes convenient to draw the fresh air from the room itself, instead of from the outside, when small fires are burned in the fireplace at irregular intervals, and insufficient heat is generated in the distributor to raise the temperature of the outer air to the required degree. But this should only be done when the fireplace draught is supplied from the warm-air flues of a furnace. Where no furnace is in use in the house, the air taken across the distributor should always be drawn from the outside. It will otherwise come into the house unwarmed through chance cracks, and the result will be that exactly that amount of heat which it could otherwise have abstracted from the distributor will be lost. If it could be done without too great expense, a metallic rod, the length of the distributor pipes, might be attached at its upper end to the masonry behind the distributor, and, heated by the latter, open and close the register by its expansion and contraction, as the fire burns or goes out. But this is a refinement the writer has not ventured to test.

The hinged panel in the chimney-breast of Fig. 190 is decorated with an oil painting, and protected on the back by tinning. The entire wooden front of the chimney-breast in this case can be made to take down, by

Fig. 190. Improved Ventilating Fireplace for Dining-Room.

removing the four large screws or bolts at the right and left corners of the mantel-shelf and under the brass warm-air registers at the top. On the right and left are two sideboards, in connection with one of which the lower square pipe of the distributor serves as a plate-warmer. Where two fireplaces built over each other in the same stack are both likely to be used, but seldom at the same time, the same distributor may be connected with both of their smoke-flues in the manner shown in longitudinal section in Fig. 191. When one of the fires is in use, it is only necessary to close the damper in the throat of the other. But both fireplaces may be used at once, because they have separate flues above the distributor. One of the flues may be the range-flue, and the Fig. 191 gives the distributor actually designed for the fireplace and range (though not so constructed). Fig. 192

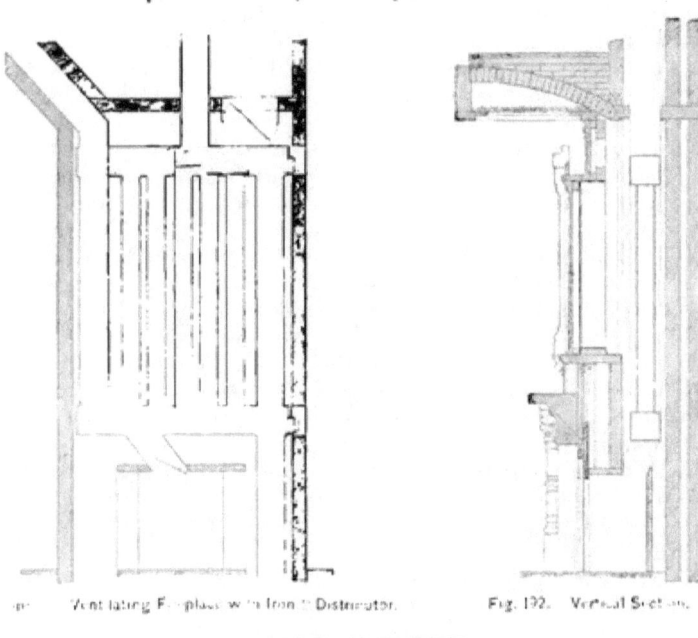

Fig. 191. Ventilating Fireplace with Iron Distributor.   Fig. 192. Vertical Section.

Fig. 193. Horizontal Section of Fireplace

gives the transverse section of the same fireplace and chimney-breast. The soapstone blower is shown in this section. Fig. 194 gives a horizontal section of the distributor and of the hinged and movable panels. The brick wall is vaulted behind the fresh-air space for the preservation of the radiated heat.

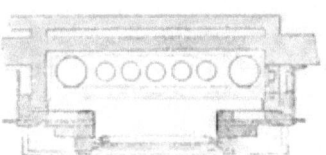

Fig. 194. Horizontal Section of Distributor.

We see by the section (Fig. 189) that the back of the hinged panel is furred out in such a manner as to bring the tin-work close up to the perpendicular pipes of the distributor, just above the lower horizontal pipe. The object of this is to direct the rising current of fresh air against and between these upright pipes. Half of the success of the apparatus depends upon the care taken in setting, so that the fresh air shall be forced to strike every part of the heating surface. But with the metallic envelope this tinning and the necessity for such care in setting are avoided. To prevent loss of heat by the radiation of the pipes upon each other, thin strips of sheet-iron should be placed between them. This greatly increases the heating-surface.

By referring to the historical division of our subject, we shall see that the peculiarities and advantages of many of the ventilating fireplaces and hot-air furnaces described have been brought together in a single apparatus.

The principle of the sloping jambs of Gauger and Rumford (Fig. 36) has been respected in the form of the fireplace itself. The fresh-air supply of Savot and Gauger at the back (Figs. 29, 30, and 34) is represented in the lower register behind the fireplace. The two-way valve (Fig. 58) may be used to regulate the admission of the fresh air from the outside, or from the room itself. The caliducts or meanders of Savot and Gauger (Fig. 37) are reproduced in a simpler form in the "distributor" pipes. The contracted throat of the fireplace, the bevelled back and its rounded upper edge, and the non-conducting, heat-radiating linings of Rumford, are found in the form and material (soapstone and tile) of our fireplace; the "soufflet" of Lhomond (Fig. 60) is given in the soapstone blower. The movable grate of Bronzac (Figs. 62 and 63) is or may be retained. For the inverted smoke-flue of Desarnod (Fig. 65) and Montalembert (Fig. 66), of Douglas Galton (Figs. 67 and 68), of Descroizilles (Fig. 69) of Peclet (Figs. 70, 71, and 72), we have substituted the simple conical damper in the upright flues, and obtained results equally good without danger of smoke or clogging. The advantages of the Taylor fireplace (Fig. 73) are retained in the use of terra-cotta, while its disadvantages are avoided by placing it where it can easily be reached for cleaning or repair. The further improvements of Leras (Fig. 75), Fondet (Figs. 84 and 85), Cordier (Figs. 86 and 87), and others, in the use of a direct smoke-flue with circulating fresh-air currents, have been adopted in the upright pipes and meandering air-passage, and in the manner in which the fresh air is brought in contact with the distributor by the sides of the air-chamber and the tin linings. The principle shown in Figs. 80, 81, 82, and in the fireplaces of Joly and Galton (Figs. 100, 101, and 103), of the increase of heating-surface by the use of iron plates intercepting or conducting radiant heat, has been followed in the use of the iron sheets placed between the upright radiating pipes. The principle of placing the heating-surface above the mantel, and of increasing it by extending the smoke-flue at this point (Fig. 125), is developed and carried to its utmost limits in the form and duplication of the distributor. The principle explained in connection with Fig. 129, by which all the heat of the smoke may be obtained without destroying the draught, is employed to advantage. Finally, the extended heating-surface of a basement furnace is emulated. The simplicity of the MacGregor or Magee drum furnace (Fig. 132), the durability and tightness of the soapstone (Fig. 144) and terra-cotta furnaces (Fig. 145), the increased heating-surface obtained by the use of separate pipes (Figs. 133, 134, 140, 141, and 142), are sought. The distribution of the smoke is accomplished with the minimum of friction and cost, and withal the artistic treatment of the fireplace and mantel is unobstructed.

Any one of the ventilating fireplaces described may be used in connection with it, and, by the combination, the maximum of effect may be reached in the minimum of space.

Figs. 195–199 give this combination with the "Fire on the Hearth" Heater. The form of the distributor as here used is objectionable on account of the reversed draught, although the particular chimney in which this was used had a powerful draught and never smoked. With an ordinary draught, however, it might be troublesome, and is not to be recommended. The lower two elbows are made to slip off for the purpose of cleaning out

Fig. 195. "Distributor" with the "Fire on the Hearth" Heater.

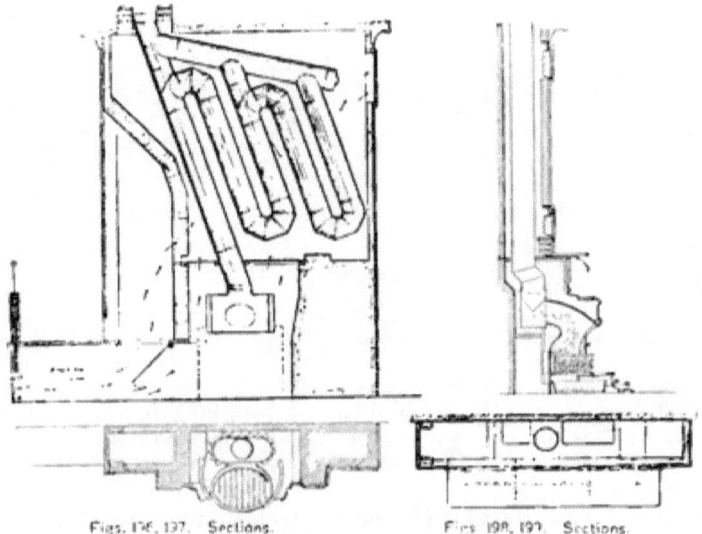

Figs. 196, 197. Sections.   Figs. 198, 199. Sections.

the pipes when necessary, but their removal will probably be attended with difficulty as soon as they become a little rusty. A damper is placed at the top of the first and third upright pipes where shown in the cuts, to direct the smoke through more or less of the pipe.

Fig. 200 gives this kind of distributor in a slightly more compact form, but open to the same, if not greater, objections.

Fig. 203 gives the effect of the combination with the Jackson fireplace in the library of a house on Marlboro' street, built by the writer in 1879. The heat of the fresh air rising from this fireplace was so great as to affect the carving on the frieze of the black-walnut mantel, and to provide against its destruction he was obliged to design the cut brass hood shown in Figs. 201 and 202, to deflect the current of hot air from the woodwork. The plate is extensible.

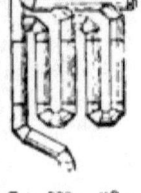

Fig. 200. "Distributor" with Downward Draft.

Figs. 204-207 represent the form of distributor designed for the Adams Nervine Hospital. In this case the openings for cleaning out and for removing the distributor were made in the side instead of the front of the chimney-breast.

Fig. 208 gives a perspective view of the writer's dining-room fireplace, above described, showing the heater behind the hinged panel. Just over

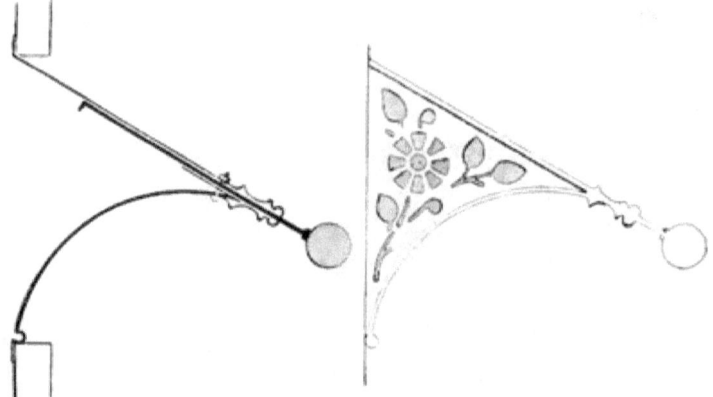

Fig. 201. Hood Section for Deflecting Heat.   Fig. 202. Hood Side View.

the mantel-shelf is the perforated panel for the admission to the air-chamber of the air of the room when the outer fresh-air register is closed. The illuminated frieze over the side-boards is of stained glass, lighted by windows behind.

Fig. 209 represents a hall chimney-piece in the house on Marlboro' street, already referred to, showing another manner of decorating the hinged panels, fresh-air registers, ventilating gas-brackets, and chandeliers.

When terra-cotta is used for the distributor, it may be cast in as many

154   THE OPEN FIREPLACE.

Fig. 203.   Library Ventilating Fireplace.

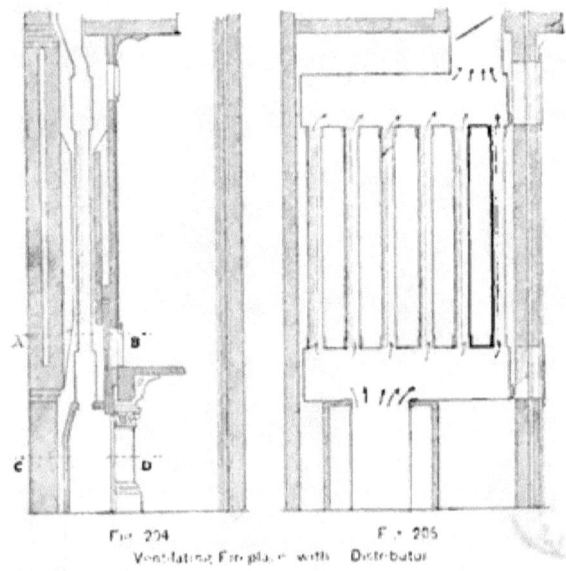

Fig. 204.   Fig. 205.
Ventilating Fireplace with Distributor.

pieces as is convenient for the baking (the pieces being made to couple together like sections of drain-pipe), and are put up with weak lime mortar in such a manner that they may be taken apart at any time, if desired, without breaking the pipe. Cement or plaster of Paris would not allow of this. A good form for the apparatus is shown in Figs. 210 and 211, where the pieces are made like common drain-pipe, except that the arms of the Y and T joints are shorter, in order to bring the transverse pipes sufficiently near together. The pipes should be so large that either one alone would suffice to carry off the smoke were the rest closed. Clean-out holes are made by using a T joint at the centre of each transverse pipe, with the opening turned toward the room. When in use these pipes are closed with earthenware covers, held in place

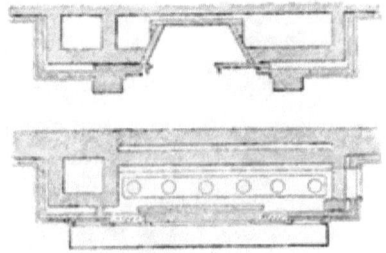

Figs. 206, 207. Horizontal Sections.

Fig. 208. Perspective View of Improved Dining-room Fireplace.

with just enough lime mortar to keep them in and the air out. They may then be easily removed, and the flues cleaned with an ordinary chimney brush or scraper.

As before said, in order to prevent the loss of heat by absorption in the brickwork, and also to direct the fresh air upon the pipes, the distributor should be encased by the manufacturer in a tin box, blackened

156   THE OPEN FIREPLACE.

on the inside with lamp or ivory black, to better guide the fresh air, to prevent the loss of heat by absorption in the masonry, and as an extra

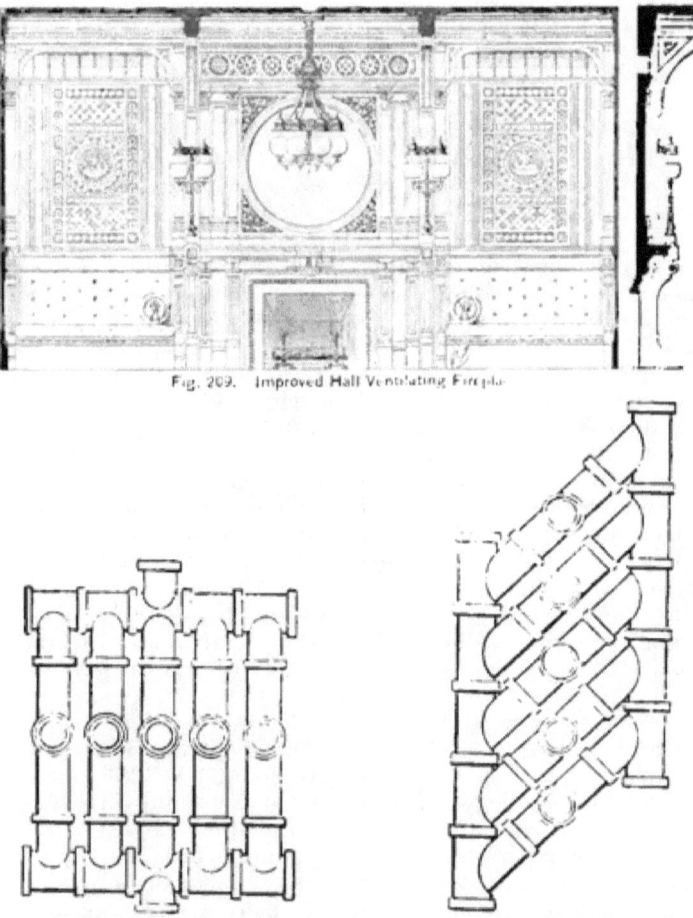

Fig. 209.   Improved Hall Ventilating Fireplace.

Fig. 210.   Drain-pipe "Distributor."

Fig. 211.   Drain-pipe "Distributor."

precaution against fire from old or damaged distributor pipes, and with an opening below for the admission of the cold air, and another above for the emission of the warm; otherwise the most careful supervision will hardly suffice to ensure correct setting by an ordinary mason. The side of this tin box towards the room should be made to open, to allow of inspection of the distributor pipes. If a furnace be used, it need only be a small one, — say a portable furnace of the smallest size, — with a large cold-air box, to heat the hall or temper the fresh-air supply on festal occasions, when open fires are inadmissible. A much more convenient heater in this case would be steam-pipes connecting with a central boiler, under the control of a special company or of the public, like gas and water pipes, because the amount of heat required would be comparatively small, only that actually used would have to be paid for, and a great first cost, and the care of running a basement furnace at irregular intervals would be dispensed with.

A lower register, to admit air to the distributor from the room, instead of from the outside of the house, should always be provided, either below the mantel, as in Fig. 208, or just above the shelf, as in Fig. 208, or through registers at the sides of the chimney-breast, and near the floor, not shown in the drawings. This is necessary, because when but a very small or no fire is burned in the fireplace, or when a basement furnace is used in the house, it may be found convenient to keep the outer fresh-air supply register closed; and the air for circulation about the distributor must then be obtained from the room. The hot air should be conveyed to its destination by tin flues, not brick flues.

Where one has the audacity to diverge so far from the beaten track as to omit the panelled or plastered front of the chimney-breast altogether, the convector may be enjoyed also as a radiator; and in the attempt to treat it decoratively a new field is opened for the pencil of the artist. Its surface may be legitimately ornamented, at the junctions of the pipes, by brass bands and fillets, and the clean-out caps may be treated as bosses and rosettes. In this case, for the material of the radiator terra-cotta would have the advantage of producing a more monumental and durable appearance. By placing strips of sheet-iron between the upright pipes, and bending the strips on the front edges to the right and left, the fresh air may be made to circulate completely around the pipes before it enters the room. These strips, when heated through, become themselves radiators, and greatly add to the heating power of the device. This form of radiator was tried in the room referred to in the first chapter as ineffectually warmed by an ordinary open fireplace. As there described, 3 kilograms of wood burned therein were able to raise its temperature but a single degree Centigrade. After the introduction of the radiator, the room, standing at 40° (F.) at the start, was heated in 60 minutes to 105° (F.), or about a degree for every minute during which the wood was burned. It might have been raised still higher by burning more wood. Contrary to what might be expected, the direct radiation of the elevated pipes upon the heads of the occupants causes no discomfort. Nevertheless, ornamental screens rising above the mantel-shelf may be used to deflect the rays from the heads of those standing nearest the fire, and from the clock or delicate mantel ornaments. Figs. 212 and 213 are intended to suggest methods of decorating the open radiator. In the former, the triangular form of the upper horizontal pipe, by which the smoke of the various upright pipes is collected and directed into the single flue above, is exposed as part of the design. The lower end of the flue above is also shown at

Fig. 212. "Distributor" as Open Radiator

Fig. 213. "Distributor" as Open Radiator.

the top of the triangle. The slip-joint for the removal of the radiator is formed at this point. In the latter design the perforated panel containing the large arch and the central screen must be unscrewed before the radiator can be removed. Fig. 214 gives a section through this fireplace, in

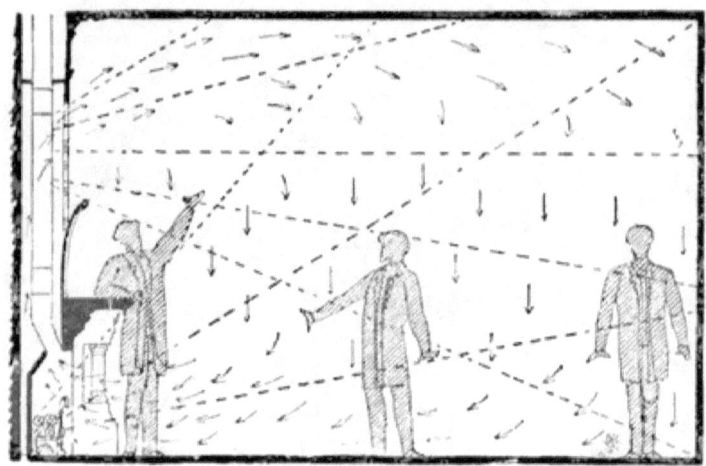

Fig. 214. Diagram showing the Distribution of Heat Rays and Air Currents.

order to show the manner in which the rays of heat from the fire and the radiator above distribute themselves throughout the room. The head of a person standing near the mantel is protected by the screen from the hottest rays of the radiator, which can only be felt at this point by raising the hand above the head. Persons standing at the middle and further end of the room are warmed all over equally by the rays from the fire and radiator both, and experience no greater warmth at the head than at the feet. Moreover, the rays are reflected from the opposite walls back again so as to strike the backs of all three when looking toward the fire.

The arrows show the actual movement of the fresh air coming from the distributor chamber, giving the occupants in every part of the room a continual supply of pure, and only pure, air. The breath from the nostrils follows the general movement, so that no portion of the air is ever twice inhaled. Fig. 215 gives a plan of this radiator, showing the horizontal pipes and the intervening strips of sheet-iron in section. The bent ends of the strips for deflecting the currents of air upon the front surfaces of the pipes are also shown. The clean-out caps in both these designs are ornamented with carving and gold.

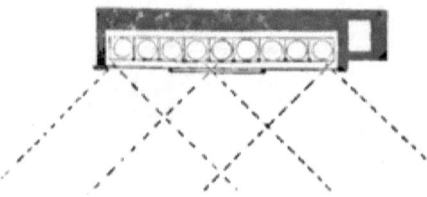

Fig. 215. Diagram Showing Plan of Heat Rays.

Fig. 216. "Distributer" as Open Radiator.

Fig. 217. "Distributer" as Open Radiator.

In 213 they follow the curve of the large arch. The screens in both are circular in form, and rise from the centre of the backboard of the mantel. In 213 it echoes the large arch above, and the outer edge bends slightly forward, as shown in section in 214, to allow more room for the heat rays to pass from the pipes. Solar radiation is represented symbolically in the painting of the frieze above the radiator. In Fig. 216 a screen of a different form, extending across the entire front of the radiator, is given. Here again the genial rays of the sun are conventionally represented extending over the entire upper part of the chimney-breast, the sun himself rising at the centre of the arch. A still greater heating effect is obtained by throwing the radiator entirely out into the room, as in Fig. 217. But the difficulty of the artistic handling is proportionately increased, and the rough sketch is presented merely as a suggestion for development under more careful study or a more skilful hand. The screen here surrounds the entire base of the radiator, and the upright flues unite at the top in a single flue which may enter a second radiator with or without a second fireplace directly above it in the next story. The plan of this radiator is given in Fig. 218, and the movement of the

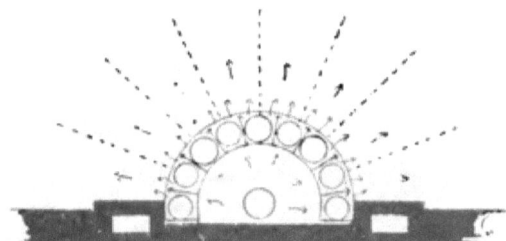

Fig. 217. "Distributor" as Open Radiator. Horizontal Section.

fresh air and of the heat-rays is clearly indicated by arrows and dotted lines. In all but one of the above designs, though the majority of the chimney-breast is taken up by the radiator, a certain amount of space is still left for picture-hanging.

COST.

It remains to determine the practical value of the distributor as far as it is dependent upon its cost; for if the cost of manufacture, instalment, and management does not compare favorably with that of the ordinary furnace and fireplace, the instrument for practical purposes is valueless.

The cost includes, first, that of manufacture and setting, and second, that of management, and involves, of course, the consideration of the exact amount of its heating and ventilating power.

Taking first the enclosed distributor we have as items of expense. —
(1.) The distributor itself.
(2.) The sheet-iron strips between the pipes.
(3.) The tin casing.
(4.) The two dampers, lower and upper.

(5.) The two register plates, lower and upper.
(6.) The flagging to support the chimney-breast above.
(7.) The hot-air flues between the distributor in question and the rooms above.
(8.) The panelled front of the chimney-breast.

The cost varies with the size of the distributor, but the cost of any size may be easily calculated, as follows: —

(1.) The cost of the distributor depends upon its material and the form and extent of its heating surface. The best material is sheet-iron of the weight of 28 oz. per square foot (8 kilograms per square meter), or what is called No. 20 sheet-iron, of about a millimeter in thickness. The upright pipes may be made of common iron, at say 5 cents a pound, or 10 cents a kilogram. The horizontal pipes should be made of the best bloom iron, at say 20 cents[1] a kilogram. The best form for the distributor is given in Fig. 188. Here we have 6 upright round pipes 20 centimeters in diameter each and 2 meters long, between 2 horizontal square pipes 25 centimeters on each side. The pipes are 10 centimeters apart. This makes the horizontal pipes 1.80 meters long. The distributor contains 5 conical dampers 15 centimeters in diameter, and 20 centimeters on the side, made of the same thickness of *common* iron, and hung in place on two stout wires passing through the plane of the base at right angles with each other, and one ordinary disk damper 20 centimeters in diameter, revolving on an axis above the hinged panel, to be operated from the room.

The amount of iron in the 6 upright pipes is, then, 7.6 square meters.

That in the 2 horizontal pipes and their 4 ends is 3.85 square meters.

That in the 5 conical dampers is 0.32 square meters.

That in the remaining dampers is 0.03 square meters.

The weight of the upright pipes is, then, $7.6 \times 8 = 60.8$ kilograms, and the cost would be \$6.08.

The weight of the horizontal pipes is $3.85 \times 8 = 30.8$ kilograms, and the cost $= \$6.16$.

The weight of the dampers is $0.35 \times 8 = 2.80$, and the cost $= \$.28$.

Making a total cost of \$12.52 for the material, or, allowing for lap and waste, say \$13.00.

If the weight of the iron were reduced to one-half the above, the cost of the material would be \$6.50.

The distributor described would be, however, unusually large. One two-thirds the size would be more usual, and the cost would be \$8.66 or \$4.33. Allowing for the labor of manufacturer (the estimate of the furnace-maker by whom the apparatus was made), from \$4.00 to \$10.00, according to the size and number ordered, we have a total cost of from \$17.00 to \$23.00 for the largest and heaviest distributors, and from \$8.33

---

[1] The variations in the iron market render it impossible to make an accurate estimate for all time, but accuracy at any time may be obtained by substituting for the round number here given the real price of iron at the time the estimate is made.

to $11.33 for the smaller ones. Made of terra-cotta the largest size costs from $25.00 to $30.00 each, when made singly. What the reduction would be where several were made cannot yet be ascertained, but terra-cotta is, as said, only to be recommended in exceptional cases.

(2.) The 5 sheet-iron strips, 20 centimeters wide and 2 meters long, would be worth $.80, or, with the labor of cutting the strips, say $1.00.

(3.) The tin casing should have a width of 1.80 meters, a height of 2.70 (10 centimeters clear space above and 10 centimeters below the distributor, for the free circulation of the fresh air), and a depth of 35 centimeters at the bottom and at the top where it surrounds the horizontal pipes, so as to give 5 centimeters free space on each side of these pipes for the circulation of the fresh air. Where it comes against the perpendicular pipes the depth of the casing should be diminished to 22 centimeters, so as to leave but 1 centimeter between the perpendicular pipes and the sides of the casing. This forces the air to pass between the pipes and completely envelop each. Where no tin casing is used these proportions should be given to the masonry, so that it may direct the air in the same manner. It is of the utmost importance that the form and dimensions specified for the envelope of the distributor should be carefully observed, otherwise a large part of the heat will be lost.

The amount of tin in the casing will therefore be about 13 square meters, and the cost we may put now at about $15.00, painted on the inside. Then for a distributor two-thirds as large, the cost of the casing would be about $11.00.

(4.) The two dampers with frames and cords would cost about $6.00.

(5.) The two register plates (ordinary black japanned), the lower one 25 centimeters square and the upper one 1.50 meters long and 30 centimeters wide, would cost $1.20 and $6.00 respectively.

(6.) The flagging, as before stated, need not cost more than the ordinary form of hearth.

(7.) The hot-air flues connecting the hot-air chamber with the 3d and 4th stories will not exceed 12 meters in length, or $18.00 in cost.

(8.) The panelled front of the chimney-breast is more than offset in the saving in masonry, studding, lath and plaster, and papering.

The total cost of the largest radiator and all its appurtenances for heating and ventilating four rooms would, therefore, be $60.50. For the ordinary size (two-thirds as large) the outside cost would be $47.00.

The labor of setting the above when the tin casing is used is no greater than that of building an ordinary flue, including the brick trimmer-arch. No pargeting is needed on the inside of the flue. Two of these distributors, one at each end of the house, are sufficient (with a stove in the basement for heating the hall and for festal occasions) for thoroughly heating and ventilating a four-story city house, 8 meters wide and 20 meters deep, in the manner already described.

In the ordinary city private house but two distributors would generally be required, one over the range and one over a fireplace at the opposite end of the house.[1]

The cost of the two distributors, say one large and one small, being $107.00, add cost of small portable furnace and 10 feet of pipe for the hall (say $80.00) (price list for McGregor Portable Furnace No. 1, and 10 feet of pipe, registers, etc.), and the total cost is $187.00.

To do the same work with an ordinary basement McGregor Furnace would, according to maker's estimate, require a No. 5 Furnace. Cost of No. 5 Portable Furnace per price list is $225.00. If a soapstone furnace were used, the size, according to maker's estimate, required would be No. 36, of which the cost per price list is $350.00. To this must be added the cost of piping and registers. Taking the same number and price of registers required in the case of the distributors, we have for these and the soapstone frames at the very least cost $27.00, allowing a minimum of 3 meters of pipe for hall register; 7 meters for front room, 1st story; 7 meters for rear room, 1st story; 11 meters for front room, 2d story, 11 for rear room; 15 for front room, 3d story, and 15 for rear room; 19 for front room, 4th story, and 19 for rear room, — we have a total of 107 meters of tin pipe. Estimating the value of this pipe at the same rate we did in the case of the distributors, we have $160.00. Add at least $50.00 for labor on furnace, piping and for double piping, collars, etc., and we have a total of $412.00 for the iron furnace work and $537.00 for the soapstone furnace work, against $187.00 for distributors and small furnace.

There will, of course, be other and incidental expenses, such as cold-air box, furnace smoke-pipes, gas-pipe ventilators, etc.; but these will be the same in both cases, or greatly in favor of the distributor, and need not therefore be considered. That the consideration of these would be in favor of the distributor will readily be seen when we recollect that both supply and exhaust openings are included in the arrangements of the distributors, while, with the furnace, only supply-openings are estimated upon. The estimates of cost are in all cases taken from the price lists without consideration of discounts. Where the distributor is exposed, as in Figures 212-217, the cost of decorating the radiator may, for a corresponding degree of ornamental work, be taken as offset by the saving in omitting the hinged panel, so that the above figures may be taken as roughly to cover either kind.

Such being the saving in the first cost, we have now to compare the cost of management in the two cases. The heating surface of the large distributor we found to be 11.60 square meters. Add 1.4 square meter for fireplace back and connecting-pipe, and we have 13 square meters.

The McGregor furnace No. 4 has, according to measurements, 9 square

---

[1] In private houses and in buildings of but a few stories in height, it is, as a general rule, best not to attempt to have two encased distributors over each other, because the movement of the fresh air around the upper one would be slow, on account of the shortness of the hot-air flue leading from it. But upper distributors may be used as *open radiators*. They may be encased in plain or ornamental wire netting of mesh fine enough to obscure the radiator partially or completely.

meters of heating surface. No. 5 has about the same as the large distributor.

The Soapstone furnace No. 18 has about 12 square meters; Sanford's Challenge No. 10, about 9 square meters; the Dunkler No. 8, about 10 square meters; the Peerless No. 16, about 8 square meters; the Chilson No. 8, about 6 square meters, — all according to the writer's measurements. With the same amount of coal burned, therefore, a single distributor is capable of warming an equal amount of fresh air to the same extent with any of the above-mentioned furnaces. But, since in the case of the distributor the fuel used is the same as that which supplies the open fires, while with the ordinary furnace other fuel is burned, and seven-eighths of that used in the open fireplaces is lost, the annual saving in the former case is equal to about half the total cost of the fuel burned in the open fireplaces used in connection with the basement furnace. A Boston coal-dealer, taking at random from his books 20 houses on the Back Bay of Boston supplied by him with fuel, found the average annual amount of furnace, range, and cannel coal (for open fireplaces) consumed in each was 14, 15, and $3\frac{1}{2}$ tons respectively, which, at a cost of $4, $5, and $14 respectively, made $56 for the cost of furnace, $75 for the range, and $49 for the open fireplace. The use of the distributors would, therefore, give us in each of these 20 houses an annual saving of say $25. Where, however, one of the distributors is used with the range-flue, we have an additional saving of say $32, making a total annual saving of $57, or more than enough in 2 years to pay for the entire first cost of both distributors and their necessary accessories.

"The cost of fuel annually required in the United States for mechanical and manufacturing purposes, mainly for the generation of steam, cannot fall short of $60,000,000. Estimating it at $50,000,000, an invention or discovery which would save one-fourth of this amount would increase the national wealth by $12,500,000 per annum. The cost of fuel for culinary purposes, warming dwellings, etc., *is of course much greater.*"[1]

According to Table XI., taken from the Smithsonian Reports, we see that a metal stove with vertical pipes, with circulation of air taken from the outside or inside, is capable of utilizing 93 per cent. of the heat generated by the fuel. The "distributor" is such a stove, and is, therefore, following the authority quoted, able to save nearly all the heat of the fuel. In practice, however, such a result will rarely be obtained, and the greatest percentage reached by the writer with the distributor, during the summer months, has been a little under 80 per cent. In winter, when the air brought in contact with the pipes is much colder, a greater saving can be made; but no opportunity has as yet been presented to make experiments in the winter, the apparatus suited for accurate test having been completed only in the spring of the present year.

The distributor is connected with the masonry of the fireplace by simply embedding its lower connecting pipe in mortar and brickwork for sev-

---

[1] J. Jenkins's Improvements in Heating.

TABLE XI.

CLASSIFICATION OF HEATING-APPARATUS IN REGARD TO HEATING EFFECT.

(See Smithsonian Reports, 1873, p. 308.)

Forms of Apparatus.		Percentage of heating effect.	Remarks.
Ordinary Fireplaces		10–12	Carry off foul air, but do not directly bring in fresh air. Effect of system healthful.
Ventilating Fireplaces		33–35	Carry off foul air, and directly introduce moderately warmed fresh air. Healthful system of heating.
Common stoves without circulation of air.	Cast-iron, Coal burning Coke	90	Produce a very insufficient change of air. Unhealthful system.
		83	
	Porcelain, burning wood, slightly healthful	87	
Metal stoves, with circulation of air taken from the outside or inside.	Model in use in schools in Paris, with vertical pipes, Chaussenot's model	68	Do not produce sufficient change of air, and heat too much the air they introduce. Very injurious system of warming if pipes be of cast-iron; slightly healthful if of sheet-iron.
		93	
Heaters with pipes for circulation of hot air.	Horizontal	63	Cannot directly produce a sufficient removal of foul air, and in general supply overheated air, but may easily be modified so as to give out air at 86° or 104°. System injurious when not combined with means of ventilation.
	Vertical	80	
Apparatus for circulation of hot water.	When the pipes and radiators are very numerous, with large surface compared with that of the heater	65–75	Easily adapted for the establishment of regular direct ventilation.
	When the boiler, furnace, and all the radiators or pipes are contained in the place to be warmed	85–90	

eral courses. The expansion and contraction of the metal must then take place upwards. To allow of this, at the top, where the iron pipe rejoins the brick flue, it should be fitted into a piece of tin pipe half a meter long, with just room enough to slip in it when heated. The tin pipe should be firmly bedded in the brick flue with cement. The iron should enter the tin flue a distance at least equal to its own diameter. When the tin pipe rusts away, the smooth cement in which it was set will have become hard enough to take its place, and serve the same purpose. The tin pipe should be built in by the mason when the chimneys are built. Copper may be substituted for tin where it is thought that the unprotected cement would be likely to be decomposed by the smoke and moisture.

EFFECT ON THE DRAUGHT OF ABSTRACTION OF HEAT FROM THE FLUE.

It may be asked whether the utilization of the heat of the smoke-flue, by means of the distributor, would not injure the draught of the chimney in direct proportion to the amount of heat abstracted from the flue.

The heat abstracted from the distributor is not lost by immediate dissipation in the outer air, as is the case with that taken from the surface of an ordinary flue of brick or iron, especially when exposed, but is at once returned again to the flue through the open fireplace, after warming the rooms of the house. The entire house becomes the chimney, the rooms and outside walls forming, as it were, a kind of outside coating, and the heat is simply transferred from the outside to the inside of the flue, after passing through the rooms, or double coating, in its passage. Were the foul air removed from the house through independent flues, and from the ceilings of the various rooms to be ventilated, as is customary, the case would be different. We have presupposed that the walls of the house are rendered as impervious as may be to heat. This can, of course, be only partially accomplished, by vaulting the walls, doubling the windows, back plastering, etc. Even then a certain amount of heat will be lost through them, but the interior of the house will always be warmer than the exterior, and the draught in the chimney strong in proportion to the excess.

Even without this it is clear that the abstraction of the heat alone could not be sufficient to destroy the draught, because, if it were, no fire in any ordinary chimney could ever be *lighted* without smoking, since the brick flue has at the time of lighting received absolutely no heat from its own fireplace, and experience shows that, with properly constructed flues, the difference between the ordinary temperature of the house and the exterior air is, in winter, sufficient to produce a chimney draught of 50 or 60 meters a minute. Indeed, with good chimneys a difference of one or two degrees is sufficient to produce a good initial draught. The friction against the smooth sides of the distributor slightly diminishes the *rapidity* of the current, but hardly more than that in an ordinary chimney against the rough flues of brickwork.

To illustrate the movement of the warm air currents formed in heat-

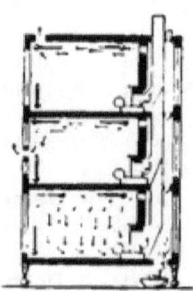

Fig. 219. Model of House to Show Air Currents with Ventilating Chimney

ing and ventilating rooms by direct and indirect radiation, the writer had a model of a house made of glass, wood, and metal. The model was about .75 m. high, and contained 3 rooms, with fireplaces and independent flues, as shown in section, Fig. 219. The glass sides were made double at all openings to exclude the outer air. Small oil lamps served as fires. The smoke-flues were constructed of metal from top to bottom, and passed through a fresh-air chamber just large enough to contain all the flues, and allow of a free circulation of air about them when the fires were lighted. The fresh air entered this chamber at the bottom of the stack, was heated around the flues, and then entered the various rooms through registers in the chimney-breast near the ceilings, as indicated by the arrows. Thermometers placed along the ceilings and floors of the rooms showed a remarkable equality of temperature, in different parts of each, with a gradual increase in ascending from the lowest to the highest room, and in all as long as the fires were burned in any one.

The movement of the currents could be followed with the greatest accuracy by tinging the air with ammonia fumes, generated over nitric acid, or with the smoke of damp gunpowder ignited. When the flues in the top and middle rooms were cold, or stopped with corks, the hot-air currents in these two rooms were interrupted, no ventilation was effected, and their temperature immediately began to fall. Upon uncorking openings at the top and sides of these rooms, the currents again started through them, but the air and heat escaped before it reached the lower parts of the rooms, and at these points the mercury remained nearly stationary, showing clearly the folly of the common mode of exhaust ventilating at or near the ceiling, in winter. In order to make certain that the currents observed in the model were similar to those found in actual buildings, the following experiment was made: cold air, made visible by the smoke of damp straw, was brought against, and heated by, the distributor, and entered the room through the upper register, as usual. The warm air acted precisely as described in the case of the furnace-flue, forming regular strata at the top of the room, which descended as they cooled, and passed out of the fireplace opening upon reaching its level, but no part of it before. The experimenter was able, by lying down, to remain in the room until the smoke strata touched the floor, after which the observations had to be made from the outside, through the glass panels of the door or window. The air colored by the smoke was cooled before entering the distributor chamber, by being conducted under the snow in a flue 10 meters long, in order that its movement should be determined solely by the heat of the distributor. Where the warm-air strata came in contact with the windows, the downward movement at these points was somewhat more rapid, but the effect was produced only on a very small quantity of air immediately in *contact* with the glass, as the column rolled up by it, no heat being given up by the air by *radiation* to the glass, so that the distortion of the layers was hardly perceptible, though the windows were not double. It is sometimes claimed that the warm air should be delivered on the window or cold side of the room, and the foul air withdrawn on the opposite side, on the ground that by this means a temperature more equal in different parts of the room can be produced. If the supply could be near the bottom of the room, under the windows, and if at the same time hot air were a *radiator* of heat, this might be the case. But neither is the fact. The fresh air cannot be introduced at the bottom, because its entrance there would be objectionable in summer, spring, and fall, on account of the draughts it would occasion, annoying and dangerous to those nearest its inlet, when the outer air introduced was cooler than the air of the room. Two supply-registers would be necessary, one below the windows for winter, and one above for summer.

Hot air is *not* a radiator of heat any more than it is a receiver of radiant heat, whereas, on the contrary, the cooling effect of window surfaces, as now constructed, is due rather to radiation than to the admission of cold air. The mere passage of a column of warm air in front of these windows does not materially warm them, nor in the least obstruct the loss of heat by radiation from the occupants of the room to the cold glass.

It is even claimed that there is a positive disadvantage, even in winter, in placing the supply under the windows, on account of the interruption to the regular flow of the air which would be occasioned by the conflict between the rising column of warm air and the cool air falling near the windows. The natural ventilating currents would be disturbed, and the regularity and amount of air change would be correspondingly reduced. Moreover, the cold air, falling from windows not particularly secured against its entrance by rubber mouldings and double sash upon the hot-air registers, sometimes obstructs the lighter column from rising. On the other hand, the two opposing currents would tend in part to neutralize each other, and the cold air entering through window-cracks, however small in amount, might still be annoying were it not tempered by mixture with a portion of the incoming warm air. So tempered, its baleful influence at the floor level would in a measure be prevented.[1]

Nevertheless, this advantage is not sufficient, in well built and tightly

---

[1] The cooling action of the windows and walls is by no means "the sole reliance in all self-acting or automatic heating apparatus." It is not a *reliance* at all, but rather a *hindrance*. The ventilation with such apparatus is determined by the height of the hot-air and exhaust flues, and the warmth or levity of the column of air they contain, as overbalanced by the density of the corresponding cold-air column of the exterior, and is *only slightly* influenced by local currents in any room. The velocity of movement of the warmer column is retarded in proportion as it is cooled by the walls of the various rooms through which it is conducted in its passage. The room of a house must be taken as merely a local enlargement of the warm-air flue, in passing through which enlargement air is cooled, and its velocity retarded in proportion to the thinness, porosity, and conductibility of the walls. To show the truth of this, we will suppose the walls of our room to be artificially cooled below the temperature of the outer air to such a degree that the warm air from the flue coming in contact with them is cooled until the levity of the warm-air column is no greater than that of the exterior. Stagnation would clearly be the result. Artificially *heat*, however, the outer walls, and notwithstanding the friction induced by irregular and conflicting local currents, the velocity of the entire column would be increased in proportion to the amount of heat imparted by the heated walls.

fitted rooms, to compensate for the extra expense and loss of carrying the warm-air flues to the outer walls of the house. This is usually considerable, because the heat generator is as a rule in the middle of the building. If two supply registers were used, one above for summer and one below for winter, the first cost would be still greater, and the difficulty of management, and the consequent liability to neglect, would be an important objection. The arrangement would lose the advantage of automatic action. Were the room warmed by direct radiation, the case would be different. A direct heat-radiator placed under the windows would radiate heat on the one hand to the occupants of the room, and on the other to the windows, and more than compensate for the return radiation to the windows from the occupants.

For the same reason fireplaces, being also direct radiators, when built on the outer walls, especially under windows, have an advantage frequently lost sight of. Where it is thought necessary to provide for a supply of fresh air in spring or autumn, for days when the outside air is too cool to allow of opening the windows, and yet not cold enough to require artificial heating, an exhaust register should be provided at the top as well as at the bottom.

Where open fires are not used, if it were possible to maintain the walls of the room at a temperature higher than that of the fresh air from the furnace flues, a greater degree of healthfulness and comfort might be attained, and the problem of the positions of supply and exhaust registers would be greatly simplified. Both registers would be near the ceiling as well in winter as in summer, and all movement of foul air, from occupants and gas-burners alike, would be simultaneously upwards. The fresh air entering would fall first to the ground, and the movement of the strata would thence be upward instead of downward. Direct radiation would be enjoyed from the surrounding walls. Although less heat would be required to warm the fresh-air supply, it does not necessarily follow that on this account the action of the heater need be the less automatic; for by using smaller hot-air flues, and mixing cold air with the hot near the registers of delivery, the same heat and velocity in them could be maintained if desired, while the exhaust-flues would be warmer. The consequent general velocity of the ventilating current would then be greater in proportion to the amount of heat supplied by an exterior source to maintain the outer walls at the required temperature. For office buildings, apartment-houses, etc., or any buildings of many stories in height where open fireplaces may be used, and rooms over each other are constantly occupied, the principle of the use of simple metal flues side by side, as illustrated by the model, may be employed most advantageously. Fig. 220 gives a section of such a chimney for a library building designed by the writer. The plans show janitor's quarters in the basement, two mezzanine stories thereover by the side of a lecture hall, two more corresponding to the library above, and an attic over all. All these small apartments have open fireplaces, except that in the basement, in which is the range.

The flues of the range, first, second, third, and fourth story fireplaces are shown constructed of sheet-iron, standing free in the fresh-air chamber formed by the walls of the chimney, as in the model. This air-chamber is in each story entirely independent of the others, being separated by horizontal platforms of brick or flagging through which the iron flues pass. These platforms bind the front and rear walls of the chimney together, and prevent the warm air from rising immediately to the top of the chimney. They also serve to prevent the passage of sound from one story to another. Each fresh-air chamber is supplied with fresh air by an independent flue, which draws its air from an air-box of brick in the basement. These supply tubes are shown at the left-hand side of the stack. They do not increase the width of the stack because they diminish in number in each story as the smoke-flues increase, and therefore occupy only waste space, and are actually necessary to serve as withes to strengthen the lower half of the chimney. In short, they take the place of the lower ends of the ordinary brick smoke-flues.

In summer the valve shown at the top of the fourth story is opened, and the fresh-air box at the bottom is closed. The range heat then passes off without heating the walls, and produces a ventilating current through the entire stack. The exhaust then takes place at the top of the rooms through the register used in winter for supply, and the fresh air is furnished through the open fireplaces, or window openings, to take its place; every current being thus reversed, throughout the entire series of rooms, by the turning of a single register in the attic once in the spring.

Where the iron smoke-flues pass through the platforms of masonry shown in the figure, at the level of each floor, short pieces of tin pipe, slightly larger than the flues, are encased in the masonry to make the joint, as shown in Fig. 221. In this manner but little air escapes. What passes up from one air-chamber to another is utilized in the latter, and the loss is confined to that which escapes through the upper junctions. This may be made inappreciable. There is no object in connecting the superimposed air-chambers one with another with valves to allow the whole, or part, of the air warmed against the lower halves of the flues to pass up to the chambers above, when not required below, because the heat which would have been abstracted by the fresh air below is carried up in the smoke, and given out to the fresh air above instead, and the first cost and complication in management of the several dampers is avoided. Moreover, less heat is lost by absorption in the masonry. But the valves are useful in summer to carry off the range heat.

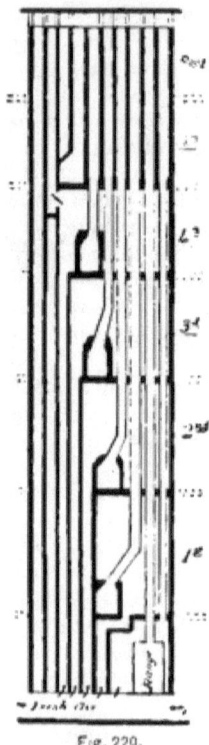

Fig. 220.
Ventilating Chimney.

Fig. 221.
Smoke-flue Joint.

By this arrangement no communication of sound from story to story is possible, as is often the case with furnace flues,—the sound passing from one room down the flue to the furnace, and up again through other flues to other rooms, so that to those standing near the registers sounds from all over the house are repeated.

Where for summer or other use it is found desirable to connect the air-chambers together, a valve, like that shown in Fig. 222, may be used

Fig. 222. Improved Simple Register and Valve Combined.

to best advantage. The three flues at the right are fresh-air supply-flues, and on the left are the fresh-air chambers containing the iron smoke-flues, or distributors, not shown in the drawing. Supposing the lower register to be for the hot-air supply of the dining-room, and the one above for the parlor, upon leaving the dining-room for the parlor the hole in the platform forming the passage between the lower and upper air-chamber may be opened more or less by sliding the valve to the right. The warm air then passes up into the upper air-chamber, and thence into the parlor or into rooms above if desired. This damper is also used to temper the incoming fresh air. With an ordinary register, if the incoming air be too warm or too cold, the only way is to close it in whole or in part. But by this method the ventilation is at the same time in whole or in part cut off. The valve under consideration, however, enables the temperature to be regulated without affecting the ventilation. Should the air from the fresh-air chamber be too warm, the valve is moved part way to the right. Part of the hot air then rises into the chamber above, while exactly the same amount of cool air enters from the cold-air flue, and mixes with the remainder of the hot air, as it enters the room through one and the same register face. The

Fig. 223. View of Register Plate.

register face is shown in Fig. 223. The handle of the sliding damper is shown in the upper part; that of the register proper below. If cold air only is wanted, the damper is moved entirely to the right, and all the hot air passes up above. When the room is left empty, as in the case of a dining-room after the feast, and neither heat nor ventilation is wanted, the valve is pushed entirely to the right, and the register proper is closed. When but little ventilation is wanted, the register is closed partially, more or less, according to the amount. The various iron flues above described may be constructed of short pieces, the upper pieces always fitting inside the next below. Cement is hardly necessary, as the joints will soon cement themselves with iron oxide and soot. Any section may be removed and replaced, through the hinged panels, by hammering and cutting the joints with shears.

The top of the chimney should be protected from the rain by flagging, or by ventilating caps where it is desirable that the wind should be made to improve the draught. These ventilators should not be made of metal, which is rapidly destroyed by dampness, but rather of terra-cotta. The most effective and simplest form is the ordinary Emerson chimney-cap, or the Van Noorden, Fig. 224, which is similar to the Emerson, except that the under side of the cover is formed of an inverted cone, instead of a plane. When the wind strikes the top of these caps an upward current, strong in proportion to the strength and direction of the wind, is induced in the flues with unerring certainty. No chimney-cap yet invented is able to do more than these, or to prevent the chimney from smoking under certain conditions, as when the top is surrounded by air condensed by pressure, while the air below is in its normal condition. This happens when a chimney stands near an object higher than itself. A strong gust of wind may, without touching the chimney itself, strike this object, and by its pressure so condense the air below as to drive it down the mouth of the chimney and in every other direction where no resistance is offered. The simple Emerson or Van Noorden ventilator, especially when constructed of a durable material, unlike the complicated and ungainly patent chimney-tops of uncertain parentage and design, forms a permanent ornament to the edifice. Nor is a chimney-cap able to prevent a chimney from smoking

Fig. 224. Van Noorden Chimney-Cap.

under the conditions illustrated by Fig. 225. The upper room is closed tight, and no provision is made for the supply of air to take the place of that ascending the chimney. The cold-air supply will therefore descend the chimney in waves, as shown, in spite of the "ventilator" at the top, "warranted to cure smoking in every case," and will puff into the room and bring smoke along with it. Nor will any chimney-cap prevent smoking under the conditions illustrated by the lower part of the figure. The lower room is connected with a hall or tower, with ventilator at the top. When the sun beats on this tower, and not on the chimney, or when the tower is in any way made warmer than the chimney, the column of air in the former will be lighter than that in the latter, so that, if there be no independent air-supply for the room

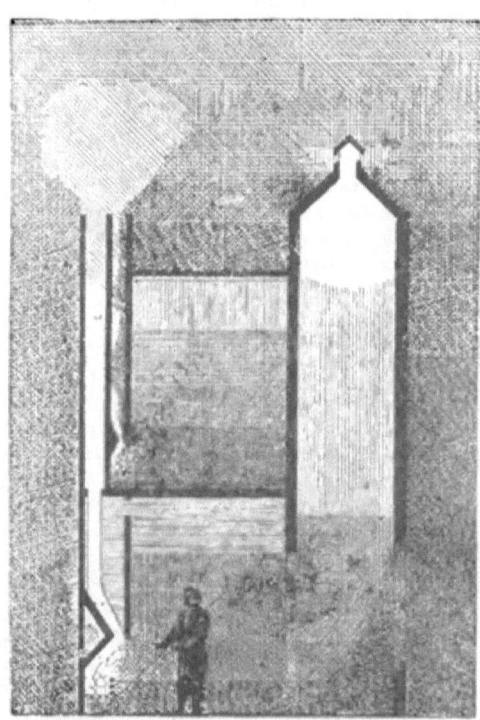

Fig. 225. Diagram Showing Movement of Air Currents with Fireplaces.

or tower, and no wind at the top of the chimney to act as motive power on the cap, the air will descend in the chimney-flue, and cause it to smoke when the fire is first lighted, and as long after as the want of equilibrium continues.

If sufficient cold air be supplied directly from the window, through intentional openings and unintentional cracks, the evil will be cured at once, but at the peril of the occupants, whose legs will be bathed in a frigid zone.

The ventilating fireplace provides against this by warming the air-supplies, as shown in the left-hand side of the lower room, through an opening behind its back. The fresh warm air is here, as usual, represented as entering the room at the ceiling. The movement of the air in strata of various degrees of warmth is represented by various degrees of shading.

RANGE-FLUE.

The following simple arrangement for the improvement of the range-flue, in dwelling-houses, has frequently been tried by the writer with success, — the particular form illustrated by Fig. 226 having been adopted in a wooden cottage built by him at Nahant during the present year. The flue proper is constructed of tile, and around it is built an ordinary brick flue, leaving an air-space between, in such a manner that it may act in summer as a hot and foul air exhaust, both ventilating the room and carrying off the heat of the range-flue, and in winter as a warm-air supply. In the ceiling of the upper bed-chamber a bent pipe containing a damper is constructed as shown, the damper register-faces being in the ceiling close up to the chimney-breast. The flue in this case stands between two bedrooms. The right-hand valve is shown closed, and illustrates the manner in which the flue acts as a fresh-air supply. The left-hand valve is shown open, and the flue acting as an exhaust, removing the troublesome heat of the range from the walls.

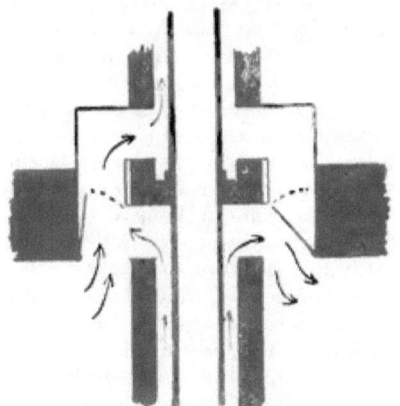

Fig. 226. Range-Flue Ventilating Registers.

FURNACE-FLUE.

In Fig. 129 a model of a furnace is sketched, constructed after the principle of the distributors shown in Fig. 187. The furnace-flue shown in this latter figure was connected with the lower pipe of the lower distributor, and valves were so arranged that the smoke of the furnace could be turned into the distributor, or allowed to ascend direct in the furnace-flue proper, as desired. When the smoke was caused to pass through the distributors, the furnace became at once an example of the one represented in Fig. 129, and described in connection therewith. The heat of the smoke was saved without injury to the draught. By using a furnace regulator in connection with this arrangement the combustion is automatically controlled, and the maximum of safety and economy obtained without the necessity of constant supervision.

DECORATIVE TREATMENT OF THE VENTILATING REGISTERS.

Like the open fireplace, regarded from an economical stand-point, the ventilating register, index of the popular feeling in sanitary matters, remains, from an artistic point of view, in a worse than primitive state of rudeness. Its design is left to the care of the furnace-maker and foundry-man. The artist appears to consider it generally unworthy of his notice in the decorative treatment of the room. It is put in anywhere, in an obscure corner if possible, and painted black, so as to attract no unnecessary attention. The utmost notice that is taken of it, in the usual building specification, is a wholesale summary of sizes for the several rooms. Had Nature, in the design of the human frame, given so little attention to the inlets for the supply of fresh air, throwing them in anywhere at random, and covering every opening with a casting taken from the same mould, of indifferent design and color, we should have lost the features most prominent in giving the wonderful power of ever-varying expression, the distinguishing characteristic of human beauty. If an amount of care were given to each object corresponding to its importance, the ventilating register would no longer stand at the foot of the list. No time spent in elaborating its design would be considered wasted, and solid gold would scarcely appear too costly for its material.

After so much of a peroration, allusion to the following examples should only be made, protected by the knowledge that even failure in an attempt made in the right direction is better than no attempt at all. Figs. 203, 208, and 209, give three methods of treating the registers in cut brass. Fig. 227 shows the effect of three square registers of brass, fire-gilt, over a fireplace in the parlor of the Hotel Cluny, Boston, built by the writer in 1878; and Fig. 228 of three larger registers over the sideboard of the house on Marlboro' street referred to in connection with Figs. 203 and 209. The fresh air is in this case warmed by an iron range-flue behind the breast of the fireplace, of corresponding design, opposite this sideboard. It is conducted across the ceiling in tin flues, shown in section in the beams over the registers to the right and left. By this means the china-closet behind the sideboard may also be warmed by the same flues.

Fig. 227. Parlor Fireplace in the Hotel Cluny, Boston.

IMPROVED SMOKE-CONSUMING FIREPLACE.

Having found that it is no longer necessary to throw away nine-tenths of the heat generated by the consumption of our fuel, we may now reasonably interest ourselves in the one-tenth unconsumed, — namely, that which escapes in the form of smoke. In reviewing the various forms of smoke-consuming fireplaces hitherto invented, the best for modern purposes, all things considered, seems to be that of Touet-Chambor (Figs. 42 and 43). But in this the two upper openings to the flue are not well placed, either for appearance or for use. It would be better to adopt here the ordinary long and narrow chimney-throat at the top of the fire. In other respects the form of the fireplace might remain as it is, except that of course the fresh-air pipes behind, forming no necessary part of the device, may be omitted, or placed above the mantel in the form of a distributor. When the fire is first lighted the upper outlet may be opened, if necessary, by means of a simple damper, arranged to operate easily from the front of the mantel, after the principle of that shown in Fig. 83. But if the draught is good this may always remain closed, and the smoke will then pass out behind and below the coals and be consumed in its passage. Such a form of smoke-consuming fireplace has the great advantage of being simple and practically automatic. The lower outlet is always open ready for use, and with a good draught the upper one need never be opened, or it may be left partially open, enough for the first moments when the heat of the fire and flue is feeble, but not enough to carry off the products of full combustion, which will then find their outlet chiefly through the lower opening.

LARGE FIREPLACES.

When some admirer of the manners and customs of the olden time yearns for the colossal proportions of the mediaeval fireplace to produce in his modern cottage the effect of the baronial hall, he does it with heroic indifference to personal comfort, believing that the use of such a fireplace necessarily implies blackening his timbered ceilings and tapestried walls with smoke, at the least provocation.

But this annoyance is quite unnecessary. With proper construction one may be assured of a good draught at all times, even when but small quantities of fuel are burned in the fireplace. The peculiar construction necessary to secure this result is as follows: We will suppose the fireplace to be 2 meters square. In the first place the chimney-flue should be of the proper size in proportion to the opening, to allow of a free passage of the products of combustion and the accompanying air. The top of the chimney should be surmounted by a Van Noorden ventilator. A portion of the back of the fireplace should be recessed slightly, so as to form a smaller shallow fireplace within the large one. A recess similar in form

178　　　THE OPEN FIREPLACE.

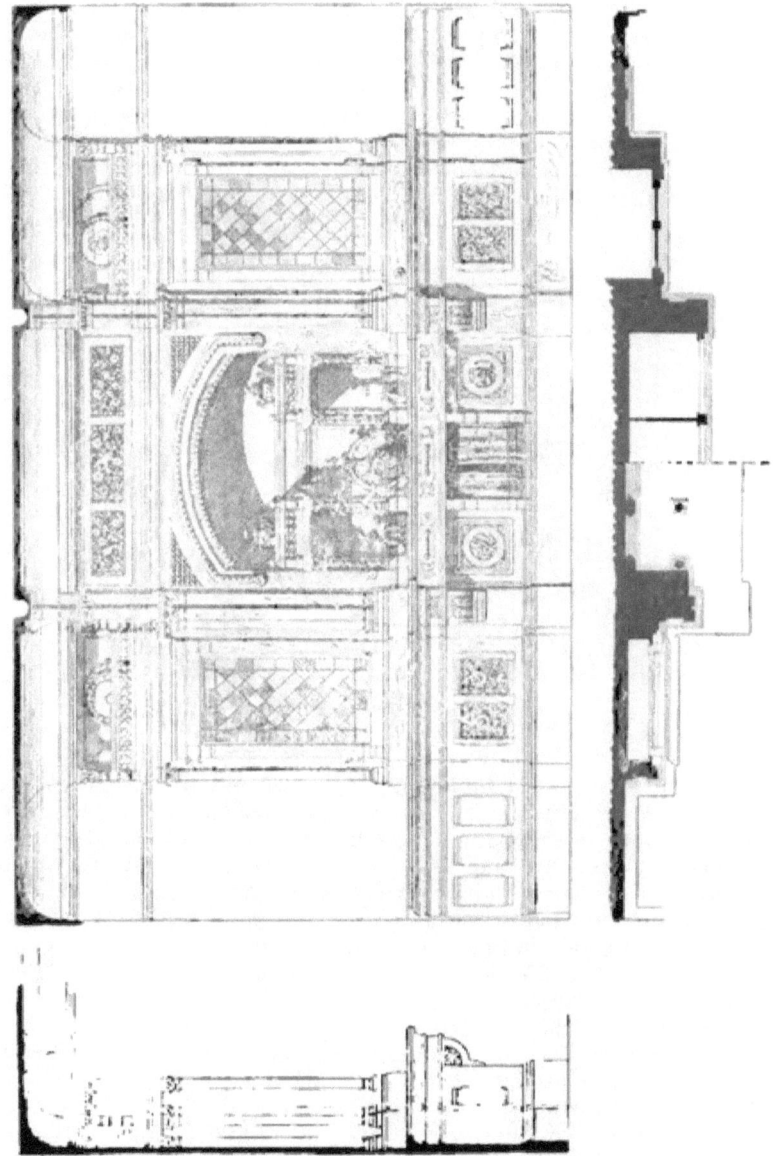

Fig. 229. Dining-Room Ventilating Registers over Sideboard.

to this is sometimes formed in the backs of mediæval fireplaces to receive an ornamental slab carved with heraldic or other devices. The small fireplace then has its own independent chimney-throat and flue connecting with the main flue above the level of the top of the larger fireplace. A damper operated like that shown in Figs. 69, 71, 80, or 83, is built in the throat of the larger fireplace, so that it may be closed when but a small fire is wanted, and the lower chimney-throat (also provided with a damper) only is in use. An improved form of smoke-consuming fireplace is the result. The appearance of the large fireplace so arranged is shown in Fig. 229,

Fig. 229. Large Fireplace for Reading-Room.

designed for the library building before referred to. This recess in the back of the large fireplace may be made an ornamental feature, but when a fire is burning in the large one proportionate to its size, the recess will be covered by the fire and fuel. An arched alcove at the end of the reading-room encloses both fireplaces, and forms a retired and sheltered niche, lighted by windows at the right and left, for the convenience of readers. The small fireplace is .80 meters, the large 1.80 meters, and the alcove 3 meters high to the springing of the arch. The depth of the alcove is 2 meters. The large fireplace is 1 meter, and the small .33 meters deep, decorated with a carved slab of terra-cotta at the back. The entire floor of the alcove is tiled, forming a large hearth for both fireplaces. The alcove is entirely constructed of stone, including the sculptured arch. The fireplaces are of terra-cotta, tile, and mosaic work.

The frontispiece (reprinted on the cover) gives another illustration of this arrangement, with a fire burning in the large fireplace. Ventilating registers are shown above, extending across the entire front of the chimney-breast. Thus, by using a distributor with a large old-fashioned fireplace constructed in this manner, both dangerous draughts and liability to smoke are avoided, while all the advantages enjoyed by our forefathers are retained.

FORMULÆ FOR DISCOVERING THE CAUSE AND EFFECTING THE CURE OF SMOKY CHIMNEYS.

It is customary for the public to imagine that the certain cure of the smoking of chimneys surpasses the capability of the average intellect, that the causes are legion, shrouded in impenetrable mystery. The reason for this belief is that in nine cases out of ten no systematic method is followed to discover the cause, and the cure is often difficult to apply. The simplest and most natural method is to tabulate a list of all the possible causes of smoke arranged in the order of easiest detection, and with this in hand to examine the chimney thoroughly for each defect in succession. In some cases the fault is in open sight, and the cure is simple and close at hand. In others important demolitions will be necessary to discover it, and still more expensive reparations to effect its cure. Therefore, in making our list the defects easiest to see should come first in order, so that no unnecessary expense may be incurred.

(1.) The subject of inquiry which should first occupy us, as being the one most easily answered, concerns the supply of air necessary to furnish the draught. The opening or openings for the supply of air to the room should be as large in area as those for the exhaust, including both fireplace, smoke-flue, and all special exhaust ventilating-flues. If this precaution be not taken the result will be as shown in Fig. 225. One chimney is said to "overpower" another when both are built in the same room, or in rooms adjoining, and insufficient fresh-air supply is provided. When the doors separating these rooms from the hall or other rooms are closed, the hotter flue will overpower the cooler and draw from it its supply of air, bringing the smoke with it. The action of the overpowering chimney is exactly the same with that of the tower in Fig. 225. Even the range-flue, or the flue of some fireplace in the house quite remote, has been known to overpower all the other flues in the house from this cause.

In order to make certain whether or not the want of a sufficient supply of fresh air is the true and only cause of the smoking, it is only necessary to open a door or window in such a manner as to admit the required amount of the air without allowing it to blow on the fire in gusts.

To cure this defect, furnish a supply of air as large as the exhaust. This may be done (*a*) by bringing outer air into the room through some kind of ventilator over the windows, or in the cornice, which may be perforated all round and so arranged as to admit the air in a thin film along all the four sides; (*b*) by carrying a hot-air flue from the furnace to the room, but the flue should not open directly in front of the fire, where hot-air registers are sometimes placed, because a powerful hot-air current from the furnace register, shooting up in front of a feeble fire, acts often as a baffle, preventing the proper supply of air entering the fireplace, and even drawing air *from* the flue, and whisking out the smoke by suction; or (c) by building a ventilating fireplace in place of the old one.

(2.) The position of a door in a room, when standing at certain angles, may, by allowing draughts to strike across the fire, be such as to drive the smoke into the room.

The cure is to hinge the door on the opposite side of its frame, or to provide proper fire-screens.

(3.) The size of the smoke-flue is too small, or too large for that of the fireplace. A flue too small will not allow of free passage of the products of combustion. One too large allows its movement to be too sluggish, and less able to resist any unfavorable influence, and gives opportunity for troublesome eddies. The flue should be somewhat larger than the throat to allow for clogging by soot, friction against its walls, the disadvantageous form of its section (the circular or best section being seldom practicable), and for the bends more or less abrupt in its course. Roughly speaking, a brick flue of the usual form should have a sectional area equal to $\frac{1}{7}$ of the size of the fireplace opening. For a round iron flue $\frac{1}{12}$ would be sufficient. More accurate formulæ could be, and have been given; but such formulæ are usually too complicated, and too difficult of application to be of any service to the general public. According to our rule a small fireplace .80 meters wide and .75 meters high (32 by 30 inches) would require a brick flue of 600 square centimeters in sectional area, which is equivalent to an ordinary 8 by 12 inch flue. A large fireplace of 1 meter square should have a brick flue of 1,000 square centimeters area, equivalent to a little over 144 square inches, or an ordinary 12 by 12 inch flue. A very large fireplace of 2 meters wide by 1 meter high would have a flue, say 10 by 50 centimeters, or 12 by 24 inches, and an old-fashioned fireplace of extraordinary size, say 2 meters high and 2 meters wide, or large enough to contain a dozen tall men standing, or " to roast an ox whole," should have a flue of 100 square centimeters, or 1 foot by 3 feet. Such a fireplace and flue built for use at the present day would have to be constructed in the manner shown in Fig. 224, to ensure a good draught under all circumstances. To ascertain the size of the flue, measure it at the top, or just above the throat.

Generally the only cure for a flue too small is to diminish the size of the fireplace to correspond. To enlarge the flue is usually too serious an undertaking to be attempted.

For a flue too large, — a defect seldom met with, and one little likely to cause inconvenience if the throat be of the proper size, — the simplest treatment is to increase the height of the chimney, and top out with a Van Noorden ventilator; but the best method is to make a virtue of necessity, and, by introducing within the large flue a smaller one of tile or sheet-iron, to construct a ventilating flue on the Douglas Galton principle, as already described, and utilize the heat of the smoke in heating and ventilating the house. Either a tile or an iron flue may be easily lowered into the large flue, cementing the pieces one to the other as they are lowered, and connecting the lowest joint with the fireplace with masonry. To make the lower connection an opening may have to be made in the chimney-breast above the mantel. The ventilating openings and details of the construction have already been described.

(4.) The chimney-throat is too large, allowing an unnecessary amount of cold air from the room to enter the flue along with the products of combustion. By this the column of air becomes cooled, and its movement consequently sluggish. Measure first the size of the throat, and see how far it varies from the rule we have established, then test the effect of diminishing the throat temporarily with dry bricks, or other non-combustible materials.

The cure is to brick up the chimney-throat so as to give it a sectional area equal to one-twelfth of the area of the fireplace opening, and the shape shown in, and described in connection with, Fig. 52.

(5.) The throat is too small to admit freely the products of combustion.

The cure may then be effected by diminishing the size either of the fireplace itself, by relining its back and sides, or of its opening by means of sliding blowers, or new facing. If there are objections to diminishing the fireplace, increase the size of the throat. First measure the throat and fireplace to ascertain as before the amount of diminution of fireplace, or of enlargement of throat necessary, then test the effect of diminishing the size of the fireplace opening with card-board, or of removing bricks, one by one, from the throat.

(6.) The air in an unused chimney may, when the temperature of the outer air becomes, for a time, warmer than that in the house, sink in the chimney until the equilibrium is restored. In so doing the smoke from an adjacent flue may be drawn down with the reversed air-current. The only remedy is to close the fireplace with a damper as long as it remains unused, unless it is found that the flue may be raised in height without injury to the draught of the adjacent flues.

(7.) The length of the smoke-flue may be less or more than is sufficient or desirable. If the flue be too short the difference of weight of the column of smoke and the exterior air column will be insufficient to produce a movement of the requisite velocity or strength.

If the flue be too long compared with the size of the fire, the loss of heat and the friction against its sides may reduce the velocity to too great an extent, though this is a cause rarely met with.

The cure for the former is to lengthen the chimney, and for both to diminish the size of the fireplace and its throat, so as to cause less cool air to enter the flue.

(8.) The flue of one fireplace entering that of another sometimes leads to the cooling of the hot current by the air from the fireplace not in use, to such an extent as to destroy the power of the draught.

The fact of whether or not the flue of one fireplace enters that of another may be ascertained at the chimney-top by means of smoke made successively in each fireplace, and the effect of one flue entering another may be learned by closing each fireplace successively while the other is in use.

The cure is to build another flue; or, if this be impracticable, to close one fireplace by means of a damper in the throat while the other is in use.

(9.) A sudden bend in the flue, especially near the fireplace throat, may cause the smoke to rebound into the room. The presence and position of such a bend may be ascertained by means of a weight tied to a string and dropped down the flue.

The cure is either to diminish the fireplace or straighten the flue by rebuilding.

(10.) Bricks, mortar, vermin, or other obstructions, may have become deposited in the flue. Rats and birds sometimes build obstructions in flues long unused.

Ascertain the position of the obstructions with weight and cord. If a bend in the flue prevents examination in this way, the flue must be opened below the bend, and the weight dropped from this opening.

The obstruction, when discovered, if it cannot be raised with a hook from above, may be removed either by firing the chimney, or by opening it at the point where the obstruction occurs.

(11.) A wind passing horizontally over the top of a chimney may have the effect of closing the flues like a plank placed upon them. A Van Noorden ventilator on each flue will form an effectual cure.

(12.) The flue runs up on the outside of the building, unprotected from the cold throughout its entire height. In this case it will contain a column of air difficult to heat, and the result will be that it will frequently have a motion the reverse of what is desired. The only cure is to lower into the flue a second flue of iron or tile pipe, to form a double flue with dead-air space, or else to use a stove instead of an open fireplace.

(13.) The chimney-top is commanded by higher buildings or hills. The air condensed by a gust of wind falling against these higher objects descends the chimney in expanding or rebounding.

The only cure is to raise the flue beyond the influence of the commanding surfaces.

No bonnets, cowls, or patent ventilators can prevent this except in so far as they increase the height of the flue; because no such device can prevent the expansion of compressed air in every direction in which a free opening is left for its passage.

It is no small source of comfort to the architect to feel that every evil to which chimneys are heirs can be cured without recourse to the patent cowls and ventilators by which the summits of so many of our noblest buildings are disfigured; "some looking like Dutch ovens come up to see the world; some like half-sections of sugar-loaves; some like capital H's, and sundry other pleasing objects." Some looking like a pile of inverted milk-cans, laid out on the roof for an airing; some radiating in every direction long arms, and flourishing them about like demons clutching for prey, or armed with wings gyrating with terrible energy and clamor in squally weather, and when the pivot becomes a little rusty. These "seem perpetually whizzing round for the mere fun of the thing, since any good they do is extremely apt to escape detection."

The Archimedian Screw ventilator is designed to *wind up*, as it were, the air and smoke from below; but it also acts as an impediment in calm weather, and, when rusty, in all weathers. A peculiarly hideous monster frowns upon the writer through his office window from the roof of a neighboring shed. It resembles a huge cuttle-fish, with an awkward, writhing body, and a hundred eyes covering the whole surface of the main trunk and head in the form of large lenses, designed to concentrate the heat of the sun and throw it into the flue. The idea is ingenious, but the effect produced, though striking enough to dismay the beholder without, is inappreciable to the owner within. Though but lately built, and though braced and clamped with plenty of iron stays, it has already a battered and miserable appearance, and seems destined rather to provoke than to appease the wrath of the elements.

"In casting one's eye down the long streets of a smoky city, in taking a survey of the roofs and their tormented chimneys, the infinity of other contrivances is so great that it is scarcely a poetical hyperbole to say our pen starts back from it. Here is patent upon patent, scheme after scheme, each doing its best, no doubt, to obtain the mastery over that simple thing — smoke; and each with a degree of success of a very hopeless amount. There appears to me something intensely ludicrous in these struggles against what seems to be an absurd, but invincible foe, the very element of whose success against us lies in our not strangling him in his birth. Many obstacles are in the way, no doubt; there are obstacles in the way of every good; but I have little doubt that had the perverted ingenuity which has misspent itself upon the chimney-pots been directed to the fireplace, we might have now had a different tale to tell. The smoke nuisance is laughed at as a minor evil, by a great practical people like ourselves, who heroically make up our minds to put up with it; but when it is considered as an item in the comfort, cleanliness, and health of a whole nation, it assumes, or should assume, a different position."[1]

The simple Emerson Ventilator, or the late Van Noorden improvement on the same, when built of durable materials, serves to adorn rather than to disfigure the building. When several flues side by side are topped with these ventilators, care should be taken to have their mouths or smoke-outlets *on the same level*, to avoid injury by one to the draught of another. To relieve the monotony, and produce a picturesque effect, the forms of the caps may then be varied to any extent desirable.

Fig. 230 represents the narrow or entrance front of the Library Building already described in connection with Figs. 220 and 229. The effect of a row of eight of these terra-cotta chimney-tops with turned shafts is seen in the central chimney. The tower chimney is treated as a prominent feature, and richly decorated with sculpture. Fig. 231 (one of several designs for the extension of an old country house shown in the upper corner) gives the effect of a chimney surmounted with terra-cotta tops of the same height, showing the manner in which the monotony may be relieved, and the cen-

---

[1] Tomlinson.

Fig. 230. Ornamental Terra-Cotta Chimney-Tops on Public Building.

tral top made to appear higher and more prominent than the rest, by simply varying the form and height of the caps.

Fig. 231. Ornamental Terra-Cotta Chimney-Tops on Private Houses.

RECAPITULATION.

We saw in our first chapter how great a waste of fuel is incurred in attempting to heat by means of the open fireplace as it is now constructed. Absurd as it may sound, it is easily demonstrated by reasoning from the experiments there described, that to heat the rooms of a public building, like, say, our State House, to the temperature given by the present apparatus, a thousand tons of coal a day burned in open fireplaces, without help of other heaters, would not suffice, because the draught has to be supplied entirely by the air at zero from without. If one single immense fireplace could be used to do the work, it would have to be as large as the United States Senate Chamber, a raging fire kept burning in it at a white heat, while the draught induced, if brought through a single opening a couple of meters square, would sweep everything before it with the fury of a hurricane. A fireplace built on such a grand scale would almost pay for its construction in presenting us with a picture of our extravagance vivid enough to lead us to attempt a saving; while small fireplaces scattered in different buildings, but burning the same amount of fuel at an equal disadvantage, leave us still indifferent.

Returning again, with the improvements in mind which we have here before described, to our "ideal fireplace," to see how far such a saving is possible, and to what extent the ideal may be realized, we find a

REAL FIREPLACE,

giving us the following: —

(1.) All the heat generated by the combustion of the fuel may be utilized in heating and ventilating the house by the use of the distributors, and the combustion of the fuel may be made complete by using the modified form of the fireplace of Tomet-Chambor in combination with the distributors.

(2.) The supply of fresh air introduced into the house, to take the place of the foul air removed, is as pure as the source without from which it is drawn. It is warmed in winter to a temperature somewhat below that of the room; may be moistened enough (with ordinary furnace evaporating-pans attached to the distributor if necessary) to give it its proper hygrometric condition; abundant enough to supply amply the fire, occupants, and gas-burners; so distributed and located at its entrance as to cause no perceptible draught at any point; the gentle air-current so directed that it reaches every part of the room; so steady that no part of it passes twice over the same spot, or can be twice breathed by the occupants; and so regulated by simple valves, like that shown in Figs. 222 and 223, as to be under perfect control.

(3.) The flues include a special gas-ventilator (the left-hand flue in Fig. 220) so arranged that the heat generated by the combustion of the gas is as far as possible retained in the room, and utilized by radiation from the ventilating-pipes attached to the chandeliers (Figs. 149 to 157), while the injurious products of combustion are removed at their source.

(4.) A complete ventilation of the room is effected, both in summer and in winter, without opening doors and windows, by the use of a simple valve.

(5.) The chimney being supplied with fresh air, and properly capped when necessary with a Van Noorden ventilator (Fig. 224), and properly constructed as to height and form as described, never smokes.

(6.) Finally, the construction of the fireplace and flues is simple: they are sufficiently durable, easily repaired in any part likely to require it, inexpensive, safe, and unobjectionable in appearance.

PLATES.

PLATE XXXII.

Fireplace in the dining-room of the second story of the Hotel Cluny, Boston, built by the writer in 1877–78. The room is finished in cherry, and the work is elaborately carved; but this is lost in the reproduction on account of the smallness of the scale.

PLATE XXXII.

PLATE XXXIII.

Plates XXXIII. and XXXIV. are two unexecuted designs. They are for a country house in stone, shown in perspective in the *American Architect* for June 10, 1876.

Plate XXXIII. is for a fireplace of stone and brick combined. The ceilings and sideboards are from Talbert.

PLATE XXXIII.

PLATE XXXIV.

Rustic fireplace in stone between two window niches.

PLATE XXXIV.

PLATE XXXV.

Designs for two simple and inexpensive fireplaces in wood. The upper figure represents the hall mantel of a house in Salem, reconstructed in 1876. The finish of this hall is in chestnut, which was the wood originally used. The panels are ornamented with carving of natural foliage (chestnut-leaves) and birds. The facing is of buff tiles moulded to correspond with the floral decoration. The opening is 1.^{m} 30 square.

The lower figure gives the mantel in the hall of a house in Andover, built in 1877. It is constructed of face-brick and ash wood.

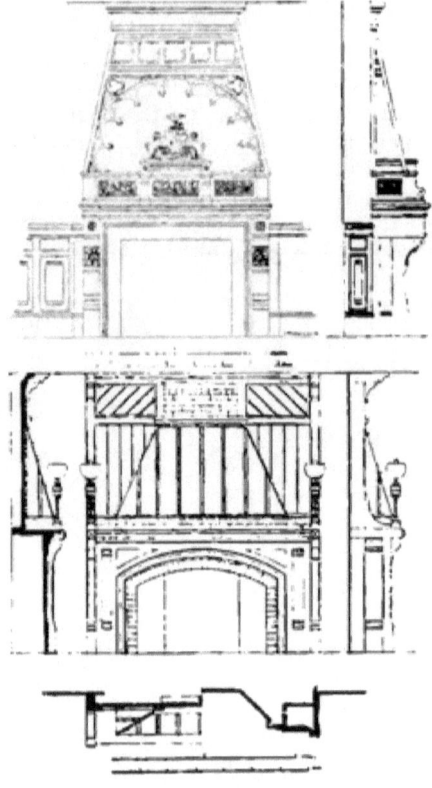

PLATE XXXV.

PLATE XXXVI.

Library mantel in house on Commonwealth Avenue. The large lamp brackets have ventilating caps, the educt flues being shown in the section and in plan. The material of this fireplace and of the rest of the standing-finish in this room is cherry.

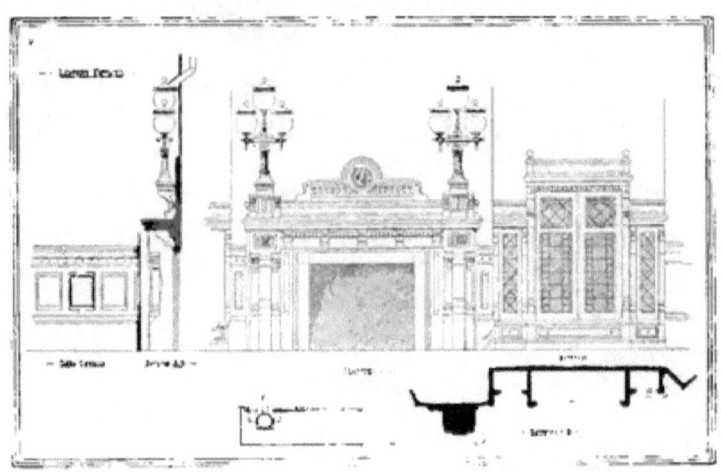

PLATE XXXVI.

PLATE XXXVII.

Simple design for mantel and coat closets opposite main staircase in the hall of a sea-side cottage, built in 1880. The material is ash. Fireplace in face brick, with tile facings and hearth.

PLATE XXXVII.

PLATE XXXVIII.

Fireplace in the parlor of a house on Commonwealth Avenue. *American Architect* for April 29, 1880.

PLATE XXXVIII.

PLATE XXXIX.

Fireplace in the dining-room of the same house. The room is finished in oak throughout.

PLATE XXXIX.

PLATE XL.

Hall fireplace in the house of Mr. Marcus Sayer, Montrose, N. Y. Mr. W. Halsey Wood, architect, Newark, N. J. From *The American Architect and Building News*, May 7th, 1881.

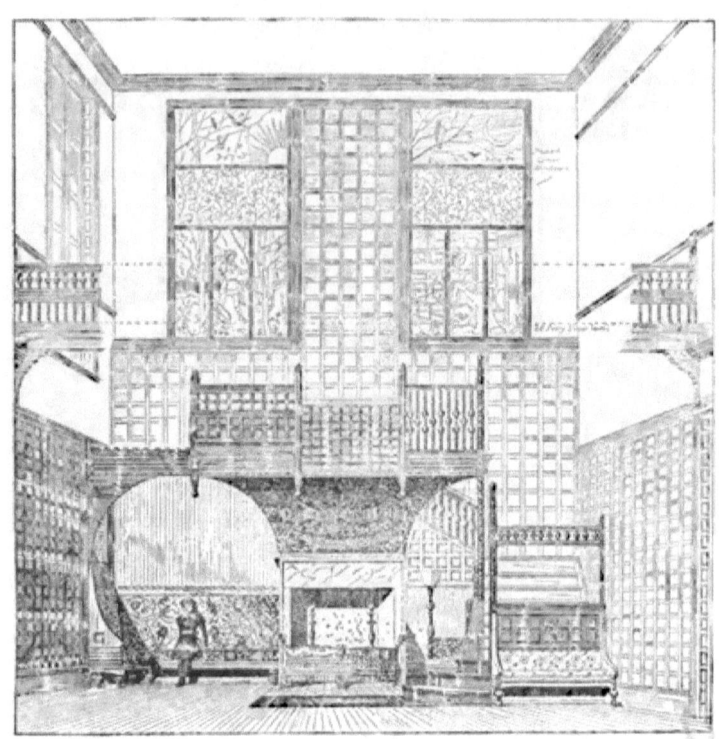

PLATE XL.

PLATE XLI.

Fireplace in the house of Mr. Pierre Lorillard, Newport, R. I. Messrs. Peabody & Stearns, architects, Boston. From the original drawing.

PLATE XLI.

PLATE XLII.

Fireplace in a private residence. Messrs. Potter & Robertson, architects, N. Y. From the original drawing.

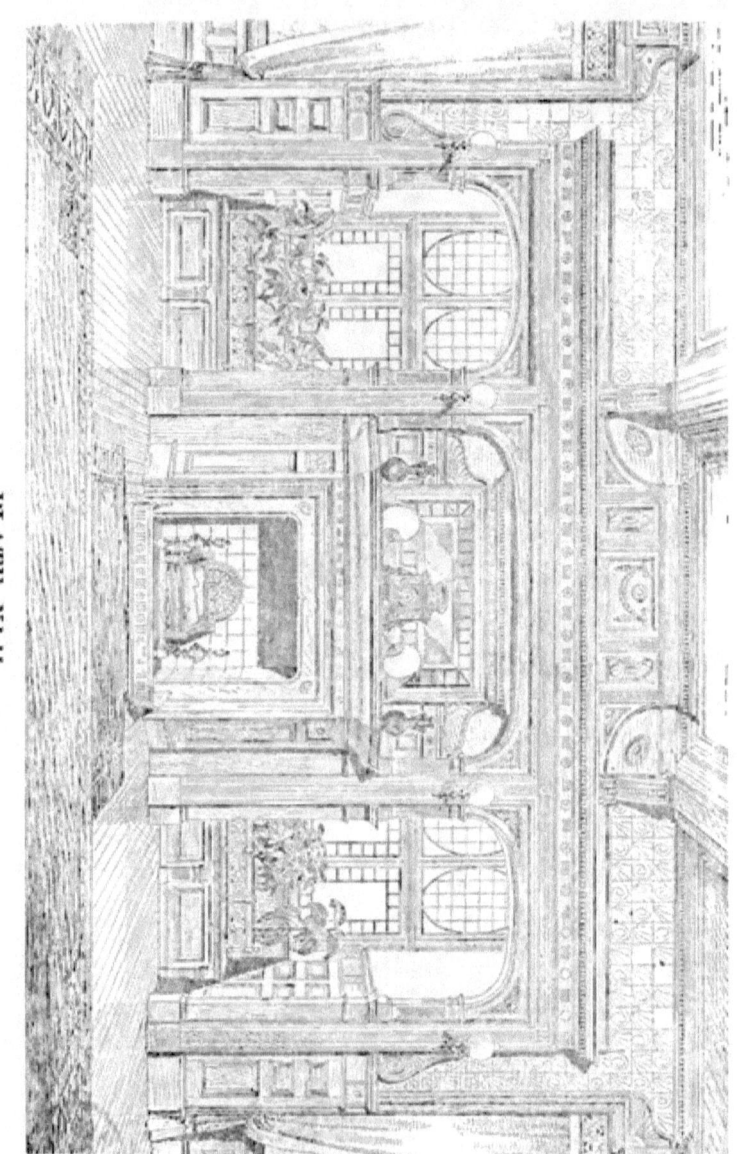

PLATE XLII.

PLATE XLIII.

Dining-room alcove fireplace. Messrs. Rotch & Tilden, architects, Boston. From the original drawing.

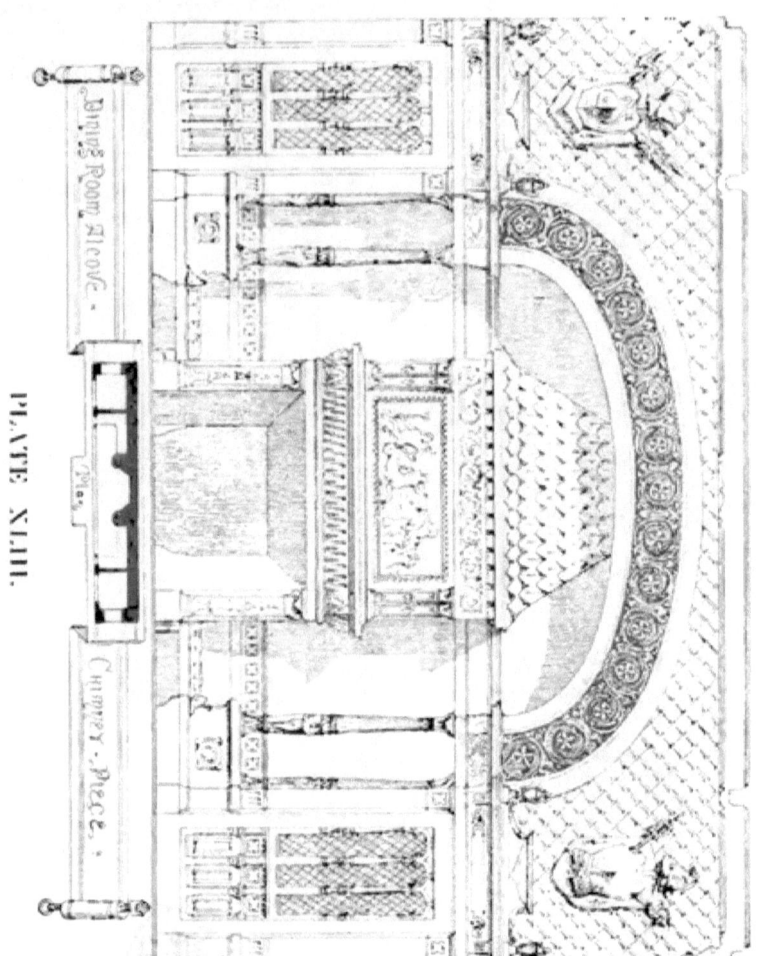

PLATE XLIV.

Fireplace at Lenox, Mass. Messrs. G. R. & R. G. Shaw, architects, Boston. From the original drawing.

PLATE XLIV.

PLATE XLV.

Hall fireplace designed for a residence at Chestnut Hill, near Philadelphia. T. P. Chandler, Jr., architect, Philadelphia. From the original drawing.

PLATE XLV.

PLATE XLVI.

Fireplace in the private "Counting-room" of Messrs. Harper & Brothers, publishers, N. Y., called the "Dutch Room," on account of its architectural character. The fireplace is built of Philadelphia face brick, the ornamental portions being carved. The only stone-work is in the two shelves, which are of Belgian marble. The opening is lined with iron casings, in Flemish patterns, and finished with wrought-iron crane, and brass water-pots, and tea-pots of old Dutch character. The walls of the room are of mahogany and the timbered ceiling of oak. The frieze on the walls illustrates the history of printing and the early history of New York City. Mr. J. Cleveland Cady, architect, N. Y. From the original drawing.

PLATE XLIX.

PLATE XLVII.

Hall fireplace in the house of C. H. Joy, Esq., Boston. Messrs. Sturgis & Brigham, architects, Boston. From the original drawing.

PLATE XLVII.

PLATE XLVIII.

Fireplace in a residence in Boston. W. Whitney Lewis, architect, Boston. From the original drawing.

PLATE XLVIII.

PLATE XLIX.

Hooded mantel in oak, for Henry I. Sheldon, Esq., Chicago. Mr. Joseph T. Clarke, architect.

PLATE XLIX.

PLATE L.

Hall fireplace. Mr. Henry Van Brunt, architect, Boston.

PLATE L.

PLATE LI.

Saloon fireplace in the house of D. Jackson Steward, Goshen, N. Y. Mr. Daniel Atwood, architect, N. Y. From the original drawing.

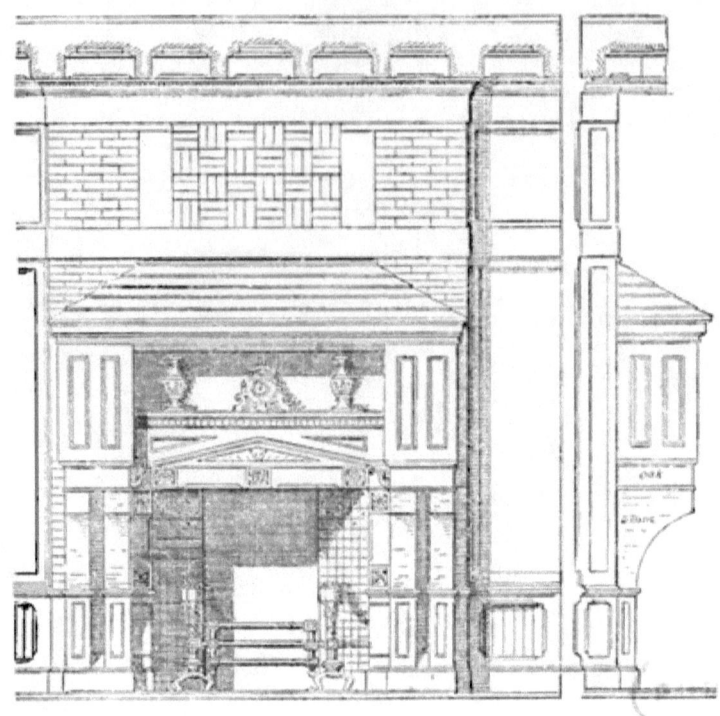

PLATE LI.

PLATE LII.

Fireplace in house of Dr. Greenleaf, Lenox, Mass. Mr. Carl Fehmer, architect, Boston. From the original drawing.

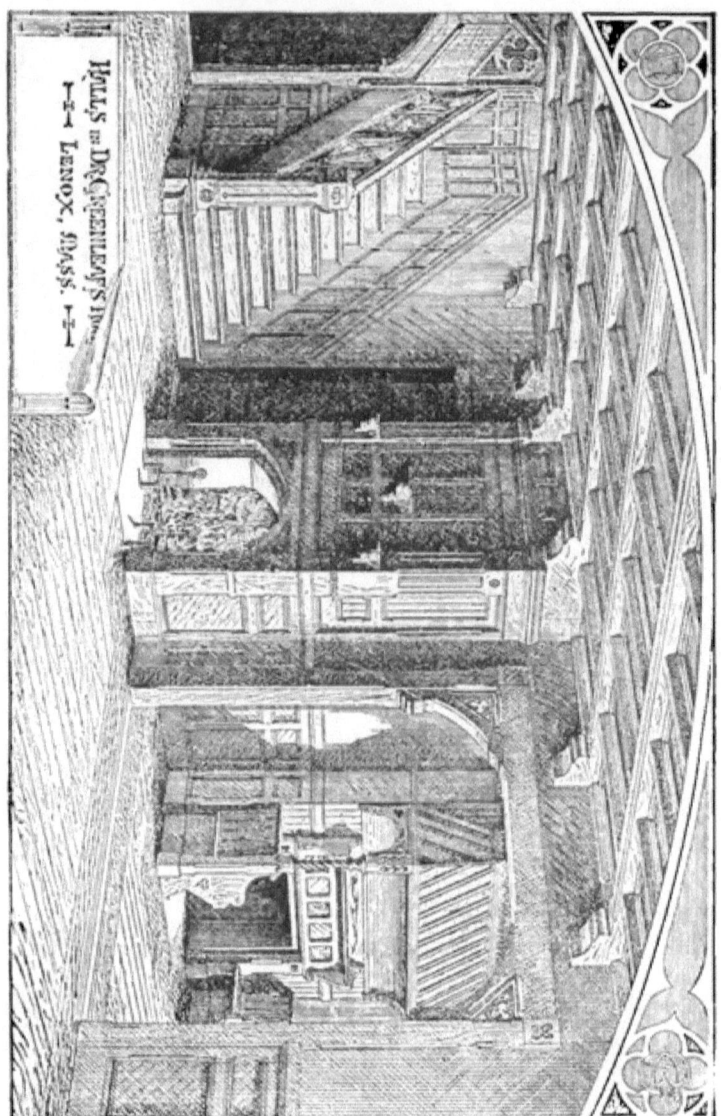

PLATE LII.

PLATE LIII.

Dining-room fireplace.   Mr. Henry Van Brunt, architect, Boston.

PLATE LIII.

PLATE LIV.

Hall fireplace. Messrs. Cabot & Chandler, architects, Boston. From the original drawing.

PLATE LIV.

PLATE LV.

Fireplace in the reading-room of the Equitable Life Insurance building, Boston. Mr. Carl Fehmer, architect, Boston. From the original drawing.

PLATE LV.

Side.

Section.

APPENDIX.

HEATING AND VENTILATION OF PRIVATE HOUSES.

FIGS. 177 to 180 give the first three stories and basement of a four-storied dwelling-house, of which the front elevation is shown in Fig. 183, as previously stated.

In planning the heating and ventilating of a house three rules should be observed as of vital importance: —

(1.) Every room requiring ventilation should have special and independent provision for *both supply and exhaust*.

(2.) Every exhaust-flue should be provided with a certain and constant supply of heat to act as motive power for such time as it is intended that it should be operative.

(3.) This motive heat should be the waste heat used for warming the rooms, cooking, drying, lighting, or performing the regular work of the household independent of the ventilating.

Starting with the *Sub-Basement* or air-space under the floors, the supply is obtained from the basement hall through perforations in the floors. The exhaust is accomplished by means of a pipe 10 centimeters in diameter passing through the basement W. C. and connecting with the exhaust of this closet.

In the *Basement* (Fig. 179), to begin with the kitchen, the *supply* of fresh air should be brought in at the hottest point, *i.e.*, near the range. An opening in the outer wall, over the range, connects with the sheet-iron range hood, which is made double to receive it. The lower piece of iron is painted black to absorb the heat rising from the range. The cold air flows over this, takes up the heat, and enters the kitchen in a thin film or shower from the entire circumference of the hood. The air-supply is regulated by the expansion and contraction of a metallic rod passing through the range, fire, and ovens, constructed on the principle of an ordinary furnace regulator rod, so that as the fire goes out at night the cold-air supply is cut off, and the danger of freezing avoided. The register is opened and shut by means of a simple lever rod, pivoted so that a very minute expansion of the metal suffices. If made at the same time with the range, the cost would be trifling. But after the range is set the device cannot be applied without an outlay greater than is justified by the end; in which case the kitchen supply will have to be obtained in the usual way through door and window-cracks. The lower sheet of the range hood should be lipped up around the edge in the manner shown in the lower rim of the section of the ventilating bell over the chandelier globes shown in Fig. 151. The entrance of the air may then be partially or entirely cut off in very cold weather when the range is in use, by rubber strips or window sand-bags laid over the opening. The kitchen exhaust-pipe starts at the hood, and rises alongside of the kitchen smoke-flue its entire length, as shown in Fig. 187. The pipe should not be less than 30 cm. in diameter, and should be painted black, so as to absorb as much heat from the range-flue as possible. The hood will then collect all the steam, gases, and smells arising from the cooking, and direct them into this exhaust-flue, whose powerful draught will carry them at once to the roof.

As ordinarily constructed, the range hood connects with some so-called brick ventilating flue of insufficient size, built in a cold wall, and is consequently valueless. An ordinary iron hood over a range is liable to become inconveniently hot, and if the head of the cook gets overheated the whole household is likely to suffer. By building it double and allowing the cold air to pass between the surfaces, a part of this heat is taken up in warming the entering air.

A gas-ventilating flue in the south-east corner of the kitchen over the sink gas-burner serves as an extra exhaust when this gas is lighted. This burner is provided with a ventilating bell on the principle of that shown in Fig. 168.

Laundry Supply. — The fresh-air supply is provided by a furnace hot-air flue.

The *exhaust* is a brick flue adjoining the boiler flue, from which it receives its heat. (The drawing incorrectly represents this flue at some distance from the boiler flue, and not in contact with it, as it should be.) The gas-burner over the wash-tubs is ventilated into this exhaust-flue in the same manner with the kitchen gas-burner.

Drying Room. — The *supply* is from the laundry. The *exhaust* is a large brick flue in the side wall heated by the flat-iron heater, smoke-pipe of tile contained within it, and by a gas-jet ventilated like that in Fig. 170.

Furnace Room. — The *supply* is from the cold-air box, which starts in the front vestibule, as shown in Fig. 178, descends in the waste space of the chimney stack, Fig. 179, and passes under the brick steps leading from the basement hall to the furnace room.

The *exhaust* is a 10 cm. tin flue, connecting with the drying-room exhaust.

W. C. The *supply* is from the back hall through perforations in the lower panels of the door.

The exhaust is a tin flue 12 cms. in diameter, which passes along the ceiling of the laundry and connects with the exhaust flue of the first story W. C. The gas-burner with bell is ventilated into this flue.

The *Soil-Pipe* is ventilated by a 4-inch iron pipe passing up through the roof.

The *First Floor* (Fig. 178) is ventilated as follows: —

Dining-Room Supply. — Fresh air is supplied by a furnace hot-air flue and by a register in the chimney-breast, connecting with the fresh-air chamber around the distributor. Figs. 190, 208, 191, 192, 193, and 194.

The *exhaust* is the open fireplace, whose flue is warmed by the range distributor and flue.

Toilet Room. — The *supply* is a hot-air flue from furnace, and also from distributor chamber of the library fireplace.

The *exhaust* is a continuation of the exhaust-pipe of the W. C. below, enlarged to 15 cms. in diameter.

The gas-burner is also ventilated into this pipe.

The *Soil-Pipe Supply*. — The soil-pipe is supplied with air through the manhole over the yard cesspool trap.

The *exhaust* is effected through a 4-inch iron soil-pipe passing through the roof.

The *Study Supply.* — From the distributor chamber over the study ventilating fireplace; also from a hot-air flue of the furnace.

Exhaust. — The open fireplace.

The gas-burner is ventilated as shown in Fig. 168.

The *Parlor* is ventilated in the same way with the dining-room, and as shown in Figs. 181, 182, 187, 188, and 189, the fireplace, whose flue is heated by the range-flue when it is not itself in use, acts as exhaust.

The *Hall.* — The *supply* is the hot-air register from furnace.

The *exhaust* is formed by the exhaust-flues generally throughout the house.

The *Upper Stories* are ventilated throughout, after the same principles, as shown in Figs. 177, 180, and 187.

Double windows should be used throughout for winter houses, especially on corner-lots. With single windows, the waste of heat is very great, and the leakage of cold air interferes materially with the proper working of the heating and ventilating apparatus; one of the windows in each room may be left single, if desired, for convenience.

THE "FIRE ON THE HEARTH" HEATER. NO. 2.

Since the first edition of this work was written, the "Fire on the Hearth" heater has been materially improved. Figs. 232 and 233 represent the apparatus as it is now used.

The heater is enclosed in a metallic shell or air-chamber which insures close contact of the fresh air with all the heating surfaces and leaves nothing to the care of the mason. The design of the front has also been much improved, making the fireplace one of the best manufactured, especially for offices.

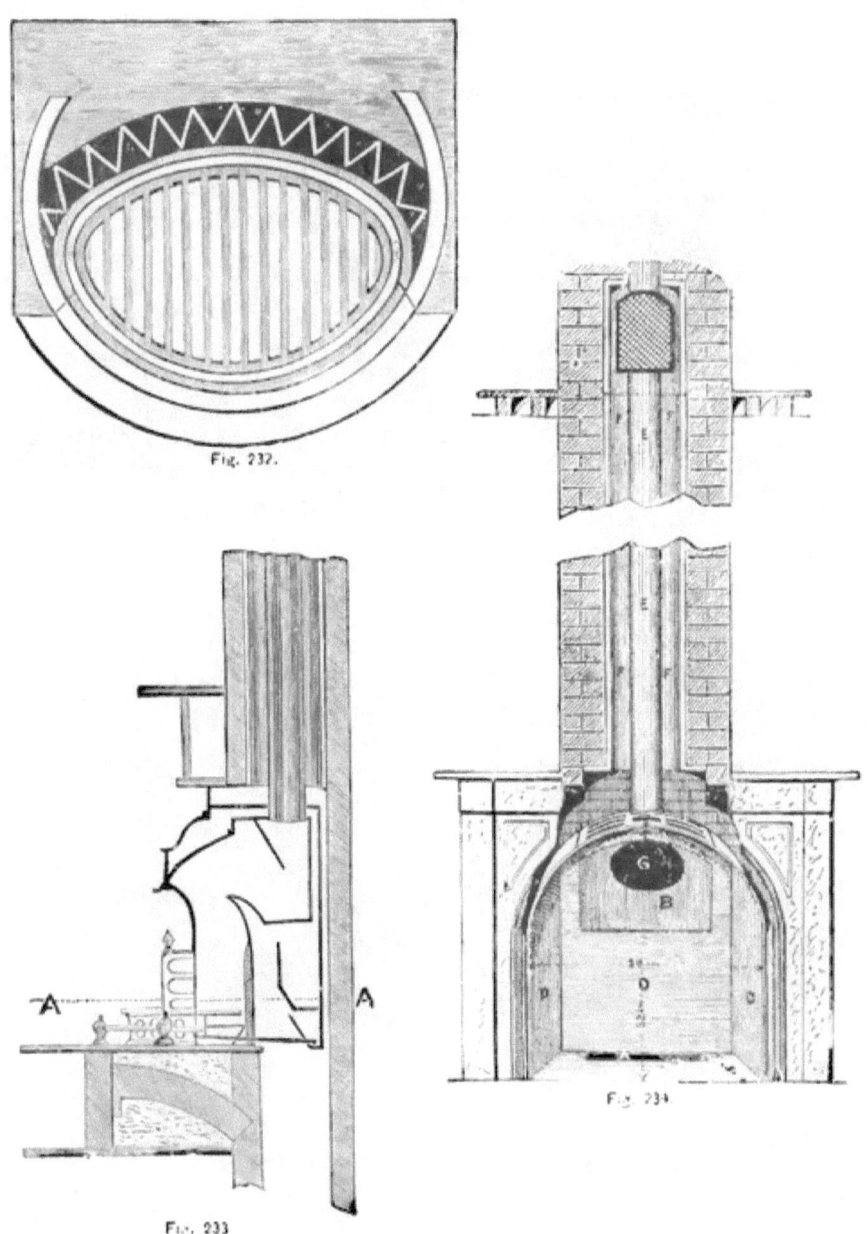

Fig. 232.

Fig. 233.

Fig. 234.

Figs. 235-238. The Jackson Ventilating Fireplace.

Figures Nos. 235–238 represent some of the improved forms of the Jackson Ventilating Fireplace, described on page 78.

Figure No. 235 shows one of the designs of the fronts, which are made in the various styles of finish of the modern fireplace.

Figure No. 236 shows the construction of the heat-saving chambers, — the outer shell being in part broken away. The pure air from out-doors entering the chambers and impinging upon the heated surfaces of the back, — gills and spurs, — in its passage into the room, as before described, performs a double service of utility and healthfulness through the agency of the heat that is lost in the ordinary grate. The air thus heated enters in sufficient volume to replace the whole atmospheric contents of a large room every twenty or twenty-five minutes.

Figure No. 237 shows the method adopted for obtaining an air-supply when the grate is set in an interior wall. When the grate is set in an exterior wall it is better to dispense with the cold air-box in the cellar, shown at the left at base of cut, and carry the fresh air-duct the opposite way through the wall to the outer air.

Figure No. 238 shows the method of adapting the fireplace to a flue for disposing of the ashes in a pit below.

Another form of the Jackson Ventilating Fireplace is made, in which the conserved heat may, at pleasure, be directed, in whole or in part, to a room on the floor above, passing from the upper heat-saving chamber through a pipe inserted in the chimney flue, and entering the room on the floor above through a register. By this arrangement all the advantages of the cheerful, open fire are afforded to the room in which the grate is set, with the addition of a largely increasing heating capacity there; while, with a part of the conserved heat directed above, a room on an upper floor can be comfortably heated with pure, warm air.

Figure 239 represents the front view, and Fig. 240 the rear view, of the "Sanitary" Grate manufactured by William H. Jackson & Co., Union Square, New York. In the latter figure the casing is represented cut away to show the interior construction and air-chambers. This fireplace is similar to the last in general principles of construction, and is artistically designed. In order to test its heating power the writer has made a series of experiments extending from September 20 to October 8, 1883. The tests were made in the evening, between 6 and 12 o'clock, in a large studio at the writer's house, No. 277 Dartmouth street. The usual precautions were taken against direct radiation and other adverse influences.

Table X. represents, in an abbreviated form, one of the tests, which may be accepted as typical of the rest. This table gives only the difference between the temperature of the air before and after passing through the heater. By these tests we found that the combustion of the first three kilograms of fuel would have yielded, before the fire went out, over 1,248 units of heat in each experiment, or $\frac{1248}{10750}$, = nearly 12 per cent. of the total available heat possible with the wood used. This is the best result attained by any of the grates tested during the combus-

Fig. 239. The "Sanitary" Grate. Front View.

Fig. 240. The "Sanitary" Grate. Rear View.

tion of the first three kilograms of fuel; showing the grate to be a very rapid heater.

It is claimed that, by the use of heavy wrought-iron tubes for the carrying of the air across the fireplace, a larger area is gained for the absorption of heat from the products of combustion, and a smoother passage and more rapid flow of the fresh-air current.

In this fireplace an anti-clinker bottom grate is used for convenience in keeping a continuous fire and managing the ashes, and a double blower for better control of the grate and avoidance of dust in shaking up the coals.

The arrangement for conducting the hot air from this grate into rooms above is also excellent, and well designed for abstracting from the heater the maximum amount of heat, and transporting it with the least loss in its passage.

One form of this grate is especially designed to take its supply of fresh air from the room in which it is placed; and where the halls are heated by a furnace this is probably the most convenient method, all things considered, because, when the fire burns low, or is allowed to go out entirely, there is no danger of cooling the house in case of neglect of closing the fresh-air inlet register.

But I am informed that the manufacturers are prepared to provide, with each grate, a flue and register, so arranged that either the outer or inner air may be used, in whole or in part, at pleasure, — a device which would prove very useful, and a great saver of heat, particularly when the rest of the house is heated by furnace.

APPENDIX.

THE METRIC SYSTEM.

MONEY.

10 mills (0.518 centimes) make a cent.
10 cents (5.18 centimes) . make a dime.
10 dimes (0.518 francs) . make a dollar.
10 dollars (5.18 francs) . make an eagle.

LENGTH.

10 milli-meters (.039 inches) . make a centimeter.
10 centi-meters (0.39 inches) . make a decimeter.
10 decimeters (0.328 feet) . make a meter.
10 meters (3.28 feet) . make a dekameter.
10 deka-meters (32.80 feet) . make a hectometer.
10 hecto-meters (328.09 feet) . make a kilometer.
10 kilo-meters (0.621 miles) . make a myriameter.

WEIGHTS.

10 milli-grams (0.015 grains Troy) . make a centigram.
10 centi-grams (0.154 grains Troy) . make a decigram.
10 deci-grams (1.543 grains Troy) . make a gram.
10 grams (15.432 grains Troy) . make a dekagram.
10 deka-grams (0.321 ounces Troy) . make a hectogram.
10 hecto-grams (3.215 ounces Troy). make a kilogram.
10 kilo-grams $\begin{cases} (2.679 \text{ lbs. Troy}) \\ (2.204 \text{ lbs. Avoir.}) \end{cases}$ make a myriagram.

CAPACITY.

10 milli-liters (0.008 gills) make a centiliter.
10 centi-liters (0.084 gills) make a deciliter.
10 deci-liters (0.845 gills) make a liter.
10 liters (1.056 quarts) . make a dekaliter.
10 deka-liter (1.134 pecks) make a hectoliter.

THE SQUARE AND CUBIC MEASURES

are nothing more than the squares and cubes of the measures of length. (Thus a square and a cubic milli-meter are the square and the cube of which one side is a milli-meter in length.) The *are* and *stere* are other names for the square deka-meter and the cubic meter.

TABLE I.

	Experiment No. 1. May 21, 1878. Outside Air from 15.5° C. to 19° C.								Experiment No. 2. May 25, 1878. Outside Air 15° Centigrade.							
Hours P. M.	Temperature at Top of Chimney.	Velocity of Draught by Anemometer in Meters per m.	Cubic Meters of Air passing through Chimney per m.	Diff. bet. External Air and Air at Top of Chimney.	Equivalent in Cubic Meters raised 1° Centigrade.	Temperature of Flue half-way up.	Diff. bet. External Air and Air in Middle of Flue.	Equivalent in Cubic Meters raised 1° Centigrade.	General Remarks.	Temperature at Top of Chimney.	Velocity of Draught by Anemometer in Meters per m.	Cubic Meters of Air passing through Chimney per m.	Diff. bet. External Air and Air at Top of Chimney.	Equivalent in Cubic Meters raised 1° Centigrade.	Temperature of Flue half-way up.	Diff. bet. External Air and Air in Middle of Flue.	Equivalent in Cubic Meters raised 1° Centigrade.
	1	2	3	4	5	6	7	8	9	10	11	12	13	14	15	16	17
1	17	73	3.20	2	6.40	17	2	6.40	A	20	73	3.20	7	22.40	20	7	22.40
1.1	35	88	3.96	19.5	77.22	45	29.5	116.82		25	140	6.20	12	74.40	80	67	415.40
1.2	52	98	4.41	36.5	160.96	61	45.5	200.65	B	52	212	9.54	39	362.02	105	92	877.68
1.3	60	103	4.63	44.5	206.03	80	64.5	298.63		62	197	8.73	49	427.77	100	87	759.51
1.4	66	133	5.98	50.5	303.00	95	79.5	485.41		66	194	8.73	53	462.69	100	87	759.51
1.5	70	194	8.73	54.5	475.78	100	84.5	737.68		73	200	9.06	60	540.00	101	88	792.00
1.6	75	200	9.00	59.5	535.50	106	90.5	814.50		76	203	9.13	63	575.19	102	89	812.57
1.7	80	203	9.13	64.5	588.88	110	94.5	62.78		78	218	9.60	65	624.00	103	90	864.00
1.8	86	212	9.54	70.5	672.57	111	95.5	911.07		80	224	10.00	67	670.00	104	91	910.00
1.9	87	254	11.43	71.5	817.24	115	99.5	1137.28		82	254	11.43	69	788.70	106	93	1061.99
1.10	90	2-5	12.82	74.5	955.09	120	104.5	1339.69		84	186	8.15	71	578.60	110	97	790.55
.11	89	227	10.00	73.5	735.00	115	99.5	995.00		84	194	8.73	71	619.83	105	92	803.16
.12	85	224	10.00	69.5	695.00	95	79.5	795.00	C	83.5	194	8.73	70.5	685.46	100	87	759.51
.13	80	212	9.54	64.5	615.33	80	64.5	615.33	c	80	194	8.73	67	584.91	90	77	672.21
.14	76	200	9.00	60.5	544.50	79	63.5	571.50		78	210	9.65	65	627.25	80	67	656.55
.15	66	194	8.73	50.5	440.86	70	51.5	475.78		68	172	7.74	55	425.70	75	62	479.88
.16	60	194	8.73	41.5	399.48	64	48.5	423.49	d	63	170	7.70	60	462.00	66	53	408.10
.17	56	180	8.10	40.5	328.05	60	44.5	400.45		59	159	7.20	46	331.20	60	47	338.40
.18	54	165	7.39	38.5	284.51	55	3.5	231.90	D	55	148	6.66	42	279.72	55	42	279.72
.19	49	163	7.20	33.5	241.20	52	36.5	262.80		51	142	6.25	38	237.50	53	40	250.00
.20	46	160	7.20	30.5	219.60	50	34.5	248.40		49	141	6.20	36	223.20	50	37	229.40
.21	43	159	7.20	27.5	198.00	45	29.5	212.40	e	46	140	6.20	33	204.60	48	35	217.03
.22	41	159	7.20	25.5	183.60	43	27.5	198.00		44	140	6.20	31	192.20	45	32	198.40
.23	40	140	6.20	24.5	151.90	42	26.5	164.30		42	140	6.20	29	179.80	43	30	186.00
.24	38	121	5.44	22.5	122.40	41	25.5	138.72		40	131	5.95	27	161.46	42	29	173.42
.25	37	121	5.44	21.5	116.96	40	24.5	133.28	E	38.5	129	5.75	25	146.62	40	27	155.25
.16	36	115	5.22	19.5	101.79	39	23.5	122.67		37	127	5.71	24	137.04	39	26	148.46
.27	34	115	5.22	18.5	96.57	38	22.5	117.45		36	126	5.70	23	131.10	38	25	142.50
.28	34	115	5.22	18.5	96.57	36	20.5	107.01		35	125	5.62	22	123.64	37	24	134.88
.29	33	115	5.22	17.5	91.35	35	19.5	101.80		34	124	5.58	21	117.18	36	23	128.34
.31	32.5	115	5.22	17	88.74	34	18.5	96.57		33.5	121	5.44	20	111.82	35	22	119.68
.31	32	115	5.22	16.5	85.13	33	17.5	91.35		33	115	5.22	20	104.40	34	21	109.62
.32	31.5	115	5.22	16	83.52	32	16.5	86.13		32.5	112	5.04	19.5	98.28	33	20	100.80
.33	31	114	5.20	15.5	80.60	31.5	16	83.20		32	110	5.00	19	95.00	32.5	19.5	97.50
.34	30.5	112	5.04	15	75.60	31	15.5	78.12		31.5	108	4.86	18.5	89.91	32	19	92.34
.35	30	112	5.04	14.5	73.08	30	14.5	73.08		31	107	4.80	18	86.40	31.5	18.5	88.00
.40	28	115	5.04	12.5	63.00	28	12.5	63.00		29.5	107	4.90	16.5	79.20	31	18	86.40
.45	26	112	5.01	10.5	52.60	26	10.5	52.98		29	103	4.63	15.5	71.76	29	16	74.58
.50	25	104	4.63	10	46.30	25	9.5	46.00		27.7	94	4.23	14.7	62.18	27	14	59.62
.55	24.5	99	4.45	10	44.50	25	10	44.50		27	90	4.10	14	57.40	26	13	53.30
2.	24	98	4.30	9	38.70	24	9	38.70		26.5	88	4.00	13.5	54.00	26	13	52.00
.5	23	98	4.20	8	33.60	24	9	33.60		26	86	4.00	13	52.00	25	12	48.00
.10	22.5	97	4.10	7.5	30.75	23	8	30.75		25.5	94	4.20	12.5	52.50	24.5	11.5	48.30
.15	22.5	88	4.00	7.3	29.20	23	8	29.20		25	92	4.14	12	49.68	24	11	45.54
.20	22.5	85	3.80	7.1	26.98	22	7	26.98		24.5	76	3.30	11.5	37.95	23.5	10.5	34.63
.25	22	83	3.70	7	25.90	22	7	25.90		24	66	2.97	11	32.67	23	10	29.70
.30	21.9	83	3.70	7.5	32.25	21	7	26.27		23.7	61	2.88	10.7	30.81	22.9	9.9	28.56
.35	21.5	82	3.70	7.5	27.75	21	7	26.27		23.6	69	2.70	10.5	28.35	22.8	9.8	26.41
.40	21.5	82	3.70	7.5	27.75	21	7	25.97		23.2	61	2.70	10.2	27.54	22.7	9.7	26.19
.45	21.5	82	3.70	7.3	27.75	21.5	7	22.90		23	59	2.65	10	26.50	22.6	9.6	25.44
.50	21.1	82	3.70	7.1	26.27	21	6	21.60		22.7	56	2.52	9.7	24.44	22.4	9.4	23.69
.55	21	82	3.60	7	25.20	20	6	21.60		22.5	71	3.28	9.4	31.16	22.2	9.2	30.17
3.	20.7	82	3.60	7.2	25.20	20	6.5	21.70		22.2	73	3.28	9.2	30.17	22.1	9.1	30.00
.10	20.6	82	3.60	7.1	25.20	20	6.5	21.70		22	92	4.14	9	37.26	22	9	37.26
.20	20.5	82	3.60	7	25.20	19.7	6.2	21.65		21.7	73	3.28	8.7	28.53	21	8	26.24
.30	20.4	82	3.60	7	25.20	19.7	6.7	21.60		21.5	66	2.97	8.5	25.24	20.5	7.5	22.27
.40	20.1	82	3.60	7	25.20	19.7	6.7	21.60		20.1	73	3.28	7.1	23.28	20.1	7.1	23.29
.50	20	82	3.60	7	25.20	19.5	6.5	21.60		20.1	73	3.28	7.1	23.28	20.1	7.1	23.23
4.30	19	82	3.60	6	21.60	19	6	21.60		20	73	3.28	7	22.96	20	7.1	23.29
		884.8			12695.91			18522.65				184.5		12883.16			15591.68

In column 9 of the preceding table the italic capitals refer to the first experiment, while the small italic letters refer to the second experiment. A, fire lighted; B, full blaze; C, fire declines; D, fire faint; E, fire out; F, no more heat in cinders a, fire lighted; b, full blaze; c, fire declines; fire d, faint; e, fire out; f, no more heat in cinders.

APPENDIX. 199

TABLE II.

Time.	Average Temperature of Back of Fireplace	Thermometer at 50 cm. from fire.	Thermometer at 1 m. from fire.	General Remarks.
3.32	—	19°	19°	Fire lighted.
3.37	—	45	32	Full blaze.
3.42	—	64	43	Declines.
3.47	—	75	48	
3.52	215°	60	41	Fire out.
3.58	210	45	34	
4.4	190	36	30	
4.10	155	34	27	
4.16	135	30	26	
4.22	115	27	24	
4.28	100	26	22.6	
4.34	90	24	22	
5.34	70	22	20	
6.34	40	20	20	

TABLE III.

Remarks.	Time.	Temperature of Room.	Temperature of Air entering through Left-hand Register.	Temperature of Air entering through Right-hand Register.	Velocity of Current entering through Left-hand Register, in Meters, per Minute.	Velocity of Current entering through Right-hand Register, in Meters, per Minute.	Cubic Meters of Air entering through Left-hand Register, per Minute.	Cubic Meters of Air entering through Right-hand Register, per Minute.	Equivalent in Cubic Meters raised 1° (Left-hand Register).	Equivalent in Cubic Meters raised 1° (Right-hand Register).
	1	2	3	4	5	6	7	8	9	10
Fire lighted; 2 kilograms on.	1.00	11.25°	4°	2°	72	90	.97	1.17	3.88	2.34
	5	12	10	8	99	84	1.34	1.09	13.40	8.72
	10	13	20	9	100	96	1.35	1.25	27.00	11.25
Third kilogram put on.	15	13.50	30	10	94	96	1.27	1.25	38.10	12.50
	20	14.50	31	13	96	96	1.30	1.25	40.30	16.20
	25	15	32	13	100	96	1.35	1.25	43.20	16.20
	30	15.50	32	14	102	96	1.36	1.25	43.50	17.50
	35	15	32	14	96	96	1.30	1.25	41.60	17.50
	40	15	32	14	96	96	1.30	1.25	41.60	17.50
Fourth kilogram put on.	45	15	32	15	96	96	1.30	1.25	41.60	18.70
	50	15	32	14	90	90	1.20	1.17	38.70	16.30
	55	15	31	10	90	90	1.20	1.17	37.50	11.70
Multiply by number of minutes' interval between observations.	2.00	15	30	8	85	90	1.17	1.17	35.10	9.36
							16.41	15.77	445.48	175.77
							5	5	5	5
							82.05	78.85	2,229.90	878.85

TABLE IV.

Time.	Temperature of Fresh Air entering the Room through the Register.	Velocity of the Air in Meters, per Minute.	Volume of Fresh Air in Cubic Meters, per Minute.	Difference between External Air and Air entering the Room through the Register.	Equivalent in Cubic Meters raised 1° Centigrade.[1]	General Remarks.
1	2	3	4	5	6	7
8.50		16				
51						
52	12 C.	18	.072	8	0.6	Fire lighted.
53	14	18	.072	10	0.7	
54	16	18	.072	12	0.9	
55	18	25	.1	14	1.4	
56	20	39	.136	16	2.17	
57	25	40	.13	21	3	
58	29	42	.168	25	4.2	
59	38	45	.180	34	6.1	
9.00	45	51	.204	51	10.4	
1	50	52	.20	46	11	Second kilogram put on.
2	55	53	.20	51	12	
3	60	54	.21	56	13	
4	65	55	.22	61	14	
5	70	57	.228	66	15.0	
6	77	57	.228	73	16.6	
7	83	57	.228	79	18.0	
8	88	58	.23	84	19	Third kilogram put on.
9	90	60	.240	86	20.6	
10	95	63	.254	91	22.9	
11	101	64	.24	97	24	
12	103	66	.264	99	26.1	
13	108	70	.27	104	28	
14	112	72	.288	108	31.1	
15	116	70	.27	112	30	Fire begins to decline.
16	118	68	.26	114	30	
17	120	66	.264	116	30.6	
18	121	63	.252	117	29.5	
19	120	62	.25	116	28	
20	119	61	.24	115	27	
21	118	60	.24	114	27	
22	116	60	.240	112	26.9	
23	116	59	.23	112	26	
24	115	58	.22	111	25	
25	112	57	.228	108	24.6	No more flame.
26	108	56	.22	104	23	
27	107	55	.22	103	22	
28	105	54	.21	101	22	
29	103	54	.216	99	21.4	
30	100	53	.21	96	20	
31	99	52	.20	95	19	

[1] Multiplication by 5 at lower end of the column corresponds to diminished frequency of observations.

APPENDIX. 201

TABLE IV., continued.

1	2	3	4	5	6	7
32	96	**51**	.20	92	**18**	
33	**93**	**50**	.19	**89**	**17**	
34	**91**	**49**	.19	**87**	**17**	
35	89	48	.192	9.27	85	16.3	801.1	Cinders turning
40	80	42	.168	.9	76	12.3	75	black.
45	70	**40**	.15	.8	66	**10**	55	No more sparks
50	**65**	**37**	.14	.7	**61**	**8**	45	visible; cin-
55	57	**34**	.13	.6	53	**7**	40	ders all black.
10.00	**50**	**31**	.12	.6	**46**	**5**	30	
5	**45**	**28**	.11	.5	**41**	**4**	22	
10	40	25	.100	.5	36	3.6	20	
15	**38**	**25**	.10	.5	**34**	**2**	15	
20	35	**25**	.09	.4	**31**	**2**	10	
25	**33**	**24**	.08	.4	**29**	**2**	10	
30	**31**	**23**	.07	.3	**27**	**2**	10	
35	**29**	**23**	.06	.3	**25**	**2**	10	
40	**27**	**20**	.05	.2	**23**	**1**		
45	**25**	**20**	.05	.2	**21**	**1**	7	
50	**23**	**20**	.05	.2	**19**	**1**	6	
							5	
							4	
							3	
							2	
							1	
							0.9	
				16.4			1,180	

NOTE.—Results obtained by calculation are indicated in heavy figures.

TABLE V.

Time. Evening of May 5, 1879.	Temperature of Air entering through Left-Hand Register.	Temperature of Air entering through Right-Hand Register.	Velocity of Current entering through Left-Hand Register, in Meters, per Minute.	Velocity of Current entering through Right-Hand Register, in Meters, per Minute.	Cubic Meters of Air entering through Left-Hand Register per Minute.	Cubic Meters of Air entering through Right-Hand Register per Minute.	Equivalent in Cubic Meters raised 1° (Left-Hand Register.)	Equivalent in Cubic Meters raised 1° (Right-Hand Register.)	Remarks.
1	2	3	4	5	6	7	8	9	10
9.20	12	12	36	76	.54	.98	1.08	1.98	Fire lighted.
.25	17	13	63	76	.95	.98	6.65	2.97	
.30	22	14	76	57	1.15	.74	13.80	2.96	2d kilo. put on.
.35	28	17	90	57	1.35	.74	24.30	5.18	} 3d kilo. put
.40	34	20	69	57	1.04	.74	24.96	7.4	} on.

TABLE V., continued.

1	2	3	4	5	6	7	8	9	10
.45	40	23	66	66	1.00	.86	30.00	11.2	4th kilo. put on.
.50	49	25	54	66	.81	.86	31.59	12.9	
.55	49	27	72	66	1.08	.86	33.54	14.6	5th kilo. put on.
10.	50	30	90	66	1.35	.86	54.00	17.2	
.05	55	30	90	66	1.35	.86	60.75	17.2	6th kilo. put on.
.10	57	30	90	66	1.35	.86	63.45	17.2	} 7th kilo. put
.15	59	30	36	54	.54	.70	26.46	14.0	} on.
.20	60	30	54	54	.81	.70	40.50	14.	8th kilo. put on.
.25	61	31	66	54	1.00	.70	51.00	14.7	
.30	61	31	79	54	1.19	.70	60.70	14.7	
.35	60	30	97	54	1.46	.70	73.00	14.7	
.40	56	29	66	45	1.00	.58	46.00	11.0	
.45	52	27	66	54	1.00	.70	42.00	11.9	
.50	47	26	66	66	1.00	.86	37.00	10.2	
.55	45	24	66	48	1.00	.62	35.00	8.7	
11.	40	20	66	48	1.00	.62	30.00	6.2	
.05	39	19	66	54	1.00	.70	29.00	6.3	
.10	38	18	66	57	1.00	.74	28.00	5.9	
.15	36	18	63	54	.95	.70	24.70	5.6	
.20	35	17	57	54	.86	.70	21.50	4.9	
.25	33	17	54	54	.81	.70	18.63	4.9	
.30	32	17	51	54	.76	.70	16.72	4.9	
.35	30	16	48	54	.72	.70	15.84	4.2	
.40	29	16	45	54	.67	.70	13.40	4.2	
.45	28	16	39	54	.58	.7	10.44	4.2	
.50	27	16	31	54	.47	.7	8.00	4.2	
.55	26	16	31	54	.47	.7	7.52	4.2	
12.	25	16	31	54	.47	.7	7.05	4.2	
.05	24	16	31	54	.47	.7	6.58	4.2	
.10	23	15	31	54	.47	.7	6.11	3.5	
.15	22	15	31	54	.47	.7	5.64	3.5	
.20	21	15	31	54	.47	.7	5.17	3.5	
.25	20	15	31	54	.47	.7	4.70	3.5	
.30	19	14	31	54	.47	.7	4.23	2.8	
.35	18	14	31	54	.47	.7	3.76	2.8	
.40	17	14	31	54	.47	.7	3.29	2.8	
.45	16	14	31	54	.47	.7	2.82	2.8	
.50	15	14	31	54	.47	.7	2.35	2.8	
.55	14	13	31	54	.47	.7	1.88	2.1	
1.	13	13	31	54	.47	.7	1.41	2.1	
							1034.52	325.0	
							5	5	
							5172.60	1625.0	
								5172.6	
							Total ..	6797.6	

TABLE VI.

Time; Evening of May 22, 1879.	Temperature of the Fresh Air entering Room through Register.	Velocity of Air in Meters per Minute.	Volume of Fresh Air in Cubic Meters per Minute.	Difference between external Air and Air entering Room through Register.	Equivalent in Cubic Meters raised 1°.	Remarks.
1	2	3	4	5	6	7
9.05	16°	18	.072	3°		Fire lighted.
.10	20	25	.10	7	2.12	
.15	30	30	.12	17	6.5	Second kilogram put on.
.20	64	38	.15	51	25.3	
.25	78	45	.18	65	51.4	Third kilogram put on.
.30	107	54	.22	94	82.1	
.35	116	54	.22	103	109.3	Fourth kilogram put on.
.40	128	54	.22	115	119.4	
.45	137	55	.22	124	134.2	Fifth kilogram put on.
.50	145	55	.22	132	142.0	
.55	148	55	.22	137	147.7	Sixth kilogram put on.
10.	156	55	.22	143	154.9	
.05	156	54	.22	143	157.2	Seventh kilogram put on.
.10	164	55	.22	151	163.0	Eighth kilogram put on.
.15	166	55	.22	153	166.0	
.20	168	55	.22	155	169.5	
.25	163	55	.22	150	169.5	
.30	158	57	.22	145	165.0	
.35	140	48	.19	127	159.5	
.40	108	36	.14	95	120.5	
.45	98	35	.14	85	66.5	
.50	93	35	.14	80	59.5	
.55	92	35	.14	79	56.0	
11.	85	30	.12	72	55.5	
.05	70	30	.12	57	43.0	
.10	60	30	.12	47	34.0	
.15	58	21	.12	45	28.0	
.20	50	21	.08	37	14.5	
.25	40	20	.08	27	10.5	
.30	35	20	.08	22	8.5	
.35	30	20	.08	17	6.5	
.40	25	20	.08	12	4.5	
.45	20	20	.08	7	3.0	
.50	18	20	.08	5	2.0	
.55	18	20	.08	5	2.0	
12.	18	20	.08	5	2.0	
.05	16	20	.08	3	1.0	
.10	16	20	.08	3	1.0	
.15	16	20	.08	3	1.0	
.20	16	20	.08	2	.5	
					2645.	

TABLE VII.

Time: Evening of July 30, 1879.	Temperature of the Fresh Air Current.	Velocity of the Air in Meters per Minute.	Cubic Meters of Air entering the Room per Minute.	Difference of Temperature between Outer Air, and Air entering the Room.	Equivalent in Cubic Meters raised 1°.	Weight in Kilograms.	Remarks.
1	2	3	4	5	6	7	8
6.30	25	0	0	0	0		
.40	26	21	.4	1	4	4.8	Fire lighted.
.45	34	45	.8	9	11.3	13.6	Full blaze.
.50	46	63	1.1	21	99.5	109	2d kilo. put on.
.55	62	63	1.1	37	180.4	198	
7.	85	75	1.1	60	259.6	260	3d kilo. put on.
.5	90	117	2.1	65	501.9	500	
.10	95	138	2.5	70	757.6	757	
.15	97	138	2.5	72	836.8	840	Fire declines.
.20	94	130	2.2	69	783.3	783	Fire out.
.25	86	123	2.0	61	670	730	
.30	80	120	2.0	55	602	660	
.35	75	110	1.7	50	425		
.40	71	96	1.7	46	391		
.45	65	94	1.7	40	357	1972	
.50	60	93	1.7	35	323		
.55	56	93	1.7	31	297		
8.	54	92	1.7	29	272		
.5	52	91	1.7	27	240		
.10	50	90	1.6	25	200	1184	
.15	49	87	1.6	24	190		
.20	47	85	1.6	22	175		
.25	45	80	1.6	20	160		
.30	44	77	1.6	19	140		
.35	42	75	1.5	17	120	693	
.40	40	72	1.5	15	110		
.45	39	70	1.4	14	100		
.50	38	68	1.3	13	85		
.55	37	66	1.2	12	70		
9.	37	64	1.2	12	65	396	
.5	36	63	1.2	11	60		
.10	36	62	1.2	11	55		
.15	35	61	1.1	10	48		
.20	35	61	1.1	10	45		
.25	34	60	1.1	9	40	256	
.30	34	60	1.1	9	40		
.35	33	59	1.1	8	38		
.40	33	59	1.0	8	35		
.45	32	58	1.0	7	30		
.50	32	58	1.0	7	28	174	
.55	31	57	0.9	6	25		
10.	30	56	0.8	5	23		
.10	29	55	0.8	4	18		
.20	29	54	0.7	4	13		
.30	27	53	0.7	3	10		
.40	28	52	0.6	3	8		
.50	27	51	0.6	2	6	144	
11.	26	50	0.6	1	4		
.10	26	49	0.5	1	2		
.20	26	48	0.5	1	0		
						9671	

TABLE VIII.

Temperature of the outer air, 22° Centigrade; of the room, 22° Centigrade; size of fresh-air opening, .05 square meter.

DOOR CLOSED.

Time; September 2, 1878, A.M.	Temperature of the Fresh-air Current.	Velocity of the Air in Meters per Minute.	Cubic Meters of Air entering the Room per Minute.	Difference of Temperature between Outer Air and Air entering Room.	Equivalent in Cubic Meters raised 1° Centigrade.	Weight in Kilograms.	Temperature of Room.	Thermometer in the Direct Radiation of Fireplace at one Meter distant.	Remarks.
1	2	3	4	5	6	7	8	9	10
8.10	22	0	0	0°	0	0	22½	22°	Fire lighted.
.20	19	63	3	27	294.3	294.3	22		2d kilogram.
.30	73	54	3	51	1028.8	1028.8	24	80	3d kilogram.
.40	83	78	4	61	1893	1704	26	81	
.50	68	36	2	46	1178	1178	26¼	80	
9.	54	30	1.5	32	723	723	26	77	
.10	48	27	1.3	26	351	386	26	76	
.20	42	25	1.3	20	258	283	26		
.30	37	25	1.3	15	191	210	25	75	
.40	36	25	1.3	14	178	196			
.50	35	22	1.1	13	136	150			
10.	33	22	1.1	11	125	137			
.10	32	22	1.1	10	111	125			
						6415			

TABLE IX.

Temperature of the outer air, 25° Centigrade; of the room at the beginning of the experiment, 26° Centigrade; size of fresh-air opening, .05 square meter.

DOOR OPEN.

Time; September 2, 1879, P.M.	Temperature of the Fresh-air Current.	Velocity of the Air in Meters per Minute.	Cubic Meters of Air entering the Room per Minute.	Difference of Temperature between Outer Air and Air entering Room.	Equivalent in Cubic Meters raised 1° Centigrade.	Weight in Kilograms.	Temperature of Room.	Thermometer in the Direct Radiation of Fireplace at one Meter distant.	Remarks.
1	2	3	4	5	6	7	8	9	10
3.32	27°	0	0	2°	0	0	27°	27°	Fire lighted.
.42	49	39	1.9	24	239.7	263.7	29	88	2d kilogram.
.52	67	57	2.8	42	861.0	861.0	30	94	3d kilogram.
4.02	91	78	3.9	66	2002.8	1802.5	32	107	
.12	65	52	2.6	40	1240.0	1240.0	29	84	
.22	54	36	1.8	29	582.4	582.4	29	83	
.32	50	34	1.7	25	450.5	450.5	29	82	
.42	45	29	1.4	20	324.5	357.0	28	82	
.52	42	27	1.3	17	234.5	258.0	28		
5.02	39	21	1.0	14	176.1	194.0	28		
.12	36	21	1.0	11	59.4	65.3	28		
.22	33	14	0.7	8	28.8	34.5	27		
.32	30	7	0.3	5	9.0	11.0	27		
						6120			

TABLE X.

Time, evening, Oct. 8, 1853.	Temperature of fresh air entering the room through the Register.	Difference between external air and air from Register.	Remarks.
6.00	12 degrees.		First kilogram put on.
6.05	13 "	1 degree.	
6.07	27 "	15 "	Full blaze.
6.10	59 "	47 "	
6.13	66 "	54 "	Declines.
6.15	65 "	53 "	Second kilogram put on.
6.17	63 "	51 "	Full blaze.
6.20	93 "	81 "	
6.23			Third kilogram put on.
6.24	97 "	85 "	Full blaze.
6.28	116 "	104 "	
6.30	108 "	96 "	Fourth kilogram put on.
6.36	118 "	106 "	
6.38	115 "	103 "	Fifth kilogram put on.
6.42	120 "	108 "	
6.45	117 "	105 "	Sixth kilogram put on.
6.50	127 "	115 "	
6.54	120 "	108 "	Seventh kilogram put on.
6.59	135 "	123 "	
7.02	131 "	119 "	Eighth kilogram put on.
7.07	129 "	117 "	
7.10	122 "	110 "	Small blaze.
7.15	103 "	91 "	Bright embers.
7.20	84 "	73 "	Few bright embers.
7.35	53 "	42 "	
7.40	48 "	37 "	All out.
8.35	20 "	9 "	

www.ingramcontent.com/pod-product-compliance
Lightning Source LLC
Chambersburg PA
CBHW031859220426
43663CB00006B/688